2009 | THE LITTLE DATA BOOK ON GENDER

THE WORLD BANK

ISBN: 978-0-8213-7872-4
E-ISBN: 978-0-8213-7873-1
DOI: 10.1596/ 978-0-8213-7872-4

The Little Data Book on Gender 2009 is a product of the Development
Data Group of the Development Economics Vice Presidency and
the Gender and Development Group of the World Bank.

Editing, design, and layout by Communications Development Incorporated,
Washington, D.C. Cover design by Peter Grundy Art & Design, London, U.K.

Contents

Acknowledgments

The Little Data Book on Gender 2009 is a collaborative effort between the Development Data Group of the Development Economics Vice Presidency and the Gender and Development Group.

Richard Fix, with the assistance of Mehdi Akhlaghi and Beatriz Prieto-Oramas, coordinated all stages of production. Meta de Coquereaumont, Christopher Trott, and Elaine Wilson of Communications Development Incorporated, provided design, editing, and layout. Staff from External Affairs oversaw publication and dissemination of the book.

Introduction

The *Little Data Book on Gender 2009* is a pocket edition of *World Development Indicators 2009* with a focus on gender-related statistics. It is intended as a quick reference for users of the *World Development Indicators 2009* book and CD-ROM and *WDI Online*, our electronic subscription database. Together, they cover more than 800 indicators and span more than 40 years.

The 209 country tables in *The Little Data Book on Gender* present the latest available data for World Bank member countries and other economies with populations of more than 30,000. The 14 summary tables cover regional and income group aggregates.

For more information about these data or other World Bank data publications, visit our data Web site at www.worldbank.org/data, e-mail us at data@worldbank.org, call our data hotline 800.590.1906 or 202.473.7824, or fax us at 202.522.1498.

To order *World Development Indicators 2009* or the *World Development Indicators 2009* CD-ROM, visit the publications Web site at www.worldbank.org/publications, call 800.645.7247 or 703.661.1580, or fax 703.661.1501.

Data notes

The data in this book are for 1990 and 2007 or the most recent year unless otherwise noted in the table or the *Glossary*.

- Growth rates are proportional changes from the previous year unless otherwise noted.

- Regional aggregates include data for low- and middle-income economies only.

- Figures in *italics* indicate data for years or periods other than those specified.

Symbols used:

- **..** indicates that data are not available or that aggregates cannot be calculated because of missing data.

- **0 or 0.0** indicates zero or small enough that the number would round to zero at the displayed number of decimal places.

- **$** indicates current U.S. dollars.

Data are shown for economies with populations greater than 30,000 or for smaller economies if they are members of the World Bank. The term *country* (used interchangeably with *economy*) does not imply political independence or official recognition by the World Bank but refers to any economy for which the authorities report separate social or economic statistics.

The selection of indicators in these pages includes some of those being used to monitor progress towards the Millennium Development Goals. For more information about the eight goals—halving poverty and increasing well-being by 2015—please visit our Web site www.developmentgoals.org or see *World Development Indicators 2009*.

Regional tables

The country composition of regions is based on the World Bank's analytical regions and may differ from common geographic usage.

East Asia and Pacific

American Samoa, Cambodia, China, Fiji, Indonesia, Kiribati, Democratic Republic of Korea, Lao People's Democratic Republic, Malaysia, Marshall Islands, Federated States of Micronesia, Mongolia, Myanmar, Palau, Papua New Guinea, Philippines, Samoa, Solomon Islands, Thailand, Timor-Leste, Tonga, Vanuatu, Vietnam

Europe and Central Asia

Albania, Armenia, Azerbaijan, Belarus, Bosnia and Herzegovina, Bulgaria, Croatia, Georgia, Kazakhstan, Kyrgyz Republic, Latvia, Lithuania, Former Yugoslav Republic of Macedonia, Moldova, Montenegro, Poland, Romania, Russian Federation, Serbia, Tajikistan, Turkey, Turkmenistan, Ukraine, Uzbekistan

Latin America and the Caribbean

Argentina, Belize, Bolivia, Brazil, Chile, Colombia, Costa Rica, Cuba, Dominica, Dominican Republic, Ecuador, El Salvador, Grenada, Guatemala, Guyana, Haiti, Honduras, Jamaica, Mexico, Nicaragua, Panama, Paraguay, Peru, St. Kitts and Nevis, St. Lucia, St. Vincent and the Grenadines, Suriname, Uruguay, Bolivarian Republic of Venezuela

Middle East and North Africa

Algeria, Djibouti, Arab Republic of Egypt, Islamic Republic of Iran, Iraq, Jordan, Lebanon, Libya, Morocco, Syrian Arab Republic, Tunisia, West Bank and Gaza, Republic of Yemen

South Asia

Afghanistan, Bangladesh, Bhutan, India, Maldives, Nepal, Pakistan, Sri Lanka

Sub-Saharan Africa

Angola, Benin, Botswana, Burkina Faso, Burundi, Cameroon, Cape Verde, Central African Republic, Chad, Comoros, Democratic Republic of the Congo, Republic of Congo, Côte d'Ivoire, Eritrea, Ethiopia, Gabon, The Gambia, Ghana, Guinea, Guinea-Bissau, Kenya, Lesotho, Liberia, Madagascar, Malawi, Mali, Mauritania, Mauritius, Mayotte, Mozambique, Namibia, Niger, Nigeria, Rwanda, São Tomé and Principe, Senegal, Seychelles, Sierra Leone, Somalia, South Africa, Sudan, Swaziland, Tanzania, Togo, Uganda, Zambia, Zimbabwe

World

Population (millions)	6,610	Population living on less
GNI ($ billions)	52,850.4	than $1.25 a day (%) ..
GNI per capita ($)	7,995	

	1990		2007	
	Female	Male	Female	Male
Demography				
Sex ratio at birth (females per 1,000 males)	941		940	
Life expectancy at birth (years)	67	63	71	67
Child mortality rate (per 1,000)	..	..	..	..
Female-headed households (%)		..		..
Education				
Gross primary enrollment (% of relevant age group)	92	103	102	108
Gross secondary enrollment (% of relevant age group)	47	56	64	67
Gross tertiary enrollment (% of relevant age group)	..	..	25	24
Primary completion rate (% of relevant age group)	75	86	84	88
Adult literacy rate (% of population ages 15+)	70	82	79	88
Family planning and maternal health				
Total fertility rate (births per woman)	3.2		2.5	
Adolescent fertility (births per 1,000 women ages 15–19)	..		52	
Women married by age 18 (% of women ages 20–24)	..		..	
Contraceptive prevalence (% of women ages 15–49)	57		60	
Unmet need for contraception (% of women ages 15–49)	..		..	
Pregnant women receiving prenatal care (%)	..		81	
Births attended by skilled health staff (% of total)	50		65	
Maternal mortality ratio (per 100,000 live births)	430		400	
Labor force and employment dynamics				
Labor force participation (% of population ages 15+)	52	81	53	78
Women in the labor force (% of total labor force)	39		40	
Employment to population ratio (% ages 15+)	49	76	50	73
Vulnerable employment (% of employed ages 15+)	..	..	..	..
Employment in agriculture (% of employed ages 15+)	..	..	..	..
Employment in industry (% of employed ages 15+)	..	..	..	..
Employment in service (% of employed ages 15+)	..	..	..	..
Wage and salaried workers (% of employed ages 15+)	..	..	..	..
Self-employed workers (% of employed ages 15+)	..	..	..	..
Unpaid family workers (% of employed ages 15+)	..	..	..	..
Women in nonagricultural wage employment (%)	35		..	
Children in employment (% of children ages 7–14)	..	..	..	..
Unemployment (% of labor force ages 15+)	..	..	..	..
Long-term unemployment (% of total unemployment)	..	..	..	..
Youth unemployment (% of labor force ages 15–24)	..	..	..	..
Maternity leave (weeks)	..		..	
Maternal leave benefits (% of wages paid)	..		..	
Women's political participation				
Seats held by women in national parliament (%)	13		18	
Women in managerial positions (%)	..		..	

East Asia & Pacific

Population (millions)	1,912	Population living on less	
GNI ($ billions)	4,172.8	than $1.25 a day (%)	16.8
GNI per capita ($)	2,182		

	1990		2007	
	Female	Male	Female	Male
Demography				
Sex ratio at birth (females per 1,000 males)	920		903	
Life expectancy at birth (years)	69	65	74	70
Child mortality rate (per 1,000)	..	..	..	..
Female-headed households (%)	..		..	
Education				
Gross primary enrollment (% of relevant age group)	*116*	123	109	111
Gross secondary enrollment (% of relevant age group)	*42*	52	73	73
Gross tertiary enrollment (% of relevant age group)	..	..	21	22
Primary completion rate (% of relevant age group)	*97*	105	98	98
Adult literacy rate (% of population ages 15+)	94	98	90	96
Family planning and maternal health				
Total fertility rate (births per woman)	2.4		1.9	
Adolescent fertility (births per 1,000 women ages 15–19)	..		17	
Women married by age 18 (% of women ages 20–24)	..		..	
Contraceptive prevalence (% of women ages 15–49)	75		78	
Unmet need for contraception (% of women ages 15–49)	..		..	
Pregnant women receiving prenatal care (%)	..		90	
Births attended by skilled health staff (% of total)	48		87	
Maternal mortality ratio (per 100,000 live births)	*220*		150	
Labor force and employment dynamics				
Labor force participation (% of population ages 15+)	69	84	67	80
Women in the labor force (% of total labor force)	44		45	
Employment to population ratio (% ages 15+)	67	81	64	77
Vulnerable employment (% of employed ages 15+)	..	..	..	..
Employment in agriculture (% of employed ages 15+)	..	..	..	..
Employment in industry (% of employed ages 15+)	..	..	..	..
Employment in service (% of employed ages 15+)	..	..	..	..
Wage and salaried workers (% of employed ages 15+)	..	..	..	..
Self-employed workers (% of employed ages 15+)	..	..	..	..
Unpaid family workers (% of employed ages 15+)	..	..	..	..
Women in nonagricultural wage employment (%)	38		..	
Children in employment (% of children ages 7–14)	..	..	..	..
Unemployment (% of labor force ages 15+)	..	..	..	..
Long-term unemployment (% of total unemployment)	..	..	..	..
Youth unemployment (% of labor force ages 15–24)	..	..	..	..
Maternity leave (weeks)	..		..	
Maternal leave benefits (% of wages paid)	..		..	
Women's political participation				
Seats held by women in national parliament (%)	17		18	
Women in managerial positions (%)	..		..	

Europe & Central Asia

Population (millions)	446	Population living on less	
GNI ($ billions)	2,697.2	than $1.25 a day (%)	3.8
GNI per capita ($)	6,052		

	1990		2007	
	Female	Male	Female	Male
Demography				
Sex ratio at birth (females per 1,000 males)	947		943	
Life expectancy at birth (years)	73	65	74	65
Child mortality rate (per 1,000)	..	..	..	..
Female-headed households (%)	..		..	
Education				
Gross primary enrollment (% of relevant age group)	96	98	96	98
Gross secondary enrollment (% of relevant age group)	84	85	86	90
Gross tertiary enrollment (% of relevant age group)	35	31	58	47
Primary completion rate (% of relevant age group)	92	93	96	99
Adult literacy rate (% of population ages 15+)	86	88	96	99
Family planning and maternal health				
Total fertility rate (births per woman)	2.3		1.7	
Adolescent fertility (births per 1,000 women ages 15–19)	..		29	
Women married by age 18 (% of women ages 20–24)	..		..	
Contraceptive prevalence (% of women ages 15–49)	..		..	
Unmet need for contraception (% of women ages 15–49)	..		..	
Pregnant women receiving prenatal care (%)	..		..	
Births attended by skilled health staff (% of total)	..		95	
Maternal mortality ratio (per 100,000 live births)	60		44	
Labor force and employment dynamics				
Labor force participation (% of population ages 15+)	57	76	50	67
Women in the labor force (% of total labor force)	46		46	
Employment to population ratio (% ages 15+)	49	65	46	62
Vulnerable employment (% of employed ages 15+)	..	..	18	19
Employment in agriculture (% of employed ages 15+)	..	..	19	19
Employment in industry (% of employed ages 15+)	..	..	20	34
Employment in service (% of employed ages 15+)	..	..	62	47
Wage and salaried workers (% of employed ages 15+)	..	..	81	78
Self-employed workers (% of employed ages 15+)	..	..	13	20
Unpaid family workers (% of employed ages 15+)	..	..	6	2
Women in nonagricultural wage employment (%)	47		48	
Children in employment (% of children ages 7–14)	..	..	..	..
Unemployment (% of labor force ages 15+)	..	..	7	8
Long-term unemployment (% of total unemployment)	..	..	..	..
Youth unemployment (% of labor force ages 15–24)	..	..	..	..
Maternity leave (weeks)	..		..	
Maternal leave benefits (% of wages paid)	..		..	
Women's political participation				
Seats held by women in national parliament (%)	..		15	
Women in managerial positions (%)	..		..	

Latin America & Caribbean

Population (millions)	561	Population living on less	
GNI ($ billions)	3,252.1	than $1.25 a day (%)	8.2
GNI per capita ($)	5,801		

	1990		2007	
	Female	Male	Female	Male
Demography				
Sex ratio at birth (females per 1,000 males)	953		953	
Life expectancy at birth (years)	72	65	76	70
Child mortality rate (per 1,000)	..	..	..	..
Female-headed households (%)	..		..	
Education				
Gross primary enrollment (% of relevant age group)	*102*	105	116	120
Gross secondary enrollment (% of relevant age group)	*53*	49	93	86
Gross tertiary enrollment (% of relevant age group)	*16*	17	34	29
Primary completion rate (% of relevant age group)	*85*	84	101	100
Adult literacy rate (% of population ages 15+)	62	78	90	92
Family planning and maternal health				
Total fertility rate (births per woman)	3.2		2.4	
Adolescent fertility (births per 1,000 women ages 15–19)	..		77	
Women married by age 18 (% of women ages 20–24)	..		..	
Contraceptive prevalence (% of women ages 15–49)	56		..	
Unmet need for contraception (% of women ages 15–49)	..		..	
Pregnant women receiving prenatal care (%)	..		95	
Births attended by skilled health staff (% of total)	72		89	
Maternal mortality ratio (per 100,000 live births)	*180*		130	
Labor force and employment dynamics				
Labor force participation (% of population ages 15+)	38	82	53	80
Women in the labor force (% of total labor force)	32		41	
Employment to population ratio (% ages 15+)	*35*	76	48	75
Vulnerable employment (% of employed ages 15+)	28	30	31	31
Employment in agriculture (% of employed ages 15+)	*14*	21	10	21
Employment in industry (% of employed ages 15+)	*14*	30	15	27
Employment in service (% of employed ages 15+)	*71*	49	76	52
Wage and salaried workers (% of employed ages 15+)	*62*	60	65	63
Self-employed workers (% of employed ages 15+)	28	34	25	32
Unpaid family workers (% of employed ages 15+)	*11*	6	7	4
Women in nonagricultural wage employment (%)	37		..	
Children in employment (% of children ages 7–14)	..	..	..	..
Unemployment (% of labor force ages 15+)	7	6	12	7
Long-term unemployment (% of total unemployment)	..	..	..	..
Youth unemployment (% of labor force ages 15–24)	*14*	10	21	14
Maternity leave (weeks)	..		..	
Maternal leave benefits (% of wages paid)	..		..	
Women's political participation				
Seats held by women in national parliament (%)	12		20	
Women in managerial positions (%)	..		..	

Middle East & North Africa

Population (millions)	313	Population living on less
GNI ($ billions)	883.5	than $1.25 a day (%) 3.6
GNI per capita ($)	2,820	

	1990		2007	
	Female	Male	Female	Male
Demography				
Sex ratio at birth (females per 1,000 males)	952		952	
Life expectancy at birth (years)	66	63	72	68
Child mortality rate (per 1,000)	..	..	..	..
Female-headed households (%)	..		..	
Education				
Gross primary enrollment (% of relevant age group)	85	104	103	108
Gross secondary enrollment (% of relevant age group)	49	65	70	77
Gross tertiary enrollment (% of relevant age group)	9	16	25	25
Primary completion rate (% of relevant age group)	72	84	88	93
Adult literacy rate (% of population ages 15+)	46	70	65	82
Family planning and maternal health				
Total fertility rate (births per woman)	4.8		2.8	
Adolescent fertility (births per 1,000 women ages 15–19)	..		30	
Women married by age 18 (% of women ages 20–24)	..		..	
Contraceptive prevalence (% of women ages 15–49)	42		62	
Unmet need for contraception (% of women ages 15–49)	..		..	
Pregnant women receiving prenatal care (%)	..		76	
Births attended by skilled health staff (% of total)	48		80	
Maternal mortality ratio (per 100,000 live births)	260		200	
Labor force and employment dynamics				
Labor force participation (% of population ages 15+)	21	77	26	74
Women in the labor force (% of total labor force)	21		26	
Employment to population ratio (% ages 15+)	17	68	22	67
Vulnerable employment (% of employed ages 15+)	..	..	52	34
Employment in agriculture (% of employed ages 15+)	..	..	..	..
Employment in industry (% of employed ages 15+)	..	..	..	..
Employment in service (% of employed ages 15+)	..	..	..	..
Wage and salaried workers (% of employed ages 15+)	..	..	..	..
Self-employed workers (% of employed ages 15+)	..	..	..	..
Unpaid family workers (% of employed ages 15+)	..	..	..	..
Women in nonagricultural wage employment (%)	..		20	
Children in employment (% of children ages 7–14)	..	..	..	..
Unemployment (% of labor force ages 15+)	22	11	18	10
Long-term unemployment (% of total unemployment)	..	..	..	..
Youth unemployment (% of labor force ages 15–24)	..	..	..	..
Maternity leave (weeks)	..		..	
Maternal leave benefits (% of wages paid)	..		..	
Women's political participation				
Seats held by women in national parliament (%)	4		9	
Women in managerial positions (%)	..		..	

South Asia

Population (millions)	1,522	Population living on less	
GNI ($ billions)	1,338.7	than $1.25 a day (%)	40.3
GNI per capita ($)	880		

	1990		2007	
	Female	**Male**	**Female**	**Male**
Demography				
Sex ratio at birth (females per 1,000 males)	936		934	
Life expectancy at birth (years)	59	59	66	63
Child mortality rate (per 1,000)	42	29	13	9
Female-headed households (%)	..		..	
Education				
Gross primary enrollment (% of relevant age group)	75	99	104	111
Gross secondary enrollment (% of relevant age group)	28	47	45	54
Gross tertiary enrollment (% of relevant age group)	..	..	8	12
Primary completion rate (% of relevant age group)	52	75	77	83
Adult literacy rate (% of population ages 15+)	33	59	52	74
Family planning and maternal health				
Total fertility rate (births per woman)	4.2		2.9	
Adolescent fertility (births per 1,000 women ages 15–19)	..		67	
Women married by age 18 (% of women ages 20–24)	..		..	
Contraceptive prevalence (% of women ages 15–49)	40		53	
Unmet need for contraception (% of women ages 15–49)	18		14	
Pregnant women receiving prenatal care (%)	47		69	
Births attended by skilled health staff (% of total)	32		41	
Maternal mortality ratio (per 100,000 live births)	650		500	
Labor force and employment dynamics				
Labor force participation (% of population ages 15+)	36	85	36	82
Women in the labor force (% of total labor force)	28		29	
Employment to population ratio (% ages 15+)	35	82	34	78
Vulnerable employment (% of employed ages 15+)	..	..	..	..
Employment in agriculture (% of employed ages 15+)	..	..	..	..
Employment in industry (% of employed ages 15+)	..	..	..	..
Employment in service (% of employed ages 15+)	..	..	..	..
Wage and salaried workers (% of employed ages 15+)	..	..	..	..
Self-employed workers (% of employed ages 15+)	..	..	..	..
Unpaid family workers (% of employed ages 15+)	..	..	..	..
Women in nonagricultural wage employment (%)	13		18	
Children in employment (% of children ages 7-14)	..	..	..	..
Unemployment (% of labor force ages 15+)	..	..	6	5
Long-term unemployment (% of total unemployment)	..	..	..	..
Youth unemployment (% of labor force ages 15–24)	..	..	12	11
Maternity leave (weeks)	..		..	
Maternal leave benefits (% of wages paid)	..		..	
Women's political participation				
Seats held by women in national parliament (%)	6		14	
Women in managerial positions (%)	..		..	

Sub-Saharan Africa

Population (millions)	800	Population living on less	
GNI ($ billions)	761.0	than $1.25 a day (%)	50.9
GNI per capita ($)	951		

	1990		2007	
	Female	**Male**	**Female**	**Male**
Demography				
Sex ratio at birth (females per 1,000 males)	968		968	
Life expectancy at birth (years)	52	49	52	50
Child mortality rate (per 1,000)	..	..	..	..
Female-headed households (%)	..		..	
Education				
Gross primary enrollment (% of relevant age group)	65	77	88	99
Gross secondary enrollment (% of relevant age group)	18	25	28	35
Gross tertiary enrollment (% of relevant age group)	..	..	4	6
Primary completion rate (% of relevant age group)	47	57	55	65
Adult literacy rate (% of population ages 15+)	45	63	54	71
Family planning and maternal health				
Total fertility rate (births per woman)	6.3		5.1	
Adolescent fertility (births per 1,000 women ages 15–19)	..		118	
Women married by age 18 (% of women ages 20–24)	..		..	
Contraceptive prevalence (% of women ages 15–49)	15		23	
Unmet need for contraception (% of women ages 15–49)	..		24	
Pregnant women receiving prenatal care (%)	..		72	
Births attended by skilled health staff (% of total)	..		45	
Maternal mortality ratio (per 100,000 live births)	920		900	
Labor force and employment dynamics				
Labor force participation (% of population ages 15+)	58	82	60	80
Women in the labor force (% of total labor force)	42		43	
Employment to population ratio (% ages 15+)	53	75	55	74
Vulnerable employment (% of employed ages 15+)	..	..	..	..
Employment in agriculture (% of employed ages 15+)	..	..	..	..
Employment in industry (% of employed ages 15+)	..	..	..	..
Employment in service (% of employed ages 15+)	..	..	..	..
Wage and salaried workers (% of employed ages 15+)	..	..	..	..
Self-employed workers (% of employed ages 15+)	..	..	..	..
Unpaid family workers (% of employed ages 15+)	..	..	..	..
Women in nonagricultural wage employment (%)	..		..	
Children in employment (% of children ages 7–14)	..	..	..	..
Unemployment (% of labor force ages 15+)	..	..	..	..
Long-term unemployment (% of total unemployment)	..	..	..	..
Youth unemployment (% of labor force ages 15–24)	..	..	..	..
Maternity leave (weeks)	..		..	
Maternal leave benefits (% of wages paid)	..		..	
Women's political participation				
Seats held by women in national parliament (%)	..		17	
Women in managerial positions (%)	..		..	

Income group tables

For operational and analytical purposes the World Bank's main criterion for classifying economies is gross national income (GNI) per capita. Each economy in *The Little Data Book on Gender* is classified as low income, middle income, or high income. Low- and middle-income economies are sometimes referred to as developing economies. The use of the term is convenient; it is not intended to imply that all economies in the group are experiencing similar development or that other economies have reached a preferred or final stage of development. Classification by income does not necessarily reflect development status.

Low-income economies are those with a GNI per capita of $935 or less in 2007.

Middle-income economies are those with a GNI per capita of more than $935 but less than $11,456. Lower middle-income and upper middle-income economies are separated at a GNI per capita of $3,705.

High-income economies are those with a GNI per capita of $11,456 or more.

Euro area includes the member states of the Economic and Monetary Union of the European Union that have adopted the euro as their currency: Austria, Belgium, Cyprus, Finland, France, Germany, Greece, Ireland, Italy, Luxembourg, Malta, Netherlands, Portugal, Slovak Republic, Slovenia, and Spain.

Low income

Population (millions)	1,296	Population living on less	
GNI ($ billions)	744.3	than $1.25 a day (%)	..
GNI per capita ($)	574		

	1990		2007	
	Female	Male	Female	Male
Demography				
Sex ratio at birth (females per 1,000 males)	962		963	
Life expectancy at birth (years)	56	53	59	56
Child mortality rate (per 1,000)	..	..	..	..
Female-headed households (%)	..		..	
Education				
Gross primary enrollment (% of relevant age group)	64	80	89	100
Gross secondary enrollment (% of relevant age group)	21	30	35	41
Gross tertiary enrollment (% of relevant age group)	..	..	5	8
Primary completion rate (% of relevant age group)	..	..	60	70
Adult literacy rate (% of population ages 15+)	45	63	55	72
Family planning and maternal health				
Total fertility rate (births per woman)	5.6		4.2	
Adolescent fertility (births per 1,000 women ages 15–19)	..		95	
Women married by age 18 (% of women ages 20–24)	..		..	
Contraceptive prevalence (% of women ages 15–49)	22		33	
Unmet need for contraception (% of women ages 15–49)	..		21	
Pregnant women receiving prenatal care (%)	..		67	
Births attended by skilled health staff (% of total)	..		42	
Maternal mortality ratio (per 100,000 live births)	790		780	
Labor force and employment dynamics				
Labor force participation (% of population ages 15+)	56	84	56	82
Women in the labor force (% of total labor force)	40		41	
Employment to population ratio (% ages 15+)	53	80	52	77
Vulnerable employment (% of employed ages 15+)	..	..	..	..
Employment in agriculture (% of employed ages 15+)	..	..	..	..
Employment in industry (% of employed ages 15+)	..	..	..	..
Employment in service (% of employed ages 15+)	..	..	..	..
Wage and salaried workers (% of employed ages 15+)	..	..	..	..
Self-employed workers (% of employed ages 15+)	..	..	..	..
Unpaid family workers (% of employed ages 15+)	..	..	..	..
Women in nonagricultural wage employment (%)	..		..	
Children in employment (% of children ages 7–14)	..	..	..	..
Unemployment (% of labor force ages 15+)	..	..	..	..
Long-term unemployment (% of total unemployment)	..	..	..	..
Youth unemployment (% of labor force ages 15–24)	..	..	..	..
Maternity leave (weeks)	..		..	
Maternal leave benefits (% of wages paid)	..		..	
Women's political participation				
Seats held by women in national parliament (%)	..		17	
Women in managerial positions (%)	..		..	

Middle income

Population (millions)	4,258
GNI ($ billions)	12,393.5
GNI per capita ($)	2,910

Population living on less than $1.25 a day (%) ..

	1990		2007	
	Female	**Male**	**Female**	**Male**
Demography				
Sex ratio at birth (females per 1,000 males)	932		926	
Life expectancy at birth (years)	67	64	72	67
Child mortality rate (per 1,000)	..	..	..	..
Female-headed households (%)	..		..	
Education				
Gross primary enrollment (% of relevant age group)	*100*	111	109	112
Gross secondary enrollment (% of relevant age group)	*45*	56	69	71
Gross tertiary enrollment (% of relevant age group)	..	..	24	23
Primary completion rate (% of relevant age group)	*79*	90	92	94
Adult literacy rate (% of population ages 15+)	66	82	80	90
Family planning and maternal health				
Total fertility rate (births per woman)	3.0		2.2	
Adolescent fertility (births per 1,000 women ages 15–19)	..		42	
Women married by age 18 (% of women ages 20–24)	..		..	
Contraceptive prevalence (% of women ages 15–49)	61		68	
Unmet need for contraception (% of women ages 15–49)	..		..	
Pregnant women receiving prenatal care (%)	..		86	
Births attended by skilled health staff (% of total)	49		74	
Maternal mortality ratio (per 100,000 live births)	*330*		260	
Labor force and employment dynamics				
Labor force participation (% of population ages 15+)	53	83	52	79
Women in the labor force (% of total labor force)	39		39	
Employment to population ratio (% ages 15+)	*50*	78	49	74
Vulnerable employment (% of employed ages 15+)	..	..	..	..
Employment in agriculture (% of employed ages 15+)	..	..	..	..
Employment in industry (% of employed ages 15+)	..	..	..	..
Employment in service (% of employed ages 15+)	..	..	..	..
Wage and salaried workers (% of employed ages 15+)	..	..	..	..
Self-employed workers (% of employed ages 15+)	..	..	..	..
Unpaid family workers (% of employed ages 15+)	..	..	..	..
Women in nonagricultural wage employment (%)	33		..	
Children in employment (% of children ages 7–14)	..	..	..	..
Unemployment (% of labor force ages 15+)	..	..	..	..
Long-term unemployment (% of total unemployment)	..	..	..	..
Youth unemployment (% of labor force ages 15–24)	..	..	..	..
Maternity leave (weeks)	..		..	
Maternal leave benefits (% of wages paid)	..		..	
Women's political participation				
Seats held by women in national parliament (%)	13		16	
Women in managerial positions (%)	..		..	

Lower middle income

Population (millions)	3,435	Population living on less
GNI ($ billions)	6,542.9	than $1.25 a day (%) ..
GNI per capita ($)	1,905	

	1990		2007	
	Female	Male	Female	Male
Demography				
Sex ratio at birth (females per 1,000 males)	928		920	
Life expectancy at birth (years)	66	63	71	67
Child mortality rate (per 1,000)	..	..	..	..
Female-headed households (%)	..		..	
Education				
Gross primary enrollment (% of relevant age group)	100	113	109	112
Gross secondary enrollment (% of relevant age group)	40	54	63	67
Gross tertiary enrollment (% of relevant age group)	..	..	19	20
Primary completion rate (% of relevant age group)	76	90	90	93
Adult literacy rate (% of population ages 15+)	60	79	77	88
Family planning and maternal health				
Total fertility rate (births per woman)	3.1		2.3	
Adolescent fertility (births per 1,000 women ages 15-19)	..		39	
Women married by age 18 (% of women ages 20-24)	..		..	
Contraceptive prevalence (% of women ages 15-49)	63		69	
Unmet need for contraception (% of women ages 15-49)	..		..	
Pregnant women receiving prenatal care (%)	..		84	
Births attended by skilled health staff (% of total)	45		69	
Maternal mortality ratio (per 100,000 live births)	380		300	
Labor force and employment dynamics				
Labor force participation (% of population ages 15+)	55	84	53	80
Women in the labor force (% of total labor force)	39		39	
Employment to population ratio (% ages 15+)	52	79	50	76
Vulnerable employment (% of employed ages 15+)	..	..	..	..
Employment in agriculture (% of employed ages 15+)	..	..	..	..
Employment in industry (% of employed ages 15+)	..	..	..	..
Employment in service (% of employed ages 15+)	..	..	..	..
Wage and salaried workers (% of employed ages 15+)	..	..	..	..
Self-employed workers (% of employed ages 15+)	..	..	..	..
Unpaid family workers (% of employed ages 15+)	..	..	..	..
Women in nonagricultural wage employment (%)	32		..	
Children in employment (% of children ages 7-14)	..	..	..	..
Unemployment (% of labor force ages 15+)	..	..	..	..
Long-term unemployment (% of total unemployment)	..	..	..	..
Youth unemployment (% of labor force ages 15-24)	..	..	..	..
Maternity leave (weeks)	..		..	
Maternal leave benefits (% of wages paid)	..		..	
Women's political participation				
Seats held by women in national parliament (%)	13		15	
Women in managerial positions (%)	..		..	

Upper middle income

Population (millions)	824	Population living on less
GNI ($ billions)	5,853.9	than $1.25 a day (%) ..
GNI per capita ($)	7,107	

	1990		2007	
	Female	**Male**	**Female**	**Male**
Demography				
Sex ratio at birth (females per 1,000 males)	952		952	
Life expectancy at birth (years)	73	65	75	67
Child mortality rate (per 1,000)	..	..	..	..
Female-headed households (%)	..		..	
Education				
Gross primary enrollment (% of relevant age group)	102	106	109	112
Gross secondary enrollment (% of relevant age group)	69	67	93	90
Gross tertiary enrollment (% of relevant age group)	23	22	46	38
Primary completion rate (% of relevant age group)	90	90	101	101
Adult literacy rate (% of population ages 15+)	89	93	93	95
Family planning and maternal health				
Total fertility rate (births per woman)	2.7		2.0	
Adolescent fertility (births per 1,000 women ages 15–19)	..		56	
Women married by age 18 (% of women ages 20–24)	..		..	
Contraceptive prevalence (% of women ages 15–49)	52		..	
Unmet need for contraception (% of women ages 15–49)	..		..	
Pregnant women receiving prenatal care (%)	..		..	
Births attended by skilled health staff (% of total)	..		95	
Maternal mortality ratio (per 100,000 live births)	98		97	
Labor force and employment dynamics				
Labor force participation (% of population ages 15+)	46	78	50	73
Women in the labor force (% of total labor force)	39		42	
Employment to population ratio (% ages 15+)	41	71	45	68
Vulnerable employment (% of employed ages 15+)	..	..	20	23
Employment in agriculture (% of employed ages 15+)	..	..	14	20
Employment in industry (% of employed ages 15+)	..	..	17	30
Employment in service (% of employed ages 15+)	..	..	68	49
Wage and salaried workers (% of employed ages 15+)	72	67	75	70
Self-employed workers (% of employed ages 15+)	17	27	16	26
Unpaid family workers (% of employed ages 15+)	11	6	7	3
Women in nonagricultural wage employment (%)	43		45	
Children in employment (% of children ages 7–14)	..	..	..	..
Unemployment (% of labor force ages 15+)	7	6	10	8
Long-term unemployment (% of total unemployment)	..	..	..	..
Youth unemployment (% of labor force ages 15–24)	14	13	26	21
Maternity leave (weeks)	..		..	
Maternal leave benefits (% of wages paid)	..		..	
Women's political participation				
Seats held by women in national parliament (%)	13		18	
Women in managerial positions (%)	..		..	

Low and middle income

Population (millions)	5,554	Population living on less	
GNI ($ billions)	13,141.1	than $1.25 a day (%)	25.3
GNI per capita ($)	2,366		

	1990		2007	
	Female	Male	Female	Male
Demography				
Sex ratio at birth (females per 1,000 males)	941		939	
Life expectancy at birth (years)	65	61	69	65
Child mortality rate (per 1,000)	..	..	..	..
Female-headed households (%)	..		..	
Education				
Gross primary enrollment (% of relevant age group)	91	104	103	109
Gross secondary enrollment (% of relevant age group)	39	50	59	63
Gross tertiary enrollment (% of relevant age group)	..	..	19	19
Primary completion rate (% of relevant age group)	73	85	83	87
Adult literacy rate (% of population ages 15+)	72	88	75	86
Family planning and maternal health				
Total fertility rate (births per woman)	3.5		2.7	
Adolescent fertility (births per 1,000 women ages 15-19)	..		56	
Women married by age 18 (% of women ages 20-24)	..		..	
Contraceptive prevalence (% of women ages 15-49)	54		60	
Unmet need for contraception (% of women ages 15-49)	..		..	
Pregnant women receiving prenatal care (%)	..		81	
Births attended by skilled health staff (% of total)	46		62	
Maternal mortality ratio (per 100,000 live births)	470		440	
Labor force and employment dynamics				
Labor force participation (% of population ages 15+)	53	83	53	79
Women in the labor force (% of total labor force)	39		40	
Employment to population ratio (% ages 15+)	50	78	50	75
Vulnerable employment (% of employed ages 15+)	..	..	..	..
Employment in agriculture (% of employed ages 15+)	..	..	..	..
Employment in industry (% of employed ages 15+)	..	..	..	..
Employment in service (% of employed ages 15+)	..	..	..	..
Wage and salaried workers (% of employed ages 15+)	..	..	..	..
Self-employed workers (% of employed ages 15+)	..	..	..	..
Unpaid family workers (% of employed ages 15+)	..	..	..	..
Women in nonagricultural wage employment (%)	32		..	
Children in employment (% of children ages 7-14)	..	..	..	..
Unemployment (% of labor force ages 15+)	..	..	..	..
Long-term unemployment (% of total unemployment)	..	..	..	..
Youth unemployment (% of labor force ages 15-24)	..	..	..	..
Maternity leave (weeks)	..		..	
Maternal leave benefits (% of wages paid)	..		..	
Women's political participation				
Seats held by women in national parliament (%)	13		16	
Women in managerial positions (%)	..		..	

Euro area

Population (millions)	324	Population living on less
GNI ($ billions)	11,611.1	than $1.25 a day (%)
GNI per capita ($)	35,818	

Population living on less than $1.25 a day (%) ..

	1990		2007	
	Female	**Male**	**Female**	**Male**
Demography				
Sex ratio at birth (females per 1,000 males)	946		946	
Life expectancy at birth (years)	80	73	83	77
Child mortality rate (per 1,000)	..	..	..	..
Female-headed households (%)	..		..	
Education				
Gross primary enrollment (% of relevant age group)	..	..	..	..
Gross secondary enrollment (% of relevant age group)	..	..	..	..
Gross tertiary enrollment (% of relevant age group)	..	..	..	..
Primary completion rate (% of relevant age group)	*100*	100	..	..
Adult literacy rate (% of population ages 15+)	..	..	..	..
Family planning and maternal health				
Total fertility rate (births per woman)	1.5		1.5	
Adolescent fertility (births per 1,000 women ages 15–19)	..		8	
Women married by age 18 (% of women ages 20–24)	..		..	
Contraceptive prevalence (% of women ages 15–49)	..		..	
Unmet need for contraception (% of women ages 15–49)	..		..	
Pregnant women receiving prenatal care (%)	..		..	
Births attended by skilled health staff (% of total)	..		..	
Maternal mortality ratio (per 100,000 live births)	*8*		5	
Labor force and employment dynamics				
Labor force participation (% of population ages 15+)	42	69	48	65
Women in the labor force (% of total labor force)	40		44	
Employment to population ratio (% ages 15+)	*38*	64	44	61
Vulnerable employment (% of employed ages 15+)	..	..	9	14
Employment in agriculture (% of employed ages 15+)	7	8	3	5
Employment in industry (% of employed ages 15+)	22	43	14	38
Employment in service (% of employed ages 15+)	*71*	49	82	56
Wage and salaried workers (% of employed ages 15+)	85	80	87	80
Self-employed workers (% of employed ages 15+)	*10*	19	10	19
Unpaid family workers (% of employed ages 15+)	*4*	1	2	1
Women in nonagricultural wage employment (%)	*40*		45	
Children in employment (% of children ages 7–14)	..	..	..	..
Unemployment (% of labor force ages 15+)	14	7	9	7
Long-term unemployment (% of total unemployment)	55	51	45	44
Youth unemployment (% of labor force ages 15–24)	28	18	21	18
Maternity leave (weeks)	..		..	
Maternal leave benefits (% of wages paid)	..		..	
Women's political participation				
Seats held by women in national parliament (%)	12		24	
Women in managerial positions (%)	..		..	

High income

Population (millions)	1,056	Population living on less
GNI ($ billions)	39,685.9	than $1.25 a day (%)
GNI per capita ($)	37,572	..

	1990		2007	
	Female	Male	Female	Male
Demography				
Sex ratio at birth (females per 1,000 males)	950		948	
Life expectancy at birth (years)	79	72	82	77
Child mortality rate (per 1,000)	..	..	..	..
Female-headed households (%)	..		..	
Education				
Gross primary enrollment (% of relevant age group)	*101*	102	101	101
Gross secondary enrollment (% of relevant age group)	*92*	91	100	101
Gross tertiary enrollment (% of relevant age group)	..	..	73	60
Primary completion rate (% of relevant age group)	..	..	97	97
Adult literacy rate (% of population ages 15+)	98	99	99	99
Family planning and maternal health				
Total fertility rate (births per woman)	1.8		1.8	
Adolescent fertility (births per 1,000 women ages 15–19)	..		22	
Women married by age 18 (% of women ages 20–24)	..		..	
Contraceptive prevalence (% of women ages 15–49)	72		..	
Unmet need for contraception (% of women ages 15–49)	..		..	
Pregnant women receiving prenatal care (%)	..		..	
Births attended by skilled health staff (% of total)	..		99	
Maternal mortality ratio (per 100,000 live births)	*12*		10	
Labor force and employment dynamics				
Labor force participation (% of population ages 15+)	49	74	52	70
Women in the labor force (% of total labor force)	41		43	
Employment to population ratio (% ages 15+)	*46*	68	49	66
Vulnerable employment (% of employed ages 15+)	..	..	..	..
Employment in agriculture (% of employed ages 15+)	5	6	3	4
Employment in industry (% of employed ages 15+)	20	39	13	34
Employment in service (% of employed ages 15+)	75	55	84	62
Wage and salaried workers (% of employed ages 15+)	86	83	89	84
Self-employed workers (% of employed ages 15+)	9	16	8	15
Unpaid family workers (% of employed ages 15+)	5	1	2	1
Women in nonagricultural wage employment (%)	*43*		46	
Children in employment (% of children ages 7–14)	..	..	..	..
Unemployment (% of labor force ages 15+)	7	6	6	5
Long-term unemployment (% of total unemployment)	18	25	23	27
Youth unemployment (% of labor force ages 15–24)	14	12	13	14
Maternity leave (weeks)	..		..	
Maternal leave benefits (% of wages paid)	..		..	
Women's political participation				
Seats held by women in national parliament (%)	12		22	
Women in managerial positions (%)	..		..	

Country tables

China

Unless otherwise noted, data for China do not include data for Hong Kong, China; Macao, China; or Taiwan, China.

Serbia and Montenegro

Montenegro declared independence from Serbia and Montenegro on June 3, 2006. When available, data for each country are shown separately. However, some indicators for Serbia continue to include data for Montenegro through 2005. Moreover, data for most indicators from 1999 onward for Serbia exclude data for Kosovo, which in 1999 became a territory under international administration pursuant to UN Security Council Resolution 1244 (1999).

Afghanistan

South Asia   **Low income**

Population (millions)	..	Population living on less	
GNI ($ billions)	8.1	than $1.25 a day (%)	..
GNI per capita ($)	..		

	1990		2007	
	Female	Male	Female	Male
Demography				
Sex ratio at birth (females per 1,000 males)	..		..	
Life expectancy at birth (years)	..	..	..	..
Child mortality rate (per 1,000)	..	..	..	..
Female-headed households (%)	..		..	
Education				
Gross primary enrollment (% of relevant age group)	..	..	..	..
Gross secondary enrollment (% of relevant age group)	..	..	..	..
Gross tertiary enrollment (% of relevant age group)	..	..	..	..
Primary completion rate (% of relevant age group)	..	..	..	..
Adult literacy rate (% of population ages 15+)	..	..	..	..
Family planning and maternal health				
Total fertility rate (births per woman)	..		..	
Adolescent fertility (births per 1,000 women ages 15–19)	..		..	
Women married by age 18 (% of women ages 20–24)	..		..	
Contraceptive prevalence (% of women ages 15–49)	..		..	
Unmet need for contraception (% of women ages 15–49)	..		..	
Pregnant women receiving prenatal care (%)	..		..	
Births attended by skilled health staff (% of total)	..		..	
Maternal mortality ratio (per 100,000 live births)	..		..	
Labor force and employment dynamics				
Labor force participation (% of population ages 15+)	..	..	..	..
Women in the labor force (% of total labor force)	..		..	
Employment to population ratio (% ages 15+)	..	..	..	..
Vulnerable employment (% of employed ages 15+)	..	..	..	..
Employment in agriculture (% of employed ages 15+)	..	..	..	..
Employment in industry (% of employed ages 15+)	..	..	..	..
Employment in service (% of employed ages 15+)	..	..	..	..
Wage and salaried workers (% of employed ages 15+)	..	..	..	..
Self-employed workers (% of employed ages 15+)	..	..	..	..
Unpaid family workers (% of employed ages 15+)	..	..	..	..
Women in nonagricultural wage employment (%)	..		..	
Children in employment (% of children ages 7–14)	..	..	..	..
Unemployment (% of labor force ages 15+)	..	..	..	..
Long-term unemployment (% of total unemployment)	..	..	..	..
Youth unemployment (% of labor force ages 15–24)	..	..	..	..
Maternity leave (weeks)	12		13	
Maternal leave benefits (% of wages paid)	100		100	
Women's political participation				
Seats held by women in national parliament (%)	4		27	
Women in managerial positions (%)	..		..	

Albania

Europe & Central Asia   **Lower middle income**

Population (millions)	3.2	Population living on less
GNI ($ billions)	10.5	than $1.25 a day (%) 2.0
GNI per capita ($)	3,300	

	1990		2007	
	Female	Male	Female	Male
Demography				
Sex ratio at birth (females per 1,000 males)	935		935	
Life expectancy at birth (years)	75	69	80	73
Child mortality rate (per 1,000)	..	..	1	3
Female-headed households (%)		..		..
Education				
Gross primary enrollment (% of relevant age group)	101	100	105	106
Gross secondary enrollment (% of relevant age group)	85	93	75	78
Gross tertiary enrollment (% of relevant age group)	..	..	23	15
Primary completion rate (% of relevant age group)	..	..	96	97
Adult literacy rate (% of population ages 15+)	..	..	99	99
Family planning and maternal health				
Total fertility rate (births per woman)	2.9		1.8	
Adolescent fertility (births per 1,000 women ages 15–19)	..		16	
Women married by age 18 (% of women ages 20–24)	..		..	
Contraceptive prevalence (% of women ages 15–49)	..		60	
Unmet need for contraception (% of women ages 15–49)	..		..	
Pregnant women receiving prenatal care (%)	..		97	
Births attended by skilled health staff (% of total)	..		100	
Maternal mortality ratio (per 100,000 live births)	..		92	
Labor force and employment dynamics				
Labor force participation (% of population ages 15+)	67	84	50	71
Women in the labor force (% of total labor force)	43		42	
Employment to population ratio (% ages 15+)	43	63	42	61
Vulnerable employment (% of employed ages 15+)	..	..	..	..
Employment in agriculture (% of employed ages 15+)	..	..	..	..
Employment in industry (% of employed ages 15+)	..	..	..	..
Employment in service (% of employed ages 15+)	..	..	..	..
Wage and salaried workers (% of employed ages 15+)	..	..	..	..
Self-employed workers (% of employed ages 15+)	..	..	..	..
Unpaid family workers (% of employed ages 15+)	..	..	..	..
Women in nonagricultural wage employment (%)	..		33	
Children in employment (% of children ages 7–14)	..	..	..	..
Unemployment (% of labor force ages 15+)	..	..	..	..
Long-term unemployment (% of total unemployment)	..	..	..	..
Youth unemployment (% of labor force ages 15–24)	..	..	..	..
Maternity leave (weeks)	..		52	
Maternal leave benefits (% of wages paid)	..		80	
Women's political participation				
Seats held by women in national parliament (%)	29		7	
Women in managerial positions (%)	..		..	

Algeria

Middle East & North Africa **Lower middle income**

Population (millions)	34	Population living on less	
GNI ($ billions)	122.5	than $1.25 a day (%)	..
GNI per capita ($)	3,620		

	1990		2007	
	Female	Male	Female	Male
Demography				
Sex ratio at birth (females per 1,000 males)	952		952	
Life expectancy at birth (years)	68	66	74	71
Child mortality rate (per 1,000)	..	..	..	..
Female-headed households (%)	..		..	
Education				
Gross primary enrollment (% of relevant age group)	86	102	106	113
Gross secondary enrollment (% of relevant age group)	54	70	86	80
Gross tertiary enrollment (% of relevant age group)	..	..	28	20
Primary completion rate (% of relevant age group)	72	89	96	94
Adult literacy rate (% of population ages 15+)	36	63	66	84
Family planning and maternal health				
Total fertility rate (births per woman)	4.6		2.4	
Adolescent fertility (births per 1,000 women ages 15-19)	..		7	
Women married by age 18 (% of women ages 20-24)	..		..	
Contraceptive prevalence (% of women ages 15-49)	47		61	
Unmet need for contraception (% of women ages 15-49)	..		..	
Pregnant women receiving prenatal care (%)	58		89	
Births attended by skilled health staff (% of total)	77		95	
Maternal mortality ratio (per 100,000 live births)	..		180	
Labor force and employment dynamics				
Labor force participation (% of population ages 15+)	23	75	37	78
Women in the labor force (% of total labor force)	24		32	
Employment to population ratio (% ages 15+)	18	61	32	69
Vulnerable employment (% of employed ages 15+)	..	..	49	32
Employment in agriculture (% of employed ages 15+)	..	..	11	23
Employment in industry (% of employed ages 15+)	..	..	25	24
Employment in service (% of employed ages 15+)	..	..	64	53
Wage and salaried workers (% of employed ages 15+)	..	..	50	62
Self-employed workers (% of employed ages 15+)	..	..	37	31
Unpaid family workers (% of employed ages 15+)	..	..	14	7
Women in nonagricultural wage employment (%)	..		17	
Children in employment (% of children ages 7-14)	..	..	..	..
Unemployment (% of labor force ages 15+)	17	22	18	18
Long-term unemployment (% of total unemployment)	..	..	..	..
Youth unemployment (% of labor force ages 15-24)	..	..	46	43
Maternity leave (weeks)	14		14	
Maternal leave benefits (% of wages paid)	100		100	
Women's political participation				
Seats held by women in national parliament (%)	2		8	
Women in managerial positions (%)	..		..	

American Samoa

East Asia & Pacific   **Upper middle income**

Population (thousands)	65	Population living on less	
GNI ($ billions)	..	than $1.25 a cay (%)	..
GNI per capita ($)	..		

	1990		2007	
	Female	Male	Female	Male
Demography				
Sex ratio at birth (females per 1,000 males)	..		..	
Life expectancy at birth (years)	..	..	..	..
Child mortality rate (per 1,000)	..	..	..	..
Female-headed households (%)	..		..	
Education				
Gross primary enrollment (% of relevant age group)	..	..	..	..
Gross secondary enrollment (% of relevant age group)	..	..	..	..
Gross tertiary enrollment (% of relevant age group)	..	..	..	..
Primary completion rate (% of relevant age group)	..	..	..	..
Adult literacy rate (% of population ages 15+)	..	..	..	..
Family planning and maternal health				
Total fertility rate (births per woman)	..		..	
Adolescent fertility (births per 1,000 women ages 15–19)	..		..	
Women married by age 18 (% of women ages 20–24)	..		..	
Contraceptive prevalence (% of women ages 15–49)	..		..	
Unmet need for contraception (% of women ages 15–49)	..		..	
Pregnant women receiving prenatal care (%)	..		..	
Births attended by skilled health staff (% of total)	..		..	
Maternal mortality ratio (per 100,000 live births)	..		..	
Labor force and employment dynamics				
Labor force participation (% of population ages 15+)	..	..	..	..
Women in the labor force (% of total labor force)	..		..	
Employment to population ratio (% ages 15+)	..	..	..	..
Vulnerable employment (% of employed ages 15+)	0	0	..	..
Employment in agriculture (% of employed ages 15+)	..	..	..	..
Employment in industry (% of employed ages 15+)	..	..	..	..
Employment in service (% of employed ages 15+)	..	..	..	..
Wage and salaried workers (% of employed ages 15+)	99	97	..	..
Self-employed workers (% of employed ages 15+)	1	3	..	..
Unpaid family workers (% of employed ages 15+)	0	0	..	..
Women in nonagricultural wage employment (%)	41		..	
Children in employment (% of children ages 7–14)	..	..	..	..
Unemployment (% of labor force ages 15+)	5	5	..	..
Long-term unemployment (% of total unemployment)	..	..	..	..
Youth unemployment (% of labor force ages 15–24)	..	..	..	..
Maternity leave (weeks)	..		..	
Maternal leave benefits (% of wages paid)	..		..	
Women's political participation				
Seats held by women in national parliament (%)	..		..	
Women in managerial positions (%)	..		..	

Andorra

Population (thousands)	82	Population living on less	
GNI ($ billions)	..	than $1.25 a day (%)	..
GNI per capita ($)	..		

	1990		2007	
	Female	Male	Female	Male
Demography				
Sex ratio at birth (females per 1,000 males)	..		..	
Life expectancy at birth (years)	..	..	..	..
Child mortality rate (per 1,000)	..	..	..	..
Female-headed households (%)	..		..	
Education				
Gross primary enrollment (% of relevant age group)	..	..	87	89
Gross secondary enrollment (% of relevant age group)	..	..	86	79
Gross tertiary enrollment (% of relevant age group)	..	..	11	9
Primary completion rate (% of relevant age group)	..	..	101	104
Adult literacy rate (% of population ages 15+)	..	..	..	..
Family planning and maternal health				
Total fertility rate (births per woman)	..		..	
Adolescent fertility (births per 1,000 women ages 15–19)	..		..	
Women married by age 18 (% of women ages 20–24)	..		..	
Contraceptive prevalence (% of women ages 15–49)	..		..	
Unmet need for contraception (% of women ages 15–49)	..		..	
Pregnant women receiving prenatal care (%)	..		..	
Births attended by skilled health staff (% of total)	..		..	
Maternal mortality ratio (per 100,000 live births)	..		..	
Labor force and employment dynamics				
Labor force participation (% of population ages 15+)	..	..	..	..
Women in the labor force (% of total labor force)	..		..	
Employment to population ratio (% ages 15+)	..	..	..	..
Vulnerable employment (% of employed ages 15+)	..	..	..	..
Employment in agriculture (% of employed ages 15+)	..	..	..	..
Employment in industry (% of employed ages 15+)	..	..	..	..
Employment in service (% of employed ages 15+)	..	..	..	..
Wage and salaried workers (% of employed ages 15+)	..	..	..	..
Self-employed workers (% of employed ages 15+)	..	..	..	..
Unpaid family workers (% of employed ages 15+)	..	..	..	..
Women in nonagricultural wage employment (%)	..		46	
Children in employment (% of children ages 7–14)	..	..	..	..
Unemployment (% of labor force ages 15+)	..	..	..	..
Long-term unemployment (% of total unemployment)	..	..	..	..
Youth unemployment (% of labor force ages 15–24)	..	..	..	..
Maternity leave (weeks)	..		..	
Maternal leave benefits (% of wages paid)	..		..	
Women's political participation				
Seats held by women in national parliament (%)	..		29	
Women in managerial positions (%)	..		..	

Angola

Sub-Saharan Africa		Lower middle income

Population (millions)	17	Population living on less	
GNI ($ billions)	43.0	than $1.25 a day (%)	54.3
GNI per capita ($)	2,540		

	1990		2007	
	Female	Male	Female	Male
Demography				
Sex ratio at birth (females per 1,000 males)	971		971	
Life expectancy at birth (years)	42	39	44	41
Child mortality rate (per 1,000)	..	..	..	..
Female-headed households (%)	..		..	
Education				
Gross primary enrollment (% of relevant age group)	82	90	191	207
Gross secondary enrollment (% of relevant age group)	..	..	..	..
Gross tertiary enrollment (% of relevant age group)	..	..	..	..
Primary completion rate (% of relevant age group)	..	..	..	..
Adult literacy rate (% of population ages 15+)	..	..	..	..
Family planning and maternal health				
Total fertility rate (births per woman)	7.1		5.8	
Adolescent fertility (births per 1,000 women ages 15–19)	..		138	
Women married by age 18 (% of women ages 20–24)	..		..	
Contraceptive prevalence (% of women ages 15–49)	..		..	
Unmet need for contraception (% of women ages 15–49)	..		..	
Pregnant women receiving prenatal care (%)	..		80	
Births attended by skilled health staff (% of total)	..		47	
Maternal mortality ratio (per 100,000 live births)	..		*1,400*	
Labor force and employment dynamics				
Labor force participation (% of population ages 15+)	74	90	75	89
Women in the labor force (% of total labor force)	46		47	
Employment to population ratio (% ages 15+)	69	83	69	82
Vulnerable employment (% of employed ages 15+)	..	..	..	..
Employment in agriculture (% of employed ages 15+)	..	..	..	..
Employment in industry (% of employed ages 15+)	..	..	..	..
Employment in service (% of employed ages 15+)	..	..	..	..
Wage and salaried workers (% of employed ages 15+)	..	..	..	..
Self-employed workers (% of employed ages 15+)	..	..	..	..
Unpaid family workers (% of employed ages 15+)	..	..	..	..
Women in nonagricultural wage employment (%)	..		..	
Children in employment (% of children ages 7–14)	..	..	..	..
Unemployment (% of labor force ages 15+)	..	..	..	..
Long-term unemployment (% of total unemployment)	..	..	..	..
Youth unemployment (% of labor force ages 15–24)	..	..	..	..
Maternity leave (weeks)	12		*12*	
Maternal leave benefits (% of wages paid)	100		*100*	
Women's political participation				
Seats held by women in national parliament (%)	15		15	
Women in managerial positions (%)	..		..	

Antigua and Barbuda

Population (thousands)	85	Population living on less	
GNI ($ billions)	1.0	than $1.25 a day (%)	..
GNI per capita ($)	11,650		

	1990		2007	
	Female	**Male**	**Female**	**Male**
Demography				
Sex ratio at birth (females per 1,000 males)	..		..	
Life expectancy at birth (years)	76	71	..	..
Child mortality rate (per 1,000)	..	..	..	..
Female-headed households (%)	..		..	
Education				
Gross primary enrollment (% of relevant age group)	..	..	99	106
Gross secondary enrollment (% of relevant age group)	..	..	103	107
Gross tertiary enrollment (% of relevant age group)	..	..	..	..
Primary completion rate (% of relevant age group)	..	..	98	97
Adult literacy rate (% of population ages 15+)	..	..	..	..
Family planning and maternal health				
Total fertility rate (births per woman)	1.7		..	
Adolescent fertility (births per 1,000 women ages 15–19)	..		..	
Women married by age 18 (% of women ages 20–24)	..		..	
Contraceptive prevalence (% of women ages 15–49)	53		..	
Unmet need for contraception (% of women ages 15–49)	..		..	
Pregnant women receiving prenatal care (%)	..		100	
Births attended by skilled health staff (% of total)	..		100	
Maternal mortality ratio (per 100,000 live births)	..		..	
Labor force and employment dynamics				
Labor force participation (% of population ages 15+)	..	..	..	..
Women in the labor force (% of total labor force)	..		..	
Employment to population ratio (% ages 15+)	..	..	..	..
Vulnerable employment (% of employed ages 15+)	14	15	..	..
Employment in agriculture (% of employed ages 15+)	3	5	..	..
Employment in industry (% of employed ages 15+)	7	29	..	..
Employment in service (% of employed ages 15+)	87	63	..	..
Wage and salaried workers (% of employed ages 15+)	83	78	..	..
Self-employed workers (% of employed ages 15+)	15	20	..	..
Unpaid family workers (% of employed ages 15+)	1	1	..	..
Women in nonagricultural wage employment (%)	..		..	
Children in employment (% of children ages 7–14)	..	..	..	..
Unemployment (% of labor force ages 15+)	..	..	..	..
Long-term unemployment (% of total unemployment)	..	..	..	..
Youth unemployment (% of labor force ages 15–24)	..	..	..	..
Maternity leave (weeks)	..		13	
Maternal leave benefits (% of wages paid)	..		60	
Women's political participation				
Seats held by women in national parliament (%)	0		11	
Women in managerial positions (%)	..		..	

Argentina

Latin America & Caribbean   **Upper middle income**

Population (millions)	40	Population living on less	
GNI ($ billions)	238.7	than $1.25 a day (%)	4.5
GNI per capita ($)	6,040		

	1990		2007	
	Female	**Male**	**Female**	**Male**
Demography				
Sex ratio at birth (females per 1,000 males)	962		962	
Life expectancy at birth (years)	75	68	79	72
Child mortality rate (per 1,000)	..	..	..	..
Female-headed households (%)	..		..	
Education				
Gross primary enrollment (% of relevant age group)	108	104	112	113
Gross secondary enrollment (% of relevant age group)	..	..	89	80
Gross tertiary enrollment (% of relevant age group)	..	..	76	52
Primary completion rate (% of relevant age group)	..	..	99	95
Adult literacy rate (% of population ages 15+)	96	96	98	98
Family planning and maternal health				
Total fertility rate (births per woman)	3.0		2.3	
Adolescent fertility (births per 1,000 women ages 15–19)	..		57	
Women married by age 18 (% of women ages 20–24)	..		..	
Contraceptive prevalence (% of women ages 15–49)	..		..	
Unmet need for contraception (% of women ages 15–49)	..		..	
Pregnant women receiving prenatal care (%)	95		99	
Births attended by skilled health staff (% of total)	96		99	
Maternal mortality ratio (per 100,000 live births)	..		77	
Labor force and employment dynamics				
Labor force participation (% of population ages 15+)	29	79	50	76
Women in the labor force (% of total labor force)	28		41	
Employment to population ratio (% ages 15+)	37	72	46	72
Vulnerable employment (% of employed ages 15+)	..	..	17	22
Employment in agriculture (% of employed ages 15+)	0	1	1	2
Employment in industry (% of employed ages 15+)	18	39	11	33
Employment in service (% of employed ages 15+)	82	60	88	66
Wage and salaried workers (% of employed ages 15+)	70	68	80	73
Self-employed workers (% of employed ages 15+)	27	31	18	27
Unpaid family workers (% of employed ages 15+)	..	..	2	1
Women in nonagricultural wage employment (%)	37		45	
Children in employment (% of children ages 7–14)	..	..	12	18
Unemployment (% of labor force ages 15+)	7	7	12	8
Long-term unemployment (% of total unemployment)	..	..	..	..
Youth unemployment (% of labor force ages 15–24)	16	12	28	22
Maternity leave (weeks)	13		13	
Maternal leave benefits (% of wages paid)	60		100	
Women's political participation				
Seats held by women in national parliament (%)	6		35	
Women in managerial positions (%)	..		25	

Armenia

Europe & Central Asia		Lower middle income

Population (millions)	3.0	Population living on less
GNI ($ billions)	7.9	than $1.25 a day (%) 10.6
GNI per capita ($)	2,630	

	1990		2007	
	Female	Male	Female	Male
Demography				
Sex ratio at birth (females per 1,000 males)	931		847	
Life expectancy at birth (years)	72	66	75	68
Child mortality rate (per 1,000)	..	..	3	8
Female-headed households (%)	..		36	
Education				
Gross primary enrollment (% of relevant age group)	..	..	111	108
Gross secondary enrollment (% of relevant age group)	..	..	92	87
Gross tertiary enrollment (% of relevant age group)	..	..	37	31
Primary completion rate (% of relevant age group)	..	..	100	96
Adult literacy rate (% of population ages 15+)	98	99	99	100
Family planning and maternal health				
Total fertility rate (births per woman)	2.5		1.7	
Adolescent fertility (births per 1,000 women ages 15-19)	..		30	
Women married by age 18 (% of women ages 20-24)	..		..	
Contraceptive prevalence (% of women ages 15-49)	..		53	
Unmet need for contraception (% of women ages 15-49)	..		13	
Pregnant women receiving prenatal care (%)	..		93	
Births attended by skilled health staff (% of total)	..		98	
Maternal mortality ratio (per 100,000 live births)	..		76	
Labor force and employment dynamics				
Labor force participation (% of population ages 15+)	66	79	56	68
Women in the labor force (% of total labor force)	48		50	
Employment to population ratio (% ages 15+)	32	47	34	47
Vulnerable employment (% of employed ages 15+)	..	..	..	..
Employment in agriculture (% of employed ages 15+)	..	..	..	..
Employment in industry (% of employed ages 15+)	..	..	..	..
Employment in service (% of employed ages 15+)	..	..	..	..
Wage and salaried workers (% of employed ages 15+)	..	..	..	..
Self-employed workers (% of employed ages 15+)	..	..	..	..
Unpaid family workers (% of employed ages 15+)	..	..	..	..
Women in nonagricultural wage employment (%)	..		46	
Children in employment (% of children ages 7-14)	..	..	..	..
Unemployment (% of labor force ages 15+)	..	..	14	6
Long-term unemployment (% of total unemployment)	..	..	..	..
Youth unemployment (% of labor force ages 15-24)	..	..	..	..
Maternity leave (weeks)	..		..	
Maternal leave benefits (% of wages paid)	..		..	
Women's political participation				
Seats held by women in national parliament (%)	36		9	
Women in managerial positions (%)	..		..	

Aruba

Population (thousands)	101	Population living on less		
GNI ($ billions)	..	than $1.25 a day (%)		..
GNI per capita ($)	..			

	1990		2007	
	Female	Male	Female	Male
Demography				
Sex ratio at birth (females per 1,000 males)	952		952	
Life expectancy at birth (years)	..	..	..	..
Child mortality rate (per 1,000)	..	..	..	..
Female-headed households (%)	..		..	
Education				
Gross primary enrollment (% of relevant age group)	..	..	112	115
Gross secondary enrollment (% of relevant age group)	..	..	108	102
Gross tertiary enrollment (% of relevant age group)	..	..	39	27
Primary completion rate (% of relevant age group)	..	..	101	96
Adult literacy rate (% of population ages 15+)	..	..	98	98
Family planning and maternal health				
Total fertility rate (births per woman)	..		..	
Adolescent fertility (births per 1,000 women ages 15–19)	..		22	
Women married by age 18 (% of women ages 20–24)	..		..	
Contraceptive prevalence (% of women ages 15–49)	..		..	
Unmet need for contraception (% of women ages 15–49)	..		..	
Pregnant women receiving prenatal care (%)	..		..	
Births attended by skilled health staff (% of total)	..		..	
Maternal mortality ratio (per 100,000 live births)	..		..	
Labor force and employment dynamics				
Labor force participation (% of population ages 15+)	..	..	..	..
Women in the labor force (% of total labor force)	..		..	
Employment to population ratio (% ages 15+)	..	..	..	..
Vulnerable employment (% of employed ages 15+)	2	5	..	..
Employment in agriculture (% of employed ages 15+)	..	..	..	..
Employment in industry (% of employed ages 15+)	..	..	..	..
Employment in service (% of employed ages 15+)	..	..	..	..
Wage and salaried workers (% of employed ages 15+)	95	90	..	..
Self-employed workers (% of employed ages 15+)	4	10	..	..
Unpaid family workers (% of employed ages 15+)	1	0	..	..
Women in nonagricultural wage employment (%)	..		..	
Children in employment (% of children ages 7–14)	..	..	..	..
Unemployment (% of labor force ages 15+)	6	6	..	..
Long-term unemployment (% of total unemployment)	..	..	..	..
Youth unemployment (% of labor force ages 15–24)	..	..	..	..
Maternity leave (weeks)	..		..	
Maternal leave benefits (% of wages paid)	..		..	
Women's political participation				
Seats held by women in national parliament (%)	..		..	
Women in managerial positions (%)	..		..	

Australia

Population (millions)	21	Population living on less
GNI ($ billions)	751.5	than $1.25 a day (%) ..
GNI per capita ($)	35,760	

	1990		2007	
	Female	**Male**	**Female**	**Male**
Demography				
Sex ratio at birth (females per 1,000 males)	950		950	
Life expectancy at birth (years)	80	74	84	79
Child mortality rate (per 1,000)	..	..	..	..
Female-headed households (%)	..		..	
Education				
Gross primary enrollment (% of relevant age group)	107	108	105	105
Gross secondary enrollment (% of relevant age group)	83	80	146	154
Gross tertiary enrollment (% of relevant age group)	..	..	82	64
Primary completion rate (% of relevant age group)	..	..	..	..
Adult literacy rate (% of population ages 15+)	..	..	..	..
Family planning and maternal health				
Total fertility rate (births per woman)	1.9		1.9	
Adolescent fertility (births per 1,000 women ages 15–19)	..		14	
Women married by age 18 (% of women ages 20–24)	..		..	
Contraceptive prevalence (% of women ages 15–49)	..		..	
Unmet need for contraception (% of women ages 15–49)	..		..	
Pregnant women receiving prenatal care (%)	100		..	
Births attended by skilled health staff (% of total)	100		100	
Maternal mortality ratio (per 100,000 live births)	..		4	
Labor force and employment dynamics				
Labor force participation (% of population ages 15+)	52	76	57	72
Women in the labor force (% of total labor force)	41		45	
Employment to population ratio (% ages 15+)	47	67	55	69
Vulnerable employment (% of employed ages 15+)	9	12	7	11
Employment in agriculture (% of employed ages 15+)	4	7	3	5
Employment in industry (% of employed ages 15+)	13	34	9	31
Employment in service (% of employed ages 15+)	83	59	88	65
Wage and salaried workers (% of employed ages 15+)	88	83	91	86
Self-employed workers (% of employed ages 15+)	11	17	9	14
Unpaid family workers (% of employed ages 15+)	1	1	0	0
Women in nonagricultural wage employment (%)	45		49	
Children in employment (% of children ages 7–14)	..	..	..	..
Unemployment (% of labor force ages 15+)	7	7	5	4
Long-term unemployment (% of total unemployment)	17	24	14	17
Youth unemployment (% of labor force ages 15–24)	13	13	11	11
Maternity leave (weeks)	12		52	
Maternal leave benefits (% of wages paid)	..		0	
Women's political participation				
Seats held by women in national parliament (%)	6		25	
Women in managerial positions (%)	..		36	

Austria

Population (millions)	8.3	Population living on less	
GNI ($ billions)	348.9	than $1.25 a day (%)	..
GNI per capita ($)	41,960		

	1990		2007	
	Female	Male	Female	Male
Demography				
Sex ratio at birth (females per 1,000 males)	948		948	
Life expectancy at birth (years)	79	72	83	77
Child mortality rate (per 1,000)	..	..	..	..
Female-headed households (%)	..		..	
Education				
Gross primary enrollment (% of relevant age group)	101	101	101	102
Gross secondary enrollment (% of relevant age group)	97	105	100	104
Gross tertiary enrollment (% of relevant age group)	..	..	55	45
Primary completion rate (% of relevant age group)	..	..	102	103
Adult literacy rate (% of population ages 15+)	..	..	..	..
Family planning and maternal health				
Total fertility rate (births per woman)	1.5		1.4	
Adolescent fertility (births per 1,000 women ages 15–19)	..		12	
Women married by age 18 (% of women ages 20–24)	..		..	
Contraceptive prevalence (% of women ages 15–49)	..		..	
Unmet need for contraception (% of women ages 15–49)	..		..	
Pregnant women receiving prenatal care (%)	100		..	
Births attended by skilled health staff (% of total)	100		..	
Maternal mortality ratio (per 100,000 live births)	..		4	
Labor force and employment dynamics				
Labor force participation (% of population ages 15+)	43	70	52	68
Women in the labor force (% of total labor force)	41		45	
Employment to population ratio (% ages 15+)	42	68	50	65
Vulnerable employment (% of employed ages 15+)	..	..	9	9
Employment in agriculture (% of employed ages 15+)	9	7	6	6
Employment in industry (% of employed ages 15+)	20	49	13	40
Employment in service (% of employed ages 15+)	70	44	81	55
Wage and salaried workers (% of employed ages 15+)	..	..	88	84
Self-employed workers (% of employed ages 15+)	..	..	9	14
Unpaid family workers (% of employed ages 15+)	..	..	3	2
Women in nonagricultural wage employment (%)	41		47	
Children in employment (% of children ages 7–14)	..	..	..	..
Unemployment (% of labor force ages 15+)	4	3	5	4
Long-term unemployment (% of total unemployment)	..	..	27	27
Youth unemployment (% of labor force ages 15–24)	4	4	10	11
Maternity leave (weeks)	16		16	
Maternal leave benefits (% of wages paid)	100		100	
Women's political participation				
Seats held by women in national parliament (%)	12		32	
Women in managerial positions (%)	..		27	

Azerbaijan

Europe & Central Asia		Lower middle income

Population (millions)	8.6	Population living on less	
GNI ($ billions)	22.6	than $1.25 a day (%)	2.0
GNI per capita ($)	2,640		

	1990		2007	
	Female	Male	Female	Male
Demography				
Sex ratio at birth (females per 1,000 males)	939		855	
Life expectancy at birth (years)	70	62	71	64
Child mortality rate (per 1,000)	..	..	5	9
Female-headed households (%)	..		25	
Education				
Gross primary enrollment (% of relevant age group)	110	111	94	96
Gross secondary enrollment (% of relevant age group)	89	88	..	..
Gross tertiary enrollment (% of relevant age group)	..	..	..	..
Primary completion rate (% of relevant age group)	..	..	..	..
Adult literacy rate (% of population ages 15+)	..	..	99	100
Family planning and maternal health				
Total fertility rate (births per woman)	2.7		2.0	
Adolescent fertility (births per 1,000 women ages 15–19)	..		29	
Women married by age 18 (% of women ages 20–24)	..		..	
Contraceptive prevalence (% of women ages 15–49)	..		51	
Unmet need for contraception (% of women ages 15–49)	..		23	
Pregnant women receiving prenatal care (%)	..		77	
Births attended by skilled health staff (% of total)	..		89	
Maternal mortality ratio (per 100,000 live births)	..		82	
Labor force and employment dynamics				
Labor force participation (% of population ages 15+)	66	78	60	71
Women in the labor force (% of total labor force)	48		48	
Employment to population ratio (% ages 15+)	51	63	56	66
Vulnerable employment (% of employed ages 15+)	..	..	66	41
Employment in agriculture (% of employed ages 15+)	..	..	37	41
Employment in industry (% of employed ages 15+)	..	..	9	15
Employment in service (% of employed ages 15+)	..	..	54	44
Wage and salaried workers (% of employed ages 15+)	..	..	33	51
Self-employed workers (% of employed ages 15+)	..	..	67	49
Unpaid family workers (% of employed ages 15+)	..	..	0	0
Women in nonagricultural wage employment (%)	..		50	
Children in employment (% of children ages 7–14)	..	..	..	..
Unemployment (% of labor force ages 15+)	..	..	..	..
Long-term unemployment (% of total unemployment)	..	..	..	..
Youth unemployment (% of labor force ages 15–24)	..	..	..	..
Maternity leave (weeks)	..		18	
Maternal leave benefits (% of wages paid)	..		100	
Women's political participation				
Seats held by women in national parliament (%)	..		11	
Women in managerial positions (%)	..		..	

Bahamas, The

High income

Population (thousands)	331
GNI ($ billions)	5.4
GNI per capita ($)	17,160

Population living on less than $1.25 a day (%)	..

	1990		2007	
	Female	Male	Female	Male
Demography				
Sex ratio at birth (females per 1,000 males)	958		958	
Life expectancy at birth (years)	73	66	76	71
Child mortality rate (per 1,000)	..	..	..	..
Female-headed households (%)	..		..	
Education				
Gross primary enrollment (% of relevant age group)	97	94	103	103
Gross secondary enrollment (% of relevant age group)	94	92	96	92
Gross tertiary enrollment (% of relevant age group)	..	..	..	..
Primary completion rate (% of relevant age group)	..	..	96	98
Adult literacy rate (% of population ages 15+)	..	..	..	..
Family planning and maternal health				
Total fertility rate (births per woman)	2.6		2.0	
Adolescent fertility (births per 1,000 women ages 15–19)	..		53	
Women married by age 18 (% of women ages 20–24)	..		..	
Contraceptive prevalence (% of women ages 15–49)	62		..	
Unmet need for contraception (% of women ages 15–49)	..		..	
Pregnant women receiving prenatal care (%)	..		98	
Births attended by skilled health staff (% of total)	99		99	
Maternal mortality ratio (per 100,000 live births)	..		16	
Labor force and employment dynamics				
Labor force participation (% of population ages 15+)	64	79	67	78
Women in the labor force (% of total labor force)	46		48	
Employment to population ratio (% ages 15+)	57	70	61	73
Vulnerable employment (% of employed ages 15+)	..	..	..	..
Employment in agriculture (% of employed ages 15+)	2	9	0	6
Employment in industry (% of employed ages 15+)	5	24	5	30
Employment in service (% of employed ages 15+)	93	67	94	64
Wage and salaried workers (% of employed ages 15+)	89	82	87	82
Self-employed workers (% of employed ages 15+)	9	16	12	18
Unpaid family workers (% of employed ages 15+)	1	0	1	0
Women in nonagricultural wage employment (%)	50		50	
Children in employment (% of children ages 7–14)	..	..	..	..
Unemployment (% of labor force ages 15+)	12	12	9	7
Long-term unemployment (% of total unemployment)	40	23	..	..
Youth unemployment (% of labor force ages 15–24)	25	21	24	17
Maternity leave (weeks)	8		13	
Maternal leave benefits (% of wages paid)	100		60	
Women's political participation				
Seats held by women in national parliament (%)	4		12	
Women in managerial positions (%)	..		40	

Bahrain

High income

Population (thousands)	753	Population living on less	
GNI ($ billions)	12.6	than $1.25 a day (%)	..
GNI per capita ($)	17,390		

	1990		2007	
	Female	Male	Female	Male
Demography				
Sex ratio at birth (females per 1,000 males)	952		952	
Life expectancy at birth (years)	74	70	77	74
Child mortality rate (per 1,000)	..	..	..	..
Female-headed households (%)	..		..	
Education				
Gross primary enrollment (% of relevant age group)	110	107	119	120
Gross secondary enrollment (% of relevant age group)	98	95	104	100
Gross tertiary enrollment (% of relevant age group)	..	..	47	19
Primary completion rate (% of relevant age group)	98	96	117	117
Adult literacy rate (% of population ages 15+)	77	89	86	90
Family planning and maternal health				
Total fertility rate (births per woman)	3.6		2.3	
Adolescent fertility (births per 1,000 women ages 15–19)	..		17	
Women married by age 18 (% of women ages 20–24)	..		..	
Contraceptive prevalence (% of women ages 15–49)	53		..	
Unmet need for contraception (% of women ages 15–49)	..		..	
Pregnant women receiving prenatal care (%)	..		..	
Births attended by skilled health staff (% of total)	94		99	
Maternal mortality ratio (per 100,000 live births)	..		32	
Labor force and employment dynamics				
Labor force participation (% of population ages 15+)	28	88	34	84
Women in the labor force (% of total labor force)	17		21	
Employment to population ratio (% ages 15+)	26	84	30	81
Vulnerable employment (% of employed ages 15+)	..	..	..	..
Employment in agriculture (% of employed ages 15+)	0	3	..	..
Employment in industry (% of employed ages 15+)	7	33	..	..
Employment in service (% of employed ages 15+)	92	64	..	..
Wage and salaried workers (% of employed ages 15+)	..	..	..	..
Self-employed workers (% of employed ages 15+)	..	..	..	..
Unpaid family workers (% of employed ages 15+)	..	..	..	..
Women in nonagricultural wage employment (%)	8		10	
Children in employment (% of children ages 7–14)	..	..	..	..
Unemployment (% of labor force ages 15+)	12	5	..	..
Long-term unemployment (% of total unemployment)	..	..	..	..
Youth unemployment (% of labor force ages 15–24)	..	..	..	..
Maternity leave (weeks)	6		6	
Maternal leave benefits (% of wages paid)	100		100	
Women's political participation				
Seats held by women in national parliament (%)	..		3	
Women in managerial positions (%)	..		..	

Bangladesh

South Asia   **Low income**

Population (millions)	159	Population living on less	
GNI ($ billions)	74.9	than $1.25 a day (%)	49.6
GNI per capita ($)	470		

	1990		2007	
	Female	Male	Female	Male
Demography				
Sex ratio at birth (females per 1,000 males)	955		955	
Life expectancy at birth (years)	55	54	65	63
Child mortality rate (per 1,000)	..	..	29	24
Female-headed households (%)	..		10	
Education				
Gross primary enrollment (% of relevant age group)	73	85	105	101
Gross secondary enrollment (% of relevant age group)	14	26	45	43
Gross tertiary enrollment (% of relevant age group)	..	..	5	9
Primary completion rate (% of relevant age group)	..	..	74	70
Adult literacy rate (% of population ages 15+)	26	44	48	59
Family planning and maternal health				
Total fertility rate (births per woman)	4.3		2.8	
Adolescent fertility (births per 1,000 women ages 15–19)	..		124	
Women married by age 18 (% of women ages 20–24)	..		69	
Contraceptive prevalence (% of women ages 15–49)	40		56	
Unmet need for contraception (% of women ages 15–49)	..		11	
Pregnant women receiving prenatal care (%)	..		51	
Births attended by skilled health staff (% of total)	..		18	
Maternal mortality ratio (per 100,000 live births)	..		570	
Labor force and employment dynamics				
Labor force participation (% of population ages 15+)	62	89	57	85
Women in the labor force (% of total labor force)	40		39	
Employment to population ratio (% ages 15+)	61	87	54	82
Vulnerable employment (% of employed ages 15+)	..	..	87	85
Employment in agriculture (% of employed ages 15+)	85	54	59	50
Employment in industry (% of employed ages 15+)	9	16	18	12
Employment in service (% of employed ages 15+)	2	25	23	38
Wage and salaried workers (% of employed ages 15+)	..	..	12	15
Self-employed workers (% of employed ages 15+)	..	..	27	75
Unpaid family workers (% of employed ages 15+)	..	..	60	10
Women in nonagricultural wage employment (%)	18		..	
Children in employment (% of children ages 7–14)	..	..	6	26
Unemployment (% of labor force ages 15+)	..	..	7	3
Long-term unemployment (% of total unemployment)	..	..	..	..
Youth unemployment (% of labor force ages 15–24)	2	3	6	7
Maternity leave (weeks)	12		12	
Maternal leave benefits (% of wages paid)	100		100	
Women's political participation				
Seats held by women in national parliament (%)	10		15	
Women in managerial positions (%)	..		..	

Barbados

Population (thousands)	294	Population living on less
GNI ($ billions)	..	than $1.25 a day (%) ..
GNI per capita ($)	..	

	1990		2007	
	Female	Male	Female	Male
Demography				
Sex ratio at birth (females per 1,000 males)	965		965	
Life expectancy at birth (years)	77	72	80	74
Child mortality rate (per 1,000)	..	..	..	..
Female-headed households (%)	..		..	
Education				
Gross primary enrollment (% of relevant age group)	94	95	105	105
Gross secondary enrollment (% of relevant age group)	78	87	105	102
Gross tertiary enrollment (% of relevant age group)	..	..	73	34
Primary completion rate (% of relevant age group)	..	..	95	94
Adult literacy rate (% of population ages 15+)	..	..	..	..
Family planning and maternal health				
Total fertility rate (births per woman)	1.7		1.5	
Adolescent fertility (births per 1,000 women ages 15–19)	..		42	
Women married by age 18 (% of women ages 20–24)	..		..	
Contraceptive prevalence (% of women ages 15–49)	55		..	
Unmet need for contraception (% of women ages 15–49)	..		..	
Pregnant women receiving prenatal care (%)	100		100	
Births attended by skilled health staff (% of total)	..		100	
Maternal mortality ratio (per 100,000 live births)	..		16	
Labor force and employment dynamics				
Labor force participation (% of population ages 15+)	62	78	67	79
Women in the labor force (% of total labor force)	47		48	
Employment to population ratio (% ages 15+)	49	66	60	74
Vulnerable employment (% of employed ages 15+)	9	14	10	18
Employment in agriculture (% of employed ages 15+)	6	7	3	4
Employment in industry (% of employed ages 15+)	14	29	8	26
Employment in service (% of employed ages 15+)	70	56	78	62
Wage and salaried workers (% of employed ages 15+)	91	85	90	80
Self-employed workers (% of employed ages 15+)	9	14	10	20
Unpaid family workers (% of employed ages 15+)	1	1	0	0
Women in nonagricultural wage employment (%)	46		49	
Children in employment (% of children ages 7–14)	..	..	..	..
Unemployment (% of labor force ages 15+)	20	10	11	9
Long-term unemployment (% of total unemployment)	61	55	..	..
Youth unemployment (% of labor force ages 15–24)	41	22	29	24
Maternity leave (weeks)	12		12	
Maternal leave benefits (% of wages paid)	100		100	
Women's political participation				
Seats held by women in national parliament (%)	4		13	
Women in managerial positions (%)	..		45	

Belarus

Europe & Central Asia		Upper middle income

Population (millions)	9.7	Population living on less	
GNI ($ billions)	40.9	than $1.25 a day (%)	2.0
GNI per capita ($)	4,220		

	1990		2007	
	Female	Male	Female	Male
Demography				
Sex ratio at birth (females per 1,000 males)	939		939	
Life expectancy at birth (years)	76	66	76	65
Child mortality rate (per 1,000)	..	..	..	..
Female-headed households (%)		..	54	
Education				
Gross primary enrollment (% of relevant age group)	93	97	96	98
Gross secondary enrollment (% of relevant age group)	..	..	96	94
Gross tertiary enrollment (% of relevant age group)	..	..	80	57
Primary completion rate (% of relevant age group)	..	..	92	93
Adult literacy rate (% of population ages 15+)	97	99	100	100
Family planning and maternal health				
Total fertility rate (births per woman)	1.9		1.3	
Adolescent fertility (births per 1,000 women ages 15–19)	..		22	
Women married by age 18 (% of women ages 20–24)	..		..	
Contraceptive prevalence (% of women ages 15–49)	..		73	
Unmet need for contraception (% of women ages 15–49)	..		..	
Pregnant women receiving prenatal care (%)	..		99	
Births attended by skilled health staff (% of total)	..		100	
Maternal mortality ratio (per 100,000 live births)	..		18	
Labor force and employment dynamics				
Labor force participation (% of population ages 15+)	60	75	53	66
Women in the labor force (% of total labor force)	49		49	
Employment to population ratio (% ages 15+)	53	66	49	59
Vulnerable employment (% of employed ages 15+)	..	..	..	..
Employment in agriculture (% of employed ages 15+)	..	..	..	..
Employment in industry (% of employed ages 15+)	..	..	..	..
Employment in service (% of employed ages 15+)	..	..	..	..
Wage and salaried workers (% of employed ages 15+)	..	..	..	..
Self-employed workers (% of employed ages 15+)	..	..	..	..
Unpaid family workers (% of employed ages 15+)	..	..	..	..
Women in nonagricultural wage employment (%)	55		..	
Children in employment (% of children ages 7–14)	..	..	12	11
Unemployment (% of labor force ages 15+)	..	..	..	..
Long-term unemployment (% of total unemployment)	..	..	..	..
Youth unemployment (% of labor force ages 15–24)	..	..	..	..
Maternity leave (weeks)	..		18	
Maternal leave benefits (% of wages paid)	..		100	
Women's political participation				
Seats held by women in national parliament (%)	..		29	
Women in managerial positions (%)	..		..	

Belgium

Population (millions)	11	Population living on less
GNI ($ billions)	436.9	than $1.25 a day (%) ..
GNI per capita ($)	41,110	

	1990		2007	
	Female	Male	Female	Male
Demography				
Sex ratio at birth (females per 1,000 males)	949		952	
Life expectancy at birth (years)	79	73	83	77
Child mortality rate (per 1,000)	..	..	..	..
Female-headed households (%)	..		..	
Education				
Gross primary enrollment (% of relevant age group)	101	100	102	102
Gross secondary enrollment (% of relevant age group)	102	101	108	111
Gross tertiary enrollment (% of relevant age group)	..	..	70	56
Primary completion rate (% of relevant age group)	82	76	88	86
Adult literacy rate (% of population ages 15+)	..	..	..	..
Family planning and maternal health				
Total fertility rate (births per woman)	1.6		1.8	
Adolescent fertility (births per 1,000 women ages 15–19)	..		7	
Women married by age 18 (% of women ages 20–24)	..		..	
Contraceptive prevalence (% of women ages 15–49)	78		..	
Unmet need for contraception (% of women ages 15–49)	..		..	
Pregnant women receiving prenatal care (%)	..		..	
Births attended by skilled health staff (% of total)	100		..	
Maternal mortality ratio (per 100,000 live births)	..		8	
Labor force and employment dynamics				
Labor force participation (% of population ages 15+)	36	61	46	60
Women in the labor force (% of total labor force)	39		44	
Employment to population ratio (% ages 15+)	34	59	42	56
Vulnerable employment (% of employed ages 15+)	..	..	9	11
Employment in agriculture (% of employed ages 15+)	2	4	2	2
Employment in industry (% of employed ages 15+)	16	40	11	35
Employment in service (% of employed ages 15+)	81	56	86	62
Wage and salaried workers (% of employed ages 15+)	83	82	88	82
Self-employed workers (% of employed ages 15+)	10	18	9	17
Unpaid family workers (% of employed ages 15+)	8	1	3	0
Women in nonagricultural wage employment (%)	40		46	
Children in employment (% of children ages 7–14)	..	..	..	..
Unemployment (% of labor force ages 15+)	11	5	9	7
Long-term unemployment (% of total unemployment)	70	66	51	49
Youth unemployment (% of labor force ages 15–24)	19	10	19	21
Maternity leave (weeks)	15		15	
Maternal leave benefits (% of wages paid)	82		82	
Women's political participation				
Seats held by women in national parliament (%)	9		35	
Women in managerial positions (%)	..		31	

Belize

Latin America & Caribbean			Upper middle income	

Population (thousands)	304	Population living on less		
GNI ($ billions)	1.1	than $1.25 a day (%)		..
GNI per capita ($)	3,760			

	1990		2007	
	Female	Male	Female	Male
Demography				
Sex ratio at birth (females per 1,000 males)	971		971	
Life expectancy at birth (years)	74	71	79	73
Child mortality rate (per 1,000)	..	..	3	7
Female-headed households (%)	..		..	
Education				
Gross primary enrollment (% of relevant age group)	111	116	122	124
Gross secondary enrollment (% of relevant age group)	69	63	81	76
Gross tertiary enrollment (% of relevant age group)	..	..	4	2
Primary completion rate (% of relevant age group)	..	..	109	103
Adult literacy rate (% of population ages 15+)	70	70	..	..
Family planning and maternal health				
Total fertility rate (births per woman)	4.5		2.9	
Adolescent fertility (births per 1,000 women ages 15–19)	..		79	
Women married by age 18 (% of women ages 20–24)	..		..	
Contraceptive prevalence (% of women ages 15–49)	47		34	
Unmet need for contraception (% of women ages 15–49)	..		..	
Pregnant women receiving prenatal care (%)	96		94	
Births attended by skilled health staff (% of total)	77		96	
Maternal mortality ratio (per 100,000 live births)	..		52	
Labor force and employment dynamics				
Labor force participation (% of population ages 15+)	23	81	46	81
Women in the labor force (% of total labor force)	21		36	
Employment to population ratio (% ages 15+)	20	74	39	75
Vulnerable employment (% of employed ages 15+)	..	..	22	25
Employment in agriculture (% of employed ages 15+)	5	33	3	28
Employment in industry (% of employed ages 15+)	13	23	10	22
Employment in service (% of employed ages 15+)	79	44	86	50
Wage and salaried workers (% of employed ages 15+)	76	68	74	67
Self-employed workers (% of employed ages 15+)	21	29	22	29
Unpaid family workers (% of employed ages 15+)	3	3	4	4
Women in nonagricultural wage employment (%)	39		44	
Children in employment (% of children ages 7–14)	..	..	..	..
Unemployment (% of labor force ages 15+)	2	4	19	8
Long-term unemployment (% of total unemployment)	52	31	..	..
Youth unemployment (% of labor force ages 15–24)	..	..	33	19
Maternity leave (weeks)	12		14	
Maternal leave benefits (% of wages paid)	80		80	
Women's political participation				
Seats held by women in national parliament (%)	0		7	
Women in managerial positions (%)	..		..	

Benin

Sub-Saharan Africa		Low income

		Population living on less	
Population (millions)	9.0	than $1.25 a day (%)	47.3
GNI ($ billions)	5.1		
GNI per capita ($)	570		

	1990		2007	
	Female	Male	Female	Male
Demography				
Sex ratio at birth (females per 1,000 males)	959		959	
Life expectancy at birth (years)	55	52	58	56
Child mortality rate (per 1,000)	..	..	65	64
Female-headed households (%)	..		23	
Education				
Gross primary enrollment (% of relevant age group)	33	63	87	105
Gross secondary enrollment (% of relevant age group)	5	13	23	41
Gross tertiary enrollment (% of relevant age group)	..	..	..	..
Primary completion rate (% of relevant age group)	11	25	52	76
Adult literacy rate (% of population ages 15+)	17	40	28	53
Family planning and maternal health				
Total fertility rate (births per woman)	6.7		5.4	
Adolescent fertility (births per 1,000 women ages 15–19)	..		120	
Women married by age 18 (% of women ages 20–24)	..		..	
Contraceptive prevalence (% of women ages 15–49)	..		17	
Unmet need for contraception (% of women ages 15–49)	..		30	
Pregnant women receiving prenatal care (%)	..		84	
Births attended by skilled health staff (% of total)	..		74	
Maternal mortality ratio (per 100,000 live births)	..		840	
Labor force and employment dynamics				
Labor force participation (% of population ages 15+)	51	88	59	86
Women in the labor force (% of total labor force)	38		40	
Employment to population ratio (% ages 15+)	54	88	58	85
Vulnerable employment (% of employed ages 15+)	..	..	..	..
Employment in agriculture (% of employed ages 15+)	..	..	..	..
Employment in industry (% of employed ages 15+)	..	..	..	..
Employment in service (% of employed ages 15+)	..	..	..	..
Wage and salaried workers (% of employed ages 15+)	..	..	..	..
Self-employed workers (% of employed ages 15+)	..	..	..	..
Unpaid family workers (% of employed ages 15+)	..	..	..	..
Women in nonagricultural wage employment (%)	21		..	
Children in employment (% of children ages 7–14)	..	..	73	76
Unemployment (% of labor force ages 15+)	1	2	..	..
Long-term unemployment (% of total unemployment)	..	..	..	..
Youth unemployment (% of labor force ages 15–24)	..	..	..	..
Maternity leave (weeks)	14		14	
Maternal leave benefits (% of wages paid)	100		100	
Women's political participation				
Seats held by women in national parliament (%)	3		8	
Women in managerial positions (%)	..		..	

Bermuda

Population (thousands)	64	Population living on less	
GNI ($ billions)	..	than $1.25 a day (%)	
GNI per capita ($)	..		..

	1990		2007	
	Female	Male	Female	Male
Demography				
Sex ratio at birth (females per 1,000 males)	..		..	
Life expectancy at birth (years)	78	70	82	76
Child mortality rate (per 1,000)	..	..	..	..
Female-headed households (%)	..		..	
Education				
Gross primary enrollment (% of relevant age group)	..	..	92	108
Gross secondary enrollment (% of relevant age group)	..	..	87	82
Gross tertiary enrollment (% of relevant age group)	..	..	24	13
Primary completion rate (% of relevant age group)	..	..	105	105
Adult literacy rate (% of population ages 15+)	..	..	..	..
Family planning and maternal health				
Total fertility rate (births per woman)		..		1.8
Adolescent fertility (births per 1,000 women ages 15-19)		..		..
Women married by age 18 (% of women ages 20-24)		..		..
Contraceptive prevalence (% of women ages 15-49)		..		..
Unmet need for contraception (% of women ages 15-49)		..		..
Pregnant women receiving prenatal care (%)		..		..
Births attended by skilled health staff (% of total)		..		..
Maternal mortality ratio (per 100,000 live births)		..		..
Labor force and employment dynamics				
Labor force participation (% of population ages 15+)	..	..	..	..
Women in the labor force (% of total labor force)	..		..	
Employment to population ratio (% ages 15+)	..	..	..	..
Vulnerable employment (% of employed ages 15+)	..	..	..	..
Employment in agriculture (% of employed ages 15+)	0	3	..	..
Employment in industry (% of employed ages 15+)	4	17	..	..
Employment in service (% of employed ages 15+)	96	80	..	..
Wage and salaried workers (% of employed ages 15+)	..	..	..	..
Self-employed workers (% of employed ages 15+)	..	..	..	..
Unpaid family workers (% of employed ages 15+)	..	..	..	..
Women in nonagricultural wage employment (%)	49		49	
Children in employment (% of children ages 7-14)	..	..	..	..
Unemployment (% of labor force ages 15+)	4	7	..	..
Long-term unemployment (% of total unemployment)	..	..	..	..
Youth unemployment (% of labor force ages 15-24)	..	..	..	..
Maternity leave (weeks)		..		..
Maternal leave benefits (% of wages paid)		..		..
Women's political participation				
Seats held by women in national parliament (%)		..		..
Women in managerial positions (%)		..		..

Bhutan

South Asia		Lower middle income	

		Population living on less	
Population (thousands)	657	than $1.25 a day (%)	26.2
GNI ($ billions)	1.2		
GNI per capita ($)	1,770		

	1990		2007	
	Female	Male	Female	Male
Demography				
Sex ratio at birth (females per 1,000 males)	962		962	
Life expectancy at birth (years)	55	52	67	64
Child mortality rate (per 1,000)	..	..	..	..
Female-headed households (%)		..	28	
Education				
Gross primary enrollment (% of relevant age group)	48	63	111	111
Gross secondary enrollment (% of relevant age group)	5	21	54	58
Gross tertiary enrollment (% of relevant age group)	..	..	3	7
Primary completion rate (% of relevant age group)	..	..	86	80
Adult literacy rate (% of population ages 15+)	..	..	39	65
Family planning and maternal health				
Total fertility rate (births per woman)	5.7		2.2	
Adolescent fertility (births per 1,000 women ages 15–19)	..		37	
Women married by age 18 (% of women ages 20–24)	..		..	
Contraceptive prevalence (% of women ages 15–49)	..		35	
Unmet need for contraception (% of women ages 15–49)	..		..	
Pregnant women receiving prenatal care (%)	..		88	
Births attended by skilled health staff (% of total)	..		56	
Maternal mortality ratio (per 100,000 live births)	..		440	
Labor force and employment dynamics				
Labor force participation (% of population ages 15+)	25	84	43	80
Women in the labor force (% of total labor force)	22		32	
Employment to population ratio (% ages 15+)	24	82	40	74
Vulnerable employment (% of employed ages 15+)	..	..	76	39
Employment in agriculture (% of employed ages 15+)	..	..	..	..
Employment in industry (% of employed ages 15+)	..	..	..	..
Employment in service (% of employed ages 15+)	..	..	..	..
Wage and salaried workers (% of employed ages 15+)	..	..	18	52
Self-employed workers (% of employed ages 15+)	..	..	25	19
Unpaid family workers (% of employed ages 15+)	..	..	52	21
Women in nonagricultural wage employment (%)	..		..	
Children in employment (% of children ages 7–14)	..	..	..	..
Unemployment (% of labor force ages 15+)	..	..	3	3
Long-term unemployment (% of total unemployment)	..	..	..	..
Youth unemployment (% of labor force ages 15–24)	..	..	..	..
Maternity leave (weeks)	..		..	
Maternal leave benefits (% of wages paid)	..		..	
Women's political participation				
Seats held by women in national parliament (%)	2		3	
Women in managerial positions (%)	..		..	

Bolivia

Latin America & Caribbean		Lower middle income	

Population (millions)	9.5	Population living on less	
GNI ($ billions)	12.0	than $1.25 a day (%)	19.6
GNI per capita ($)	1,260		

	1990		2007	
	Female	Male	Female	Male
Demography				
Sex ratio at birth (females per 1,000 males)	952		952	
Life expectancy at birth (years)	61	57	68	63
Child mortality rate (per 1,000)	51	51	26	20
Female-headed households (%)	..		20	
Education				
Gross primary enrollment (% of relevant age group)	102	110	109	109
Gross secondary enrollment (% of relevant age group)	40	48	81	84
Gross tertiary enrollment (% of relevant age group)	..	..	..	..
Primary completion rate (% of relevant age group)	64	78	100	102
Adult literacy rate (% of population ages 15+)	72	88	86	96
Family planning and maternal health				
Total fertility rate (births per woman)	4.9		3.5	
Adolescent fertility (births per 1,000 women ages 15-19)	..		78	
Women married by age 18 (% of women ages 20-24)	24		26	
Contraceptive prevalence (% of women ages 15-49)	30		58	
Unmet need for contraception (% of women ages 15-49)	..		23	
Pregnant women receiving prenatal care (%)	46		79	
Births attended by skilled health staff (% of total)	43		67	
Maternal mortality ratio (per 100,000 live births)	..		290	
Labor force and employment dynamics				
Labor force participation (% of population ages 15+)	46	85	66	83
Women in the labor force (% of total labor force)	36		45	
Employment to population ratio (% ages 15+)	44	80	62	79
Vulnerable employment (% of employed ages 15+)	50	32	..	..
Employment in agriculture (% of employed ages 15+)	0	2	..	..
Employment in industry (% of employed ages 15+)	12	35	..	..
Employment in service (% of employed ages 15+)	87	63	..	..
Wage and salaried workers (% of employed ages 15+)	48	63	..	..
Self-employed workers (% of employed ages 15+)	45	34	..	..
Unpaid family workers (% of employed ages 15+)	7	4	..	..
Women in nonagricultural wage employment (%)	37		..	
Children in employment (% of children ages 7-14)	..	..	20	24
Unemployment (% of labor force ages 15+)	6	6	..	..
Long-term unemployment (% of total unemployment)	..	..	..	..
Youth unemployment (% of labor force ages 15-24)	..	..	..	..
Maternity leave (weeks)	8		12	
Maternal leave benefits (% of wages paid)	..		70	
Women's political participation				
Seats held by women in national parliament (%)	9		17	
Women in managerial positions (%)	..		..	

Bosnia and Herzegovina

Europe & Central Asia				Lower middle income

Population (millions)	3.8	Population living on less		
GNI ($ billions)	14.3	than $1.25 a day (%)		2.0
GNI per capita ($)	3,790			

	1990		2007	
	Female	Male	Female	Male
Demography				
Sex ratio at birth (females per 1,000 males)	933		933	
Life expectancy at birth (years)	75	69	77	72
Child mortality rate (per 1,000)	..	..	..	..
Female-headed households (%)	..		..	
Education				
Gross primary enrollment (% of relevant age group)	..	..	94	101
Gross secondary enrollment (% of relevant age group)	..	..	87	84
Gross tertiary enrollment (% of relevant age group)	..	..	..	..
Primary completion rate (% of relevant age group)	..	..	..	..
Adult literacy rate (% of population ages 15+)	..	..	..	..
Family planning and maternal health				
Total fertility rate (births per woman)	1.7		1.2	
Adolescent fertility (births per 1,000 women ages 15–19)	..		20	
Women married by age 18 (% of women ages 20–24)	..		..	
Contraceptive prevalence (% of women ages 15–49)	..		36	
Unmet need for contraception (% of women ages 15–49)	..		23	
Pregnant women receiving prenatal care (%)	..		99	
Births attended by skilled health staff (% of total)	97		100	
Maternal mortality ratio (per 100,000 live births)	..		3	
Labor force and employment dynamics				
Labor force participation (% of population ages 15+)	69	83	53	67
Women in the labor force (% of total labor force)	47		46	
Employment to population ratio (% ages 15+)	45	59	35	48
Vulnerable employment (% of employed ages 15+)	..	..	..	..
Employment in agriculture (% of employed ages 15+)	..	..	..	..
Employment in industry (% of employed ages 15+)	..	..	..	..
Employment in service (% of employed ages 15+)	..	..	..	..
Wage and salaried workers (% of employed ages 15+)	..	..	73	72
Self-employed workers (% of employed ages 15+)	..	..	16	25
Unpaid family workers (% of employed ages 15+)	..	..	11	3
Women in nonagricultural wage employment (%)	..		35	
Children in employment (% of children ages 7–14)	..	..	10	12
Unemployment (% of labor force ages 15+)	22	15	35	29
Long-term unemployment (% of total unemployment)	..	..	..	..
Youth unemployment (% of labor force ages 15–24)	..	..	..	..
Maternity leave (weeks)	..		..	
Maternal leave benefits (% of wages paid)	..		..	
Women's political participation				
Seats held by women in national parliament (%)	..		14	
Women in managerial positions (%)	..		..	

Botswana

Population (millions)	1.9	Population living on less	
GNI ($ billions)	11.5	than $1.25 a day (%)	..
GNI per capita ($)	6,120		

	1990		2007	
	Female	**Male**	**Female**	**Male**
Demography				
Sex ratio at birth (females per 1,000 males)	971		971	
Life expectancy at birth (years)	66	61	51	50
Child mortality rate (per 1,000)	16	18	..	..
Female-headed households (%)	..		..	
Education				
Gross primary enrollment (% of relevant age group)	108	100	106	107
Gross secondary enrollment (% of relevant age group)	42	38	78	75
Gross tertiary enrollment (% of relevant age group)	..	..	5	5
Primary completion rate (% of relevant age group)	97	80	98	91
Adult literacy rate (% of population ages 15+)	71	65	83	83
Family planning and maternal health				
Total fertility rate (births per woman)	4.6		2.9	
Adolescent fertility (births per 1,000 women ages 15-19)	..		52	
Women married by age 18 (% of women ages 20-24)	..		..	
Contraceptive prevalence (% of women ages 15-49)	33		..	
Unmet need for contraception (% of women ages 15-49)	..		..	
Pregnant women receiving prenatal care (%)	92		..	
Births attended by skilled health staff (% of total)	77		..	
Maternal mortality ratio (per 100,000 live births)	..		380	
Labor force and employment dynamics				
Labor force participation (% of population ages 15+)	44	78	48	63
Women in the labor force (% of total labor force)	38		44	
Employment to population ratio (% ages 15+)	34	65	39	54
Vulnerable employment (% of employed ages 15+)	..	..	17	7
Employment in agriculture (% of employed ages 15+)	..	..	13	29
Employment in industry (% of employed ages 15+)	..	..	17	28
Employment in service (% of employed ages 15+)	..	..	71	43
Wage and salaried workers (% of employed ages 15+)	..	..	72	74
Self-employed workers (% of employed ages 15+)	..	..	17	8
Unpaid family workers (% of employed ages 15+)	..	..	2	2
Women in nonagricultural wage employment (%)	34		42	
Children in employment (% of children ages 7-14)	..	..	..	..
Unemployment (% of labor force ages 15+)	..	..	20	15
Long-term unemployment (% of total unemployment)	..	..	..	..
Youth unemployment (% of labor force ages 15-24)	33	20	..	..
Maternity leave (weeks)	12		12	
Maternal leave benefits (% of wages paid)	25		25	
Women's political participation				
Seats held by women in national parliament (%)	5		11	
Women in managerial positions (%)	..		..	

Brazil

Latin America & Caribbean		Upper middle income

Population (millions)	192	Population living on less	
GNI ($ billions)	1,122.1	than $1.25 a day (%)	5.2
GNI per capita ($)	5,860		

	1990		2007	
	Female	Male	Female	Male
Demography				
Sex ratio at birth (females per 1,000 males)	952		952	
Life expectancy at birth (years)	70	63	76	69
Child mortality rate (per 1,000)	20	17	..	..
Female-headed households (%)	21		..	
Education				
Gross primary enrollment (% of relevant age group)	..	..	133	141
Gross secondary enrollment (% of relevant age group)	..	..	111	100
Gross tertiary enrollment (% of relevant age group)	..	..	29	22
Primary completion rate (% of relevant age group)	..	..	..	..
Adult literacy rate (% of population ages 15+)	..	..	90	90
Family planning and maternal health				
Total fertility rate (births per woman)	2.8		2.2	
Adolescent fertility (births per 1,000 women ages 15–19)	..		89	
Women married by age 18 (% of women ages 20–24)	26		..	
Contraceptive prevalence (% of women ages 15–49)	59		..	
Unmet need for contraception (% of women ages 15–49)	18		..	
Pregnant women receiving prenatal care (%)	..		97	
Births attended by skilled health staff (% of total)	72		97	
Maternal mortality ratio (per 100,000 live births)	..		110	
Labor force and employment dynamics				
Labor force participation (% of population ages 15+)	39	85	60	82
Women in the labor force (% of total labor force)	32		43	
Employment to population ratio (% ages 15+)	35	78	53	76
Vulnerable employment (% of employed ages 15+)	30	29	24	30
Employment in agriculture (% of employed ages 15+)	13	28	16	25
Employment in industry (% of employed ages 15+)	13	28	13	27
Employment in service (% of employed ages 15+)	74	44	71	48
Wage and salaried workers (% of employed ages 15+)	68	65	66	62
Self-employed workers (% of employed ages 15+)	23	31	19	31
Unpaid family workers (% of employed ages 15+)	9	4	8	5
Women in nonagricultural wage employment (%)	35		..	
Children in employment (% of children ages 7–14)	..	..	5	9
Unemployment (% of labor force ages 15+)	3	4	12	7
Long-term unemployment (% of total unemployment)	..	..	..	..
Youth unemployment (% of labor force ages 15–24)	7	7	23	14
Maternity leave (weeks)	17		17	
Maternal leave benefits (% of wages paid)	100		100	
Women's political participation				
Seats held by women in national parliament (%)	5		9	
Women in managerial positions (%)	..		..	

Brunei Darussalam

High income

Population (thousands)	389	Population living on less
GNI ($ billions)	10.2	than $1.25 a day (%)
GNI per capita ($)	26,740	..

	1990		2007	
	Female	Male	Female	Male
Demography				
Sex ratio at birth (females per 1,000 males)	948		948	
Life expectancy at birth (years)	76	72	80	75
Child mortality rate (per 1,000)	..	..	..	..
Female-headed households (%)	..		..	
Education				
Gross primary enrollment (% of relevant age group)	112	119	105	106
Gross secondary enrollment (% of relevant age group)	71	66	99	96
Gross tertiary enrollment (% of relevant age group)	..	..	20	11
Primary completion rate (% of relevant age group)	..	..	109	106
Adult literacy rate (% of population ages 15+)	82	92	93	96
Family planning and maternal health				
Total fertility rate (births per woman)	3.2		2.3	
Adolescent fertility (births per 1,000 women ages 15–19)	..		27	
Women married by age 18 (% of women ages 20–24)	..		..	
Contraceptive prevalence (% of women ages 15–49)	..		..	
Unmet need for contraception (% of women ages 15–49)	..		..	
Pregnant women receiving prenatal care (%)	..		..	
Births attended by skilled health staff (% of total)	..		100	
Maternal mortality ratio (per 100,000 live births)	..		13	
Labor force and employment dynamics				
Labor force participation (% of population ages 15+)	45	83	58	75
Women in the labor force (% of total labor force)	32		42	
Employment to population ratio (% ages 15+)	44	79	56	72
Vulnerable employment (% of employed ages 15+)	3	4	..	..
Employment in agriculture (% of employed ages 15+)	2	2	..	..
Employment in industry (% of employed ages 15+)	9	32	..	..
Employment in service (% of employed ages 15+)	90	68	..	..
Wage and salaried workers (% of employed ages 15+)	96	94	..	..
Self-employed workers (% of employed ages 15+)	3	5	..	..
Unpaid family workers (% of employed ages 15+)	1	0	..	..
Women in nonagricultural wage employment (%)	..		30	
Children in employment (% of children ages 7–14)	..	..	..	..
Unemployment (% of labor force ages 15+)	7	4	..	..
Long-term unemployment (% of total unemployment)	..	..	..	..
Youth unemployment (% of labor force ages 15–24)	..	..	..	..
Maternity leave (weeks)	..		..	
Maternal leave benefits (% of wages paid)	..		..	
Women's political participation				
Seats held by women in national parliament (%)	..		..	
Women in managerial positions (%)	..		..	

Bulgaria

Europe & Central Asia		Upper middle income

Population (millions)	7.7	Population living on less	
GNI ($ billions)	35.1	than $1.25 a day (%)	2.0
GNI per capita ($)	4,580		

	1990		2007	
	Female	Male	Female	Male
Demography				
Sex ratio at birth (females per 1,000 males)	943		943	
Life expectancy at birth (years)	75	68	76	69
Child mortality rate (per 1,000)	..	..	..	..
Female-headed households (%)	..		..	
Education				
Gross primary enrollment (% of relevant age group)	95	97	99	101
Gross secondary enrollment (% of relevant age group)	87	87	103	107
Gross tertiary enrollment (% of relevant age group)	..	..	50	41
Primary completion rate (% of relevant age group)	101	101	98	98
Adult literacy rate (% of population ages 15+)	..	..	98	99
Family planning and maternal health				
Total fertility rate (births per woman)	1.8		1.4	
Adolescent fertility (births per 1,000 women ages 15–19)	..		40	
Women married by age 18 (% of women ages 20–24)	..		..	
Contraceptive prevalence (% of women ages 15–49)	..		..	
Unmet need for contraception (% of women ages 15–49)	..		..	
Pregnant women receiving prenatal care (%)	..		..	
Births attended by skilled health staff (% of total)	..		99	
Maternal mortality ratio (per 100,000 live births)	..		11	
Labor force and employment dynamics				
Labor force participation (% of population ages 15+)	57	64	46	57
Women in the labor force (% of total labor force)	48		46	
Employment to population ratio (% ages 15+)	44	49	42	53
Vulnerable employment (% of employed ages 15+)	..	..	7	10
Employment in agriculture (% of employed ages 15+)	..	..	7	11
Employment in industry (% of employed ages 15+)	..	..	29	39
Employment in service (% of employed ages 15+)	..	..	64	50
Wage and salaried workers (% of employed ages 15–)	..	..	91	85
Self-employed workers (% of employed ages 15+)	..	..	8	14
Unpaid family workers (% of employed ages 15+)	..	..	2	1
Women in nonagricultural wage employment (%)	52		53	
Children in employment (% of children ages 7–14)	..	..	..	..
Unemployment (% of labor force ages 15+)	22	21	9	9
Long-term unemployment (% of total unemployment)	52	53	..	..
Youth unemployment (% of labor force ages 15–24)	..	..	21	23
Maternity leave (weeks)	17		19	
Maternal leave benefits (% of wages paid)	100		90	
Women's political participation				
Seats held by women in national parliament (%)	21		22	
Women in managerial positions (%)	..		30	

Burkina Faso

Sub-Saharan Africa | **Low income**

Population (millions)	15	Population living on less
GNI ($ billions)	6.4	than $1.25 a day (%) 56.5
GNI per capita ($)	430	

	1990		2007	
	Female	Male	Female	Male
Demography				
Sex ratio at birth (females per 1,000 males)	957		957	
Life expectancy at birth (years)	52	48	54	51
Child mortality rate (per 1,000)	..	..	113	110
Female-headed households (%)	..		9	
Education				
Gross primary enrollment (% of relevant age group)	25	39	60	71
Gross secondary enrollment (% of relevant age group)	4	8	13	18
Gross tertiary enrollment (% of relevant age group)	..	..	2	3
Primary completion rate (% of relevant age group)	14	24	29	37
Adult literacy rate (% of population ages 15+)	8	20	22	37
Family planning and maternal health				
Total fertility rate (births per woman)	7.3		6.0	
Adolescent fertility (births per 1,000 women ages 15–19)	..		126	
Women married by age 18 (% of women ages 20–24)	..		52	
Contraceptive prevalence (% of women ages 15–49)	8		17	
Unmet need for contraception (% of women ages 15–49)	25		29	
Pregnant women receiving prenatal care (%)	59		85	
Births attended by skilled health staff (% of total)	42		54	
Maternal mortality ratio (per 100,000 live births)	..		700	
Labor force and employment dynamics				
Labor force participation (% of population ages 15+)	76	90	77	90
Women in the labor force (% of total labor force)	47		47	
Employment to population ratio (% ages 15+)	75	87	76	87
Vulnerable employment (% of employed ages 15+)	..	..	..	..
Employment in agriculture (% of employed ages 15+)	..	..	..	..
Employment in industry (% of employed ages 15+)	..	..	..	..
Employment in service (% of employed ages 15+)	..	..	..	..
Wage and salaried workers (% of employed ages 15+)	..	..	..	..
Self-employed workers (% of employed ages 15+)	..	..	..	..
Unpaid family workers (% of employed ages 15+)	..	..	..	..
Women in nonagricultural wage employment (%)	13		..	
Children in employment (% of children ages 7–14)	..	..	51	49
Unemployment (% of labor force ages 15+)	..	..	..	..
Long-term unemployment (% of total unemployment)	..	..	..	..
Youth unemployment (% of labor force ages 15–24)	..	..	..	..
Maternity leave (weeks)	14		14	
Maternal leave benefits (% of wages paid)	100		100	
Women's political participation				
Seats held by women in national parliament (%)	..		15	
Women in managerial positions (%)	..		..	

Burundi

Sub-Saharan Africa		Low income

		Population living on less	
Population (millions)	8.5	than $1.25 a day (%)	81.3
GNI ($ millions)	923.1		
GNI per capita ($)	110		

	1990		2007	
	Female	Male	Female	Male
Demography				
Sex ratio at birth (females per 1,000 males)	971		971	
Life expectancy at birth (years)	48	44	51	48
Child mortality rate (per 1,000)	*114*	*101*	..	..
Female-headed households (%)	..		..	
Education				
Gross primary enrollment (% of relevant age group)	62	77	110	119
Gross secondary enrollment (% of relevant age group)	4	6	13	18
Gross tertiary enrollment (% of relevant age group)	..	..	1	3
Primary completion rate (% of relevant age group)	34	48	36	42
Adult literacy rate (% of population ages 15+)	28	48	..	..
Family planning and maternal health				
Total fertility rate (births per woman)	6.8		6.8	
Adolescent fertility (births per 1,000 women ages 15–19)	..		55	
Women married by age 18 (% of women ages 20–24)	*17*		..	
Contraceptive prevalence (% of women ages 15–49)	9		9	
Unmet need for contraception (% of women ages 15–49)	..		..	
Pregnant women receiving prenatal care (%)	79		92	
Births attended by skilled health staff (% of total)	*19*		*34*	
Maternal mortality ratio (per 100,000 live births)	..		*1,100*	
Labor force and employment dynamics				
Labor force participation (% of population ages 15+)	91	90	90	90
Women in the labor force (% of total labor force)	52		51	
Employment to population ratio (% ages 15+)	*85*	*83*	83	83
Vulnerable employment (% of employed ages 15+)	..	..	..	..
Employment in agriculture (% of employed ages 15+)	..	..	..	..
Employment in industry (% of employed ages 15+)	..	..	..	..
Employment in service (% of employed ages 15+)	..	..	..	..
Wage and salaried workers (% of employed ages 15+)	..	..	..	..
Self-employed workers (% of employed ages 15+)	..	..	..	..
Unpaid family workers (% of employed ages 15+)	..	..	..	..
Women in nonagricultural wage employment (%)	14		..	
Children in employment (% of children ages 7–14)	..	..	..	..
Unemployment (% of labor force ages 15+)	0	1	..	..
Long-term unemployment (% of total unemployment)	..	..	..	..
Youth unemployment (% of labor force ages 15–24)	..	..	..	..
Maternity leave (weeks)	12		*12*	
Maternal leave benefits (% of wages paid)	90		*100*	
Women's political participation				
Seats held by women in national parliament (%)	..		31	
Women in managerial positions (%)	..		..	

Cambodia

East Asia & Pacific		Low income

		Population living on less	
Population (millions)	14	than $1.25 a day (%)	40.2
GNI ($ billions)	8.0		
GNI per capita ($)	550		

	1990		2007	
	Female	Male	Female	Male
Demography				
Sex ratio at birth (females per 1,000 males)	952		952	
Life expectancy at birth (years)	57	53	62	57
Child mortality rate (per 1,000)	..	..	20	20
Female-headed households (%)		..		24
Education				
Gross primary enrollment (% of relevant age group)	81	99	115	124
Gross secondary enrollment (% of relevant age group)	18	42	38	46
Gross tertiary enrollment (% of relevant age group)	..	..	4	7
Primary completion rate (% of relevant age group)	..	..	85	85
Adult literacy rate (% of population ages 15+)	..	..	68	86
Family planning and maternal health				
Total fertility rate (births per woman)	5.7		3.2	
Adolescent fertility (births per 1,000 women ages 15–19)	..		42	
Women married by age 18 (% of women ages 20–24)	..		..	
Contraceptive prevalence (% of women ages 15–49)	..		40	
Unmet need for contraception (% of women ages 15–49)	..		25	
Pregnant women receiving prenatal care (%)	..		69	
Births attended by skilled health staff (% of total)	..		44	
Maternal mortality ratio (per 100,000 live births)	..		540	
Labor force and employment dynamics				
Labor force participation (% of population ages 15+)	77	85	75	87
Women in the labor force (% of total labor force)	52		49	
Employment to population ratio (% ages 15+)	75	82	73	85
Vulnerable employment (% of employed ages 15+)	..	..	..	..
Employment in agriculture (% of employed ages 15+)	79	71	..	..
Employment in industry (% of employed ages 15+)	3	6	..	..
Employment in service (% of employed ages 15+)	18	23	..	..
Wage and salaried workers (% of employed ages 15+)	..	..	..	..
Self-employed workers (% of employed ages 15+)	..	..	..	..
Unpaid family workers (% of employed ages 15+)	..	..	..	..
Women in nonagricultural wage employment (%)	..		52	
Children in employment (% of children ages 7–14)	..	..	..	..
Unemployment (% of labor force ages 15+)	..	..	..	..
Long-term unemployment (% of total unemployment)	..	..	..	..
Youth unemployment (% of labor force ages 15–24)	..	..	..	..
Maternity leave (weeks)	12		13	
Maternal leave benefits (% of wages paid)	100		50	
Women's political participation				
Seats held by women in national parliament (%)	..		10	
Women in managerial positions (%)	..		..	

Cameroon

Sub-Saharan Africa   **Lower middle income**

Population (millions)	19	Population living on less	
GNI ($ billions)	19.5	than $1.25 a day (%)	32.8
GNI per capita ($)	1,050		

	1990		2007	
	Female	**Male**	**Female**	**Male**
Demography				
Sex ratio at birth (females per 1,000 males)	971		971	
Life expectancy at birth (years)	56	53	51	50
Child mortality rate (per 1,000)	75	64	72	73
Female-headed households (%)	18		24	
Education				
Gross primary enrollment (% of relevant age group)	89	103	101	118
Gross secondary enrollment (% of relevant age group)	20	29	22	28
Gross tertiary enrollment (% of relevant age group)	..	..	6	8
Primary completion rate (% of relevant age group)	52	56	50	61
Adult literacy rate (% of population ages 15+)	..	..	..	..
Family planning and maternal health				
Total fertility rate (births per woman)	5.9		4.3	
Adolescent fertility (births per 1,000 women ages 15–19)	..		118	
Women married by age 18 (% of women ages 20–24)	58		47	
Contraceptive prevalence (% of women ages 15–49)	16		29	
Unmet need for contraception (% of women ages 15–49)	22		20	
Pregnant women receiving prenatal care (%)	79		82	
Births attended by skilled health staff (% of total)	58		63	
Maternal mortality ratio (per 100,000 live births)	..		1,000	
Labor force and employment dynamics				
Labor force participation (% of population ages 15+)	53	79	52	75
Women in the labor force (% of total labor force)	41		41	
Employment to population ratio (% ages 15+)	48	71	49	69
Vulnerable employment (% of employed ages 15+)	..	..	..	..
Employment in agriculture (% of employed ages 15+)	68	53	..	..
Employment in industry (% of employed ages 15+)	4	14	..	..
Employment in service (% of employed ages 15+)	23	26	..	..
Wage and salaried workers (% of employed ages 15+)	..	..	..	..
Self-employed workers (% of employed ages 15+)	..	..	..	..
Unpaid family workers (% of employed ages 15+)	..	..	..	..
Women in nonagricultural wage employment (%)	..		..	
Children in employment (% of children ages 7–14)	..	..	..	..
Unemployment (% of labor force ages 15+)	..	..	..	..
Long-term unemployment (% of total unemployment)	..	..	..	..
Youth unemployment (% of labor force ages 15–24)	..	..	..	..
Maternity leave (weeks)	14		14	
Maternal leave benefits (% of wages paid)	100		100	
Women's political participation				
Seats held by women in national parliament (%)	14		14	
Women in managerial positions (%)	..		..	

Canada

High income

Population (millions)	33	Population living on less
GNI ($ billions)	1,307.4	than $1.25 a day (%) ..
GNI per capita ($)	39,650	

	1990		2007	
	Female	Male	Female	Male
Demography				
Sex ratio at birth (females per 1,000 males)	948		948	
Life expectancy at birth (years)	81	74	83	78
Child mortality rate (per 1,000)	..	..	..	..
Female-headed households (%)	..		..	
Education				
Gross primary enrollment (% of relevant age group)	103	104	98	98
Gross secondary enrollment (% of relevant age group)	100	99	116	119
Gross tertiary enrollment (% of relevant age group)	..	..	72	53
Primary completion rate (% of relevant age group)	..	..	..	..
Adult literacy rate (% of population ages 15+)	..	..	..	..
Family planning and maternal health				
Total fertility rate (births per woman)	1.8		1.6	
Adolescent fertility (births per 1,000 women ages 15–19)	..		14	
Women married by age 18 (% of women ages 20–24)	..		..	
Contraceptive prevalence (% of women ages 15–49)	..		..	
Unmet need for contraception (% of women ages 15–49)	..		..	
Pregnant women receiving prenatal care (%)	..		..	
Births attended by skilled health staff (% of total)	..		100	
Maternal mortality ratio (per 100,000 live births)	..		7	
Labor force and employment dynamics				
Labor force participation (% of population ages 15+)	58	76	63	73
Women in the labor force (% of total labor force)	44		47	
Employment to population ratio (% ages 15+)	52	67	59	68
Vulnerable employment (% of employed ages 15+)	..	..	9	12
Employment in agriculture (% of employed ages 15+)	2	5	2	4
Employment in industry (% of employed ages 15+)	12	34	11	32
Employment in service (% of employed ages 15+)	85	61	88	64
Wage and salaried workers (% of employed ages 15+)	90	82	89	81
Self-employed workers (% of employed ages 15+)	9	18	11	19
Unpaid family workers (% of employed ages 15+)	1	0	0	0
Women in nonagricultural wage employment (%)	47		50	
Children in employment (% of children ages 7–14)	..	..	..	..
Unemployment (% of labor force ages 15+)	8	8	6	6
Long-term unemployment (% of total unemployment)	6	8	6	8
Youth unemployment (% of labor force ages 15–24)	11	14	11	14
Maternity leave (weeks)	17		18	
Maternal leave benefits (% of wages paid)	57		55	
Women's political participation				
Seats held by women in national parliament (%)	13		21	
Women in managerial positions (%)	..		35	

Cape Verde

Sub-Saharan Africa   **Lower middle income**

Population (thousands)	530	Population living on less	
GNI ($ billions)	1.3	than $1.25 a day (%)	20.6
GNI per capita ($)	2,430		

	1990		2007	
	Female	Male	Female	Male
Demography				
Sex ratio at birth (females per 1,000 males)	971		971	
Life expectancy at birth (years)	68	63	74	68
Child mortality rate (per 1,000)	..	..	..	..
Female-headed households (%)	..		..	
Education				
Gross primary enrollment (% of relevant age group)	108	116	98	105
Gross secondary enrollment (% of relevant age group)	20	21	86	73
Gross tertiary enrollment (% of relevant age group)	..	..	10	8
Primary completion rate (% of relevant age group)	51	57	88	84
Adult literacy rate (% of population ages 15+)	53	75	79	89
Family planning and maternal health				
Total fertility rate (births per woman)	5.4		3.4	
Adolescent fertility (births per 1,000 women ages 15–19)	..		83	
Women married by age 18 (% of women ages 20–24)	..		..	
Contraceptive prevalence (% of women ages 15–49)	..		61	
Unmet need for contraception (% of women ages 15–49)	..		..	
Pregnant women receiving prenatal care (%)	..		98	
Births attended by skilled health staff (% of total)	..		78	
Maternal mortality ratio (per 100,000 live births)	..		210	
Labor force and employment dynamics				
Labor force participation (% of population ages 15+)	42	86	47	75
Women in the labor force (% of total labor force)	38		41	
Employment to population ratio (% ages 15+)	39	79	44	70
Vulnerable employment (% of employed ages 15+)	..	..	..	..
Employment in agriculture (% of employed ages 15+)	..	..	..	..
Employment in industry (% of employed ages 15+)	..	..	..	..
Employment in service (% of employed ages 15+)	..	..	..	..
Wage and salaried workers (% of employed ages 15+)	..	..	..	..
Self-employed workers (% of employed ages 15+)	..	..	..	..
Unpaid family workers (% of employed ages 15+)	..	..	..	..
Women in nonagricultural wage employment (%)	..		..	
Children in employment (% of children ages 7–14)	..	..	..	..
Unemployment (% of labor force ages 15+)	23	23	..	..
Long-term unemployment (% of total unemployment)	..	..	..	..
Youth unemployment (% of labor force ages 15–24)	..	..	..	..
Maternity leave (weeks)	..		..	
Maternal leave benefits (% of wages paid)	..		..	
Women's political participation				
Seats held by women in national parliament (%)	12		15	
Women in managerial positions (%)	..		..	

Cayman Islands

		Population living on less	
Population (thousands)	54	than $1.25 a day (%)	..
GNI ($ billions)	..		
GNI per capita ($)	..		

	1990		2007	
	Female	Male	Female	Male
Demography				
Sex ratio at birth (females per 1,000 males)	..		..	
Life expectancy at birth (years)	..	..	..	..
Child mortality rate (per 1,000)	..	..	..	..
Female-headed households (%)	..		..	
Education				
Gross primary enrollment (% of relevant age group)	..	..	84	95
Gross secondary enrollment (% of relevant age group)	..	..	98	106
Gross tertiary enrollment (% of relevant age group)	..	..	..	..
Primary completion rate (% of relevant age group)	..	..	107	97
Adult literacy rate (% of population ages 15+)	..	..	99	99
Family planning and maternal health				
Total fertility rate (births per woman)	..		..	
Adolescent fertility (births per 1,000 women ages 15-19)	..		..	
Women married by age 18 (% of women ages 20-24)	..		..	
Contraceptive prevalence (% of women ages 15-49)	..		..	
Unmet need for contraception (% of women ages 15-49)	..		..	
Pregnant women receiving prenatal care (%)	..		..	
Births attended by skilled health staff (% of total)	..		100	
Maternal mortality ratio (per 100,000 live births)	..		..	
Labor force and employment dynamics				
Labor force participation (% of population ages 15+)	..	..	..	..
Women in the labor force (% of total labor force)	..		..	
Employment to population ratio (% ages 15+)	..	..	..	..
Vulnerable employment (% of employed ages 15+)	..	..	..	..
Employment in agriculture (% of employed ages 15+)	..	..	..	..
Employment in industry (% of employed ages 15+)	..	..	..	..
Employment in service (% of employed ages 15+)	..	..	..	..
Wage and salaried workers (% of employed ages 15+)	..	..	95	89
Self-employed workers (% of employed ages 15+)	..	..	5	10
Unpaid family workers (% of employed ages 15+)	..	..	..	..
Women in nonagricultural wage employment (%)	49		48	
Children in employment (% of children ages 7-14)	..	..	..	..
Unemployment (% of labor force ages 15+)	7	5	4	3
Long-term unemployment (% of total unemployment)	..	..	..	..
Youth unemployment (% of labor force ages 15-24)	13	6	..	..
Maternity leave (weeks)	..		..	
Maternal leave benefits (% of wages paid)	..		..	
Women's political participation				
Seats held by women in national parliament (%)	..		..	
Women in managerial positions (%)	..		..	

Central African Republic

Sub-Saharan Africa | **Low income**

Population (millions)	4.3
GNI ($ billions)	1.6
GNI per capita ($)	370

Population living on less than $1.25 a day (%)	62.4

	1990		2007	
	Female	**Male**	**Female**	**Male**
Demography				
Sex ratio at birth (females per 1,000 males)	971		971	
Life expectancy at birth (years)	52	47	46	43
Child mortality rate (per 1,000)	..	..	82	74
Female-headed households (%)	..		..	
Education				
Gross primary enrollment (% of relevant age group)	52	85	66	94
Gross secondary enrollment (% of relevant age group)	6	16	..	..
Gross tertiary enrollment (% of relevant age group)	..	..	0	2
Primary completion rate (% of relevant age group)	18	40	19	30
Adult literacy rate (% of population ages 15+)	20	48	..	..
Family planning and maternal health				
Total fertility rate (births per woman)	5.6		4.6	
Adolescent fertility (births per 1,000 women ages 15–19)	..		115	
Women married by age 18 (% of women ages 20–24)	..		..	
Contraceptive prevalence (% of women ages 15–49)	..		19	
Unmet need for contraception (% of women ages 15–49)	..		..	
Pregnant women receiving prenatal care (%)	..		69	
Births attended by skilled health staff (% of total)	..		53	
Maternal mortality ratio (per 100,000 live births)	..		980	
Labor force and employment dynamics				
Labor force participation (% of population ages 15+)	69	88	67	87
Women in the labor force (% of total labor force)	47		46	
Employment to population ratio (% ages 15+)	65	81	63	80
Vulnerable employment (% of employed ages 15+)	..	..	..	..
Employment in agriculture (% of employed ages 15+)	..	..	..	..
Employment in industry (% of employed ages 15+)	..	..	..	..
Employment in service (% of employed ages 15+)	..	..	..	..
Wage and salaried workers (% of employed ages 15+)	..	..	..	..
Self-employed workers (% of employed ages 15+)	..	..	..	..
Unpaid family workers (% of employed ages 15+)	..	..	..	..
Women in nonagricultural wage employment (%)	..		47	
Children in employment (% of children ages 7–14)	..	..	..	..
Unemployment (% of labor force ages 15+)	..	..	..	..
Long-term unemployment (% of total unemployment)	..	..	..	..
Youth unemployment (% of labor force ages 15–24)	..	..	..	..
Maternity leave (weeks)	14		14	
Maternal leave benefits (% of wages paid)	50		50	
Women's political participation				
Seats held by women in national parliament (%)	4		11	
Women in managerial positions (%)	..		..	

Chad

Sub-Saharan Africa			**Low income**	

Population (millions)	11	Population living on less	
GNI ($ billions)	5.8	than $1.25 a day (%)	61.9
GNI per capita ($)	540		

	1990		2007	
	Female	Male	Female	Male
Demography				
Sex ratio at birth (females per 1,000 males)	971		971	
Life expectancy at birth (years)	53	50	52	49
Child mortality rate (per 1,000)	..	..	101	96
Female-headed households (%)	..		20	
Education				
Gross primary enrollment (% of relevant age group)	30	69	61	87
Gross secondary enrollment (% of relevant age group)	2	11	12	26
Gross tertiary enrollment (% of relevant age group)	..	..	0	2
Primary completion rate (% of relevant age group)	6	26	21	41
Adult literacy rate (% of population ages 15+)	..	..	21	43
Family planning and maternal health				
Total fertility rate (births per woman)	6.7		6.2	
Adolescent fertility (births per 1,000 women ages 15-19)	..		164	
Women married by age 18 (% of women ages 20-24)	..		..	
Contraceptive prevalence (% of women ages 15-49)	..		3	
Unmet need for contraception (% of women ages 15-49)	..		21	
Pregnant women receiving prenatal care (%)	..		39	
Births attended by skilled health staff (% of total)	..		14	
Maternal mortality ratio (per 100,000 live births)	..		1,500	
Labor force and employment dynamics				
Labor force participation (% of population ages 15+)	57	84	71	77
Women in the labor force (% of total labor force)	41		49	
Employment to population ratio (% ages 15+)	56	77	66	72
Vulnerable employment (% of employed ages 15+)	98	90	..	..
Employment in agriculture (% of employed ages 15+)	86	80	..	..
Employment in industry (% of employed ages 15+)	1	3	..	..
Employment in service (% of employed ages 15+)	13	16	..	..
Wage and salaried workers (% of employed ages 15+)	1	9	..	..
Self-employed workers (% of employed ages 15+)	54	77	..	..
Unpaid family workers (% of employed ages 15+)	44	13	..	..
Women in nonagricultural wage employment (%)	4		..	
Children in employment (% of children ages 7-14)	..	..	56	64
Unemployment (% of labor force ages 15+)	0	1	..	..
Long-term unemployment (% of total unemployment)	..	..	..	..
Youth unemployment (% of labor force ages 15-24)	..	..	..	..
Maternity leave (weeks)	14		14	
Maternal leave benefits (% of wages paid)	50		50	
Women's political participation				
Seats held by women in national parliament (%)	..		7	
Women in managerial positions (%)	..		..	

Channel Islands

Population (thousands)	149	Population living on less	
GNI ($ billions)	10.2	than $1.25 a day (%)	..
GNI per capita ($)	68,640		

	1990		2007	
	Female	Male	Female	Male
Demography				
Sex ratio at birth (females per 1,000 males)	946		946	
Life expectancy at birth (years)	79	74	81	77
Child mortality rate (per 1,000)	..	..	..	..
Female-headed households (%)	..		..	
Education				
Gross primary enrollment (% of relevant age group)	..	..	..	..
Gross secondary enrollment (% of relevant age group)	..	..	..	..
Gross tertiary enrollment (% of relevant age group)	..	..	..	..
Primary completion rate (% of relevant age group)	..	..	..	..
Adult literacy rate (% of population ages 15+)	..	..	..	..
Family planning and maternal health				
Total fertility rate (births per woman)	1.5		1.4	
Adolescent fertility (births per 1,000 women ages 15–19)	..		10	
Women married by age 18 (% of women ages 20–24)	..		..	
Contraceptive prevalence (% of women ages 15–49)	..		..	
Unmet need for contraception (% of women ages 15–49)	..		..	
Pregnant women receiving prenatal care (%)	..		..	
Births attended by skilled health staff (% of total)	..		..	
Maternal mortality ratio (per 100,000 live births)	..		..	
Labor force and employment dynamics				
Labor force participation (% of population ages 15+)	..	..	..	..
Women in the labor force (% of total labor force)	..		..	
Employment to population ratio (% ages 15+)	..	..	..	..
Vulnerable employment (% of employed ages 15+)	..	..	..	..
Employment in agriculture (% of employed ages 15+)	..	..	..	..
Employment in industry (% of employed ages 15+)	..	..	..	..
Employment in service (% of employed ages 15+)	..	..	..	..
Wage and salaried workers (% of employed ages 15+)	..	..	..	..
Self-employed workers (% of employed ages 15+)	..	..	..	..
Unpaid family workers (% of employed ages 15+)	..	..	..	..
Women in nonagricultural wage employment (%)	..		..	
Children in employment (% of children ages 7–14)	..	..	..	..
Unemployment (% of labor force ages 15+)	..	..	..	..
Long-term unemployment (% of total unemployment)	..	..	..	..
Youth unemployment (% of labor force ages 15–24)	..	..	..	..
Maternity leave (weeks)	..		..	
Maternal leave benefits (% of wages paid)	..		..	
Women's political participation				
Seats held by women in national parliament (%)	..		..	
Women in managerial positions (%)	..		..	

Chile

Latin America & Caribbean		Upper middle income	

Population (millions)	17	Population living on less	
GNI ($ billions)	135.8	than $1.25 a day (%)	2.0
GNI per capita ($)	8,190		

	1990		2007	
	Female	Male	Female	Male
Demography				
Sex ratio at birth (females per 1,000 males)	962		962	
Life expectancy at birth (years)	77	71	82	75
Child mortality rate (per 1,000)	..	..	..	..
Female-headed households (%)	..		..	
Education				
Gross primary enrollment (% of relevant age group)	100	102	102	107
Gross secondary enrollment (% of relevant age group)	77	71	92	90
Gross tertiary enrollment (% of relevant age group)	..	..	46	47
Primary completion rate (% of relevant age group)	..	..	95	96
Adult literacy rate (% of population ages 15+)	94	95	96	97
Family planning and maternal health				
Total fertility rate (births per woman)	2.6		1.9	
Adolescent fertility (births per 1,000 women ages 15–19)	..		60	
Women married by age 18 (% of women ages 20–24)	..		..	
Contraceptive prevalence (% of women ages 15–49)	56		58	
Unmet need for contraception (% of women ages 15–49)	..		..	
Pregnant women receiving prenatal care (%)	95		..	
Births attended by skilled health staff (% of total)	99		100	
Maternal mortality ratio (per 100,000 live births)	..		16	
Labor force and employment dynamics				
Labor force participation (% of population ages 15+)	32	77	39	72
Women in the labor force (% of total labor force)	31		36	
Employment to population ratio (% ages 15+)	30	73	36	67
Vulnerable employment (% of employed ages 15+)	..	..	24	25
Employment in agriculture (% of employed ages 15+)	6	25	6	17
Employment in industry (% of employed ages 15+)	14	30	12	29
Employment in service (% of employed ages 15+)	80	44	83	54
Wage and salaried workers (% of employed ages 15+)	77	71	74	71
Self-employed workers (% of employed ages 15+)	20	28	23	28
Unpaid family workers (% of employed ages 15+)	..	..	3	1
Women in nonagricultural wage employment (%)	36		39	
Children in employment (% of children ages 7–14)	..	..	3	5
Unemployment (% of labor force ages 15+)	6	6	7	5
Long-term unemployment (% of total unemployment)	27	15	..	..
Youth unemployment (% of labor force ages 15–24)	12	13	21	15
Maternity leave (weeks)	18		18	
Maternal leave benefits (% of wages paid)	100		100	
Women's political participation				
Seats held by women in national parliament (%)	..		15	
Women in managerial positions (%)	..		24	

China

East Asia & Pacific · **Lower middle income**

Population (millions)	1,318
GNI ($ billions)	3,126.0
GNI per capita ($)	2,370

Population living on less than $1.25 a day (%)	15.9

	1990		2007	
	Female	Male	Female	Male
Demography				
Sex ratio at birth (females per 1,000 males)	904		870	
Life expectancy at birth (years)	70	67	75	71
Child mortality rate (per 1,000)	..	..	..	..
Female-headed households (%)		..		..
Education				
Gross primary enrollment (% of relevant age group)	122	133	111	112
Gross secondary enrollment (% of relevant age group)	32	43	76	75
Gross tertiary enrollment (% of relevant age group)	..	..	21	22
Primary completion rate (% of relevant age group)	..	..	..	..
Adult literacy rate (% of population ages 15+)	68	87	90	96
Family planning and maternal health				
Total fertility rate (births per woman)	2.1		1.7	
Adolescent fertility (births per 1,000 women ages 15–19)	..		8	
Women married by age 18 (% of women ages 20–24)	..		..	
Contraceptive prevalence (% of women ages 15–49)	85		85	
Unmet need for contraception (% of women ages 15–49)	..		..	
Pregnant women receiving prenatal care (%)	..		90	
Births attended by skilled health staff (% of total)	50		98	
Maternal mortality ratio (per 100,000 live births)	..		45	
Labor force and employment dynamics				
Labor force participation (% of population ages 15+)	73	85	71	80
Women in the labor force (% of total labor force)	45		46	
Employment to population ratio (% ages 15+)	71	81	69	77
Vulnerable employment (% of employed ages 15+)	..	..	..	..
Employment in agriculture (% of employed ages 15+)	..	..	..	..
Employment in industry (% of employed ages 15+)	..	..	..	..
Employment in service (% of employed ages 15+)	..	..	..	..
Wage and salaried workers (% of employed ages 15+)	..	..	..	..
Self-employed workers (% of employed ages 15+)	..	..	..	..
Unpaid family workers (% of employed ages 15+)	..	..	..	..
Women in nonagricultural wage employment (%)	38		..	
Children in employment (% of children ages 7–14)	..	..	..	..
Unemployment (% of labor force ages 15+)	..	..	..	..
Long-term unemployment (% of total unemployment)	..	..	..	..
Youth unemployment (% of labor force ages 15–24)	..	..	..	..
Maternity leave (weeks)	8		13	
Maternal leave benefits (% of wages paid)	100		100	
Women's political participation				
Seats held by women in national parliament (%)	21		20	
Women in managerial positions (%)		..		..

Colombia

Latin America & Caribbean	Lower middle income

Population (millions)	44	Population living on less	
GNI ($ billions)	180.4	than $1.25 a day (%)	16.0
GNI per capita ($)	4,100		

	1990		2007	
	Female	Male	Female	Male
Demography				
Sex ratio at birth (females per 1,000 males)	952		952	
Life expectancy at birth (years)	72	64	77	69
Child mortality rate (per 1,000)	6	11	3	4
Female-headed households (%)	23		19	
Education				
Gross primary enrollment (% of relevant age group)	109	95	116	117
Gross secondary enrollment (% of relevant age group)	53	47	90	81
Gross tertiary enrollment (% of relevant age group)	..	..	33	30
Primary completion rate (% of relevant age group)	82	60	109	105
Adult literacy rate (% of population ages 15+)	81	81	93	92
Family planning and maternal health				
Total fertility rate (births per woman)	3.0		2.5	
Adolescent fertility (births per 1,000 women ages 15–19)	..		76	
Women married by age 18 (% of women ages 20–24)	22		..	
Contraceptive prevalence (% of women ages 15–49)	66		78	
Unmet need for contraception (% of women ages 15–49)	11		6	
Pregnant women receiving prenatal care (%)	83		94	
Births attended by skilled health staff (% of total)	82		96	
Maternal mortality ratio (per 100,000 live births)	..		130	
Labor force and employment dynamics				
Labor force participation (% of population ages 15+)	44	77	64	79
Women in the labor force (% of total labor force)	36		46	
Employment to population ratio (% ages 15+)	38	68	55	72
Vulnerable employment (% of employed ages 15+)	26	30	41	41
Employment in agriculture (% of employed ages 15+)	1	2	8	32
Employment in industry (% of employed ages 15+)	25	35	16	21
Employment in service (% of employed ages 15+)	74	63	76	48
Wage and salaried workers (% of employed ages 15+)	71	63	56	53
Self-employed workers (% of employed ages 15+)	26	36	38	44
Unpaid family workers (% of employed ages 15+)	2	1	6	3
Women in nonagricultural wage employment (%)	42		49	
Children in employment (% of children ages 7–14)	..	..	2	6
Unemployment (% of labor force ages 15+)	13	8	14	9
Long-term unemployment (% of total unemployment)	..	..	..	..
Youth unemployment (% of labor force ages 15–24)	20	14	19	12
Maternity leave (weeks)	12		12	
Maternal leave benefits (% of wages paid)	100		100	
Women's political participation				
Seats held by women in national parliament (%)	5		8	
Women in managerial positions (%)	..		..	

Comoros

Sub-Saharan Africa		Low income

Population (thousands)	628	Population living on less
GNI ($ millions)	425.5	than $1.25 a day (%) 46.1
GNI per capita ($)	680	

	1990		2007	
	Female	Male	Female	Male
Demography				
Sex ratio at birth (females per 1,000 males)	952		952	
Life expectancy at birth (years)	59	55	67	63
Child mortality rate (per 1,000)	..	..	..	..
Female-headed households (%)	..		..	
Education				
Gross primary enrollment (% of relevant age group)	59	85	80	91
Gross secondary enrollment (% of relevant age group)	15	21	30	40
Gross tertiary enrollment (% of relevant age group)	..	..	2	3
Primary completion rate (% of relevant age group)	..	..	49	52
Adult literacy rate (% of population ages 15+)	..	..	70	80
Family planning and maternal health				
Total fertility rate (births per woman)	6.1		4.3	
Adolescent fertility (births per 1,000 women ages 15–19)	..		49	
Women married by age 18 (% of women ages 20–24)	..		..	
Contraceptive prevalence (% of women ages 15–49)	..		..	
Unmet need for contraception (% of women ages 15–49)	..		..	
Pregnant women receiving prenatal care (%)	..		75	
Births attended by skilled health staff (% of total)	..		..	
Maternal mortality ratio (per 100,000 live births)	..		400	
Labor force and employment dynamics				
Labor force participation (% of population ages 15+)	64	86	63	83
Women in the labor force (% of total labor force)	43		43	
Employment to population ratio (% ages 15+)	60	79	59	77
Vulnerable employment (% of employed ages 15+)	..	..	..	..
Employment in agriculture (% of employed ages 15+)	..	..	..	..
Employment in industry (% of employed ages 15+)	..	..	..	..
Employment in service (% of employed ages 15+)	..	..	..	..
Wage and salaried workers (% of employed ages 15+)	..	..	..	..
Self-employed workers (% of employed ages 15+)	..	..	..	..
Unpaid family workers (% of employed ages 15+)	..	..	..	..
Women in nonagricultural wage employment (%)	..		..	
Children in employment (% of children ages 7–14)	..	..	..	..
Unemployment (% of labor force ages 15+)	17	21	..	..
Long-term unemployment (% of total unemployment)	..	..	..	..
Youth unemployment (% of labor force ages 15–24)	..	..	..	..
Maternity leave (weeks)	14		14	
Maternal leave benefits (% of wages paid)	100		100	
Women's political participation				
Seats held by women in national parliament (%)	0		3	
Women in managerial positions (%)	..		..	

Congo, Dem. Rep.

Sub-Saharan Africa				Low income

Population (millions)	62	Population living on less		
GNI ($ billions)	8.6	than $1.25 a day (%)		59.2
GNI per capita ($)	140			

	1990		2007	
	Female	Male	Female	Male
Demography				
Sex ratio at birth (females per 1,000 males)	971		971	
Life expectancy at birth (years)	48	44	48	45
Child mortality rate (per 1,000)	..	..	64	70
Female-headed households (%)	..		21	
Education				
Gross primary enrollment (% of relevant age group)	45	64	76	94
Gross secondary enrollment (% of relevant age group)	14	29	23	44
Gross tertiary enrollment (% of relevant age group)	..	..	2	6
Primary completion rate (% of relevant age group)	34	58	41	61
Adult literacy rate (% of population ages 15+)	..	..	..	..
Family planning and maternal health				
Total fertility rate (births per woman)	6.7		6.3	
Adolescent fertility (births per 1,000 women ages 15–19)	..		222	
Women married by age 18 (% of women ages 20–24)	..		..	
Contraceptive prevalence (% of women ages 15–49)	8		..	
Unmet need for contraception (% of women ages 15–49)	..		24	
Pregnant women receiving prenatal care (%)	..		85	
Births attended by skilled health staff (% of total)	..		74	
Maternal mortality ratio (per 100,000 live births)	..		1,100	
Labor force and employment dynamics				
Labor force participation (% of population ages 15+)	60	86	54	90
Women in the labor force (% of total labor force)	43		39	
Employment to population ratio (% ages 15+)	55	80	50	83
Vulnerable employment (% of employed ages 15+)	..	..	..	..
Employment in agriculture (% of employed ages 15+)	..	..	..	..
Employment in industry (% of employed ages 15+)	..	..	..	..
Employment in service (% of employed ages 15+)	..	..	..	..
Wage and salaried workers (% of employed ages 15+)	..	..	..	..
Self-employed workers (% of employed ages 15+)	..	..	..	..
Unpaid family workers (% of employed ages 15+)	..	..	..	..
Women in nonagricultural wage employment (%)	26		..	
Children in employment (% of children ages 7–14)	..	..	..	..
Unemployment (% of labor force ages 15+)	..	..	..	..
Long-term unemployment (% of total unemployment)	..	..	..	..
Youth unemployment (% of labor force ages 15–24)	..	..	..	..
Maternity leave (weeks)	14		14	
Maternal leave benefits (% of wages paid)	67		67	
Women's political participation				
Seats held by women in national parliament (%)	5		8	
Women in managerial positions (%)	..		..	

Congo, Rep.

Sub-Saharan Africa		Lower middle income	

Population (millions)	3.8	Population living on less	
GNI ($ billions)	5.8	than $1.25 a day (%)	54.1
GNI per capita ($)	1,540		

	1990		2007	
	Female	Male	Female	Male
Demography				
Sex ratio at birth (females per 1,000 males)	971		971	
Life expectancy at birth (years)	59	54	57	54
Child mortality rate (per 1,000)	..	..	43	49
Female-headed households (%)		..	23	
Education				
Gross primary enrollment (% of relevant age group)	118	128	102	110
Gross secondary enrollment (% of relevant age group)	41	54	39	47
Gross tertiary enrollment (% of relevant age group)	..	..	1	6
Primary completion rate (% of relevant age group)	58	60	70	75
Adult literacy rate (% of population ages 15+)	..	..	..	..
Family planning and maternal health				
Total fertility rate (births per woman)	5.3		4.5	
Adolescent fertility (births per 1,000 women ages 15–19)	..		115	
Women married by age 18 (% of women ages 20–24)	..		..	
Contraceptive prevalence (% of women ages 15–49)	..		21	
Unmet need for contraception (% of women ages 15–49)	..		16	
Pregnant women receiving prenatal care (%)	..		86	
Births attended by skilled health staff (% of total)	..		83	
Maternal mortality ratio (per 100,000 live births)	..		740	
Labor force and employment dynamics				
Labor force participation (% of population ages 15+)	57	84	56	83
Women in the labor force (% of total labor force)	41		41	
Employment to population ratio (% ages 15+)	53	77	52	77
Vulnerable employment (% of employed ages 15+)	..	..	..	..
Employment in agriculture (% of employed ages 15+)	..	..	..	..
Employment in industry (% of employed ages 15+)	..	..	..	..
Employment in service (% of employed ages 15+)	..	..	..	..
Wage and salaried workers (% of employed ages 15+)	..	..	..	..
Self-employed workers (% of employed ages 15+)	..	..	..	..
Unpaid family workers (% of employed ages 15+)	..	..	..	..
Women in nonagricultural wage employment (%)	26		..	
Children in employment (% of children ages 7–14)	..	..	30	30
Unemployment (% of labor force ages 15+)	..	..	..	..
Long-term unemployment (% of total unemployment)	..	..	..	..
Youth unemployment (% of labor force ages 15–24)	..	..	..	..
Maternity leave (weeks)	15		15	
Maternal leave benefits (% of wages paid)	100		100	
Women's political participation				
Seats held by women in national parliament (%)	14		7	
Women in managerial positions (%)	..		..	

Costa Rica

Latin America & Caribbean		Upper middle income	

		Population living on less	
Population (millions)	4.5	than $1.25 a day (%)	2.4
GNI ($ billions)	24.6		
GNI per capita ($)	5,520		

	1990		2007	
	Female	Male	Female	Male
Demography				
Sex ratio at birth (females per 1,000 males)	952		952	
Life expectancy at birth (years)	78	74	81	76
Child mortality rate (per 1,000)	..	..	..	..
Female-headed households (%)	..		..	
Education				
Gross primary enrollment (% of relevant age group)	101	102	110	111
Gross secondary enrollment (% of relevant age group)	44	42	90	85
Gross tertiary enrollment (% of relevant age group)	..	..	28	23
Primary completion rate (% of relevant age group)	81	77	93	90
Adult literacy rate (% of population ages 15+)	..	..	96	96
Family planning and maternal health				
Total fertility rate (births per woman)	3.1		2.1	
Adolescent fertility (births per 1,000 women ages 15–19)	..		71	
Women married by age 18 (% of women ages 20–24)	..		..	
Contraceptive prevalence (% of women ages 15–49)	75		96	
Unmet need for contraception (% of women ages 15–49)	..		..	
Pregnant women receiving prenatal care (%)	95		92	
Births attended by skilled health staff (% of total)	98		99	
Maternal mortality ratio (per 100,000 live births)	..		30	
Labor force and employment dynamics				
Labor force participation (% of population ages 15+)	36	85	43	79
Women in the labor force (% of total labor force)	29		35	
Employment to population ratio (% ages 15+)	33	80	40	77
Vulnerable employment (% of employed ages 15+)	21	26	20	20
Employment in agriculture (% of employed ages 15+)	6	34	5	21
Employment in industry (% of employed ages 15+)	24	27	13	26
Employment in service (% of employed ages 15+)	69	39	82	52
Wage and salaried workers (% of employed ages 15+)	78	67	76	71
Self-employed workers (% of employed ages 15+)	16	28	21	27
Unpaid family workers (% of employed ages 15+)	6	5	3	1
Women in nonagricultural wage employment (%)	37		41	
Children in employment (% of children ages 7–14)	..	..	4	8
Unemployment (% of labor force ages 15+)	6	4	7	3
Long-term unemployment (% of total unemployment)	14	8	..	..
Youth unemployment (% of labor force ages 15–24)	10	8	22	11
Maternity leave (weeks)	17		16	
Maternal leave benefits (% of wages paid)	100		100	
Women's political participation				
Seats held by women in national parliament (%)	11		39	
Women in managerial positions (%)	..		29	

Côte d'Ivoire

Sub-Saharan Africa			Low income	

Population (millions)	19	Population living on less	
GNI ($ billions)	17.8	than $1.25 a day (%)	23.3
GNI per capita ($)	920		

	1990		2007	
	Female	Male	Female	Male
Demography				
Sex ratio at birth (females per 1,000 males)	978		978	
Life expectancy at birth (years)	56	51	49	48
Child mortality rate (per 1,000)	..	..	..	..
Female-headed households (%)	..		..	
Education				
Gross primary enrollment (% of relevant age group)	55	77	64	81
Gross secondary enrollment (% of relevant age group)	13	28	..	..
Gross tertiary enrollment (% of relevant age group)	..	..	5	11
Primary completion rate (% of relevant age group)	31	52	36	53
Adult literacy rate (% of population ages 15+)	*23*	*44*	..	..
Family planning and maternal health				
Total fertility rate (births per woman)	6.5		4.5	
Adolescent fertility (births per 1,000 women ages 15–19)	..		107	
Women married by age 18 (% of women ages 20–24)	..		..	
Contraceptive prevalence (% of women ages 15–49)	..		*13*	
Unmet need for contraception (% of women ages 15–49)	..		*29*	
Pregnant women receiving prenatal care (%)	..		*85*	
Births attended by skilled health staff (% of total)	..		*57*	
Maternal mortality ratio (per 100,000 live births)	..		*810*	
Labor force and employment dynamics				
Labor force participation (% of population ages 15+)	42	89	39	85
Women in the labor force (% of total labor force)	30		31	
Employment to population ratio (% ages 15+)	*40*	*82*	38	81
Vulnerable employment (% of employed ages 15+)	..	..	..	..
Employment in agriculture (% of employed ages 15+)	..	..	..	..
Employment in industry (% of employed ages 15+)	..	..	..	..
Employment in service (% of employed ages 15+)	..	..	..	..
Wage and salaried workers (% of employed ages 15+)	..	..	..	..
Self-employed workers (% of employed ages 15+)	..	..	..	..
Unpaid family workers (% of employed ages 15+)	..	..	..	..
Women in nonagricultural wage employment (%)	..		..	
Children in employment (% of children ages 7–14)	..	..	*44*	*48*
Unemployment (% of labor force ages 15+)	..	..	..	..
Long-term unemployment (% of total unemployment)	..	..	..	..
Youth unemployment (% of labor force ages 15–24)	..	..	..	..
Maternity leave (weeks)	14		*14*	
Maternal leave benefits (% of wages paid)	100		*100*	
Women's political participation				
Seats held by women in national parliament (%)	6		9	
Women in managerial positions (%)	..		..	

Croatia

Europe & Central Asia   **Upper middle income**

Population (millions)	4.4	Population living on less
GNI ($ billions)	46.4	than $1.25 a day (%) 2.0
GNI per capita ($)	10,460	

	1990		2007	
	Female	**Male**	**Female**	**Male**
Demography				
Sex ratio at birth (females per 1,000 males)	944		944	
Life expectancy at birth (years)	76	69	79	72
Child mortality rate (per 1,000)	..	..	..	..
Female-headed households (%)	..			
Education				
Gross primary enrollment (% of relevant age group)	..	..	99	99
Gross secondary enrollment (% of relevant age group)	..	..	93	90
Gross tertiary enrollment (% of relevant age group)	..	..	49	40
Primary completion rate (% of relevant age group)	..	..	95	97
Adult literacy rate (% of population ages 15+)	95	99	98	99
Family planning and maternal health				
Total fertility rate (births per woman)	1.6		1.4	
Adolescent fertility (births per 1,000 women ages 15–19)	..		14	
Women married by age 18 (% of women ages 20–24)	..		..	
Contraceptive prevalence (% of women ages 15–49)	..		..	
Unmet need for contraception (% of women ages 15–49)	..		..	
Pregnant women receiving prenatal care (%)	..		100	
Births attended by skilled health staff (% of total)	100		100	
Maternal mortality ratio (per 100,000 live births)	..		7	
Labor force and employment dynamics				
Labor force participation (% of population ages 15+)	52	75	45	60
Women in the labor force (% of total labor force)	43		45	
Employment to population ratio (% ages 15+)	37	56	39	56
Vulnerable employment (% of employed ages 15+)	..	..	18	18
Employment in agriculture (% of employed ages 15+)	..	..	14	12
Employment in industry (% of employed ages 15+)	..	..	18	40
Employment in service (% of employed ages 15+)	..	..	67	48
Wage and salaried workers (% of employed ages 15+)	..	..	80	77
Self-employed workers (% of employed ages 15+)	..	..	17	22
Unpaid family workers (% of employed ages 15+)	..	..	4	1
Women in nonagricultural wage employment (%)	44		44	
Children in employment (% of children ages 7–14)	..	..	..	..
Unemployment (% of labor force ages 15+)	..	..	11	8
Long-term unemployment (% of total unemployment)	..	..	62	55
Youth unemployment (% of labor force ages 15–24)	..	..	28	21
Maternity leave (weeks)	..		59	
Maternal leave benefits (% of wages paid)	..		100	
Women's political participation				
Seats held by women in national parliament (%)	..		19	
Women in managerial positions (%)	..		26	

Cuba

| Latin America & Caribbean | | | Upper middle income | |

Population (millions)	11	Population living on less	
GNI ($ billions)	..	than $1.25 a day (%)	..
GNI per capita ($)	..		

| | 1990 | | 2007 | |
	Female	Male	Female	Male
Demography				
Sex ratio at birth (females per 1,000 males)	946		946	
Life expectancy at birth (years)	77	73	80	76
Child mortality rate (per 1,000)	..	..	..	..
Female-headed households (%)		..		46
Education				
Gross primary enrollment (% of relevant age group)	98	103	100	103
Gross secondary enrollment (% of relevant age group)	101	89	93	93
Gross tertiary enrollment (% of relevant age group)	..	..	143	77
Primary completion rate (% of relevant age group)	..	..	93	93
Adult literacy rate (% of population ages 15+)	..	..	100	100
Family planning and maternal health				
Total fertility rate (births per woman)	1.7		1.5	
Adolescent fertility (births per 1,000 women ages 15–19)		..		47
Women married by age 18 (% of women ages 20–24)		..		..
Contraceptive prevalence (% of women ages 15–49)		70		77
Unmet need for contraception (% of women ages 15–49)		..		8
Pregnant women receiving prenatal care (%)		..		100
Births attended by skilled health staff (% of total)		100		100
Maternal mortality ratio (per 100,000 live births)		..		45
Labor force and employment dynamics				
Labor force participation (% of population ages 15+)	36	73	45	69
Women in the labor force (% of total labor force)	33		39	
Employment to population ratio (% ages 15+)	35	71	44	68
Vulnerable employment (% of employed ages 15+)	..	..	..	..
Employment in agriculture (% of employed ages 15+)	..	..	10	28
Employment in industry (% of employed ages 15+)	..	..	14	23
Employment in service (% of employed ages 15+)	..	..	76	50
Wage and salaried workers (% of employed ages 15+)	..	..	94	77
Self-employed workers (% of employed ages 15+)	..	..	7	23
Unpaid family workers (% of employed ages 15+)	..	..	..	..
Women in nonagricultural wage employment (%)		..		43
Children in employment (% of children ages 7–14)	..	..	..	..
Unemployment (% of labor force ages 15+)	..	..	2	2
Long-term unemployment (% of total unemployment)	..	..	..	..
Youth unemployment (% of labor force ages 15–24)	..	..	..	..
Maternity leave (weeks)	18		18	
Maternal leave benefits (% of wages paid)	100		100	
Women's political participation				
Seats held by women in national parliament (%)		34		36
Women in managerial positions (%)		..		..

Cyprus

Population (thousands)	855	Population living on less
GNI ($ billions)	19.6	than $1.25 a day (%) ..
GNI per capita ($)	24,940	

	1990		2007	
	Female	Male	Female	Male
Demography				
Sex ratio at birth (females per 1,000 males)	935		935	
Life expectancy at birth (years)	79	74	82	77
Child mortality rate (per 1,000)	..	..	..	..
Female-headed households (%)		..		..
Education				
Gross primary enrollment (% of relevant age group)	89	89	102	103
Gross secondary enrollment (% of relevant age group)	71	70	97	96
Gross tertiary enrollment (% of relevant age group)	..	..	34	33
Primary completion rate (% of relevant age group)	83	84	101	101
Adult literacy rate (% of population ages 15+)	91	98	97	99
Family planning and maternal health				
Total fertility rate (births per woman)	2.4		1.5	
Adolescent fertility (births per 1,000 women ages 15–19)	..		8	
Women married by age 18 (% of women ages 20–24)	..		..	
Contraceptive prevalence (% of women ages 15–49)	..		..	
Unmet need for contraception (% of women ages 15–49)	..		..	
Pregnant women receiving prenatal care (%)	..		..	
Births attended by skilled health staff (% of total)	..		99	
Maternal mortality ratio (per 100,000 live births)	..		10	
Labor force and employment dynamics				
Labor force participation (% of population ages 15+)	48	81	54	70
Women in the labor force (% of total labor force)	38		45	
Employment to population ratio (% ages 15+)	45	78	51	68
Vulnerable employment (% of employed ages 15+)	..	..	11	17
Employment in agriculture (% of employed ages 15+)	16	12	4	6
Employment in industry (% of employed ages 15+)	25	31	11	34
Employment in service (% of employed ages 15+)	59	55	85	59
Wage and salaried workers (% of employed ages 15+)	..	..	87	74
Self-employed workers (% of employed ages 15+)	..	..	10	25
Unpaid family workers (% of employed ages 15+)	..	..	3	1
Women in nonagricultural wage employment (%)	..		48	
Children in employment (% of children ages 7–14)	..	..	..	..
Unemployment (% of labor force ages 15+)	..	..	5	4
Long-term unemployment (% of total unemployment)	..	..	..	..
Youth unemployment (% of labor force ages 15–24)	..	..	15	14
Maternity leave (weeks)	..		16	
Maternal leave benefits (% of wages paid)	..		75	
Women's political participation				
Seats held by women in national parliament (%)	2		14	
Women in managerial positions (%)	..		18	

Czech Republic

Population (millions)	10	Population living on less	
GNI ($ billions)	150.7	than $1.25 a day (%)	..
GNI per capita ($)	14,580		

	1990		2007	
	Female	Male	Female	Male
Demography				
Sex ratio at birth (females per 1,000 males)	945		945	
Life expectancy at birth (years)	75	68	80	74
Child mortality rate (per 1,000)	..	..	..	..
Female-headed households (%)		..		..
Education				
Gross primary enrollment (% of relevant age group)	96	96	100	100
Gross secondary enrollment (% of relevant age group)	88	97	97	95
Gross tertiary enrollment (% of relevant age group)	..	..	55	45
Primary completion rate (% of relevant age group)	..	..	93	95
Adult literacy rate (% of population ages 15+)	..	..	..	..
Family planning and maternal health				
Total fertility rate (births per woman)	1.9		1.4	
Adolescent fertility (births per 1,000 women ages 15–19)	..		11	
Women married by age 18 (% of women ages 20–24)	..		..	
Contraceptive prevalence (% of women ages 15–49)	78		..	
Unmet need for contraception (% of women ages 15–49)	..		..	
Pregnant women receiving prenatal care (%)	99		..	
Births attended by skilled health staff (% of total)	..		100	
Maternal mortality ratio (per 100,000 live births)	..		4	
Labor force and employment dynamics				
Labor force participation (% of population ages 15+)	61	80	51	68
Women in the labor force (% of total labor force)	45		44	
Employment to population ratio (% ages 15+)	48	68	48	65
Vulnerable employment (% of employed ages 15+)	5	8	9	15
Employment in agriculture (% of employed ages 15+)	10	15	3	5
Employment in industry (% of employed ages 15+)	36	54	27	49
Employment in service (% of employed ages 15+)	54	31	71	46
Wage and salaried workers (% of employed ages 15+)	90	84	89	79
Self-employed workers (% of employed ages 15+)	9	15	10	21
Unpaid family workers (% of employed ages 15+)	0	0	1	0
Women in nonagricultural wage employment (%)	51		46	
Children in employment (% of children ages 7–14)	..	..	..	..
Unemployment (% of labor force ages 15+)	5	3	7	4
Long-term unemployment (% of total unemployment)	18	20	55	52
Youth unemployment (% of labor force ages 15–24)	11	7	19	19
Maternity leave (weeks)	..		28	
Maternal leave benefits (% of wages paid)	..		69	
Women's political participation				
Seats held by women in national parliament (%)	..		16	
Women in managerial positions (%)	..		..	

Denmark

High income

			Population living on less	
Population (millions)	5.5		than $1.25 a day (%)	
GNI ($ billions)	302.8			..
GNI per capita ($)	55,440			

	1990		2007	
	Female	Male	Female	Male
Demography				
Sex ratio at birth (females per 1,000 males)	949		949	
Life expectancy at birth (years)	78	72	81	76
Child mortality rate (per 1,000)	..	..	..	..
Female-headed households (%)	..		..	
Education				
Gross primary enrollment (% of relevant age group)	98	98	99	99
Gross secondary enrollment (% of relevant age group)	110	108	121	118
Gross tertiary enrollment (% of relevant age group)	..	..	93	67
Primary completion rate (% of relevant age group)	95	95	102	101
Adult literacy rate (% of population ages 15+)	..	..	..	..
Family planning and maternal health				
Total fertility rate (births per woman)	1.7		1.9	
Adolescent fertility (births per 1,000 women ages 15-19)	..		6	
Women married by age 18 (% of women ages 20-24)	..		..	
Contraceptive prevalence (% of women ages 15-49)	78		..	
Unmet need for contraception (% of women ages 15-49)	..		..	
Pregnant women receiving prenatal care (%)	..		..	
Births attended by skilled health staff (% of total)	100		..	
Maternal mortality ratio (per 100,000 live births)	..		3	
Labor force and employment dynamics				
Labor force participation (% of population ages 15+)	62	75	61	71
Women in the labor force (% of total labor force)	46		47	
Employment to population ratio (% ages 15+)	56	68	58	68
Vulnerable employment (% of employed ages 15+)	..	..	..	..
Employment in agriculture (% of employed ages 15+)	3	8	2	4
Employment in industry (% of employed ages 15+)	16	37	12	34
Employment in service (% of employed ages 15+)	81	55	86	62
Wage and salaried workers (% of employed ages 15+)	..	..	95	88
Self-employed workers (% of employed ages 15+)	..	..	4	12
Unpaid family workers (% of employed ages 15+)	..	..	1	0
Women in nonagricultural wage employment (%)	48		49	
Children in employment (% of children ages 7-14)	..	..	..	..
Unemployment (% of labor force ages 15+)	9	8	4	3
Long-term unemployment (% of total unemployment)	32	28	18	18
Youth unemployment (% of labor force ages 15-24)	12	11	10	6
Maternity leave (weeks)	18		18	
Maternal leave benefits (% of wages paid)	..		90	
Women's political participation				
Seats held by women in national parliament (%)	31		37	
Women in managerial positions (%)	..		26	

Djibouti

Middle East & North Africa		Lower middle income	

Population (thousands)	833	Population living on less	
GNI ($ millions)	907.8	than $1.25 a day (%)	18.8
GNI per capita ($)	1,090		

	1990		2007	
	Female	Male	Female	Male
Demography				
Sex ratio at birth (females per 1,000 males)	962		962	
Life expectancy at birth (years)	53	50	56	54
Child mortality rate (per 1,000)	..	..	*24*	*29*
Female-headed households (%)	..		..	
Education				
Gross primary enrollment (% of relevant age group)	30	41	52	59
Gross secondary enrollment (% of relevant age group)	9	13	24	35
Gross tertiary enrollment (% of relevant age group)	..	..	2	3
Primary completion rate (% of relevant age group)	..	..	*32*	*39*
Adult literacy rate (% of population ages 15+)	..	..	..	..
Family planning and maternal health				
Total fertility rate (births per woman)	6.1		3.9	
Adolescent fertility (births per 1,000 women ages 15-19)	..		23	
Women married by age 18 (% of women ages 20-24)	..		..	
Contraceptive prevalence (% of women ages 15-49)	..		*18*	
Unmet need for contraception (% of women ages 15-49)	..		22	
Pregnant women receiving prenatal care (%)	..		92	
Births attended by skilled health staff (% of total)	..		93	
Maternal mortality ratio (per 100,000 live births)	..		650	
Labor force and employment dynamics				
Labor force participation (% of population ages 15+)	60	82	58	77
Women in the labor force (% of total labor force)	43		43	
Employment to population ratio (% ages 15+)	..	..	..	..
Vulnerable employment (% of employed ages 15+)	..	..	..	..
Employment in agriculture (% of employed ages 15+)	0	3	..	..
Employment in industry (% of employed ages 15+)	1	11	..	..
Employment in service (% of employed ages 15+)	88	78	..	..
Wage and salaried workers (% of employed ages 15+)	79	75	..	..
Self-employed workers (% of employed ages 15+)	16	19	..	..
Unpaid family workers (% of employed ages 15+)	..	..	..	..
Women in nonagricultural wage employment (%)	..		..	
Children in employment (% of children ages 7-14)	..	..	..	..
Unemployment (% of labor force ages 15+)	*47*	*42*	..	..
Long-term unemployment (% of total unemployment)	..	..	..	..
Youth unemployment (% of labor force ages 15-24)	..	..	..	..
Maternity leave (weeks)	14		*14*	
Maternal leave benefits (% of wages paid)	50		*50*	
Women's political participation				
Seats held by women in national parliament (%)	0		11	
Women in managerial positions (%)	..		..	

Dominica

Latin America & Caribbean		Upper middle income

		Population living on less
Population (thousands)	73	than $1.25 a day (%)
GNI ($ millions)	291.7	
GNI per capita ($)	4,030	..

	1990		2007	
	Female	Male	Female	Male
Demography				
Sex ratio at birth (females per 1,000 males)	..		..	
Life expectancy at birth (years)	75	71	..	..
Child mortality rate (per 1,000)	..	..	..	..
Female-headed households (%)	..		..	
Education				
Gross primary enrollment (% of relevant age group)	..	..	87	85
Gross secondary enrollment (% of relevant age group)	..	..	105	107
Gross tertiary enrollment (% of relevant age group)	..	..	..	..
Primary completion rate (% of relevant age group)	..	..	95	97
Adult literacy rate (% of population ages 15+)	..	..	..	..
Family planning and maternal health				
Total fertility rate (births per woman)	2.7		1.9	
Adolescent fertility (births per 1,000 women ages 15–19)	..		..	
Women married by age 18 (% of women ages 20–24)	..		..	
Contraceptive prevalence (% of women ages 15–49)	50		..	
Unmet need for contraception (% of women ages 15–49)	..		..	
Pregnant women receiving prenatal care (%)	90		100	
Births attended by skilled health staff (% of total)	..		99	
Maternal mortality ratio (per 100,000 live births)	..		..	
Labor force and employment dynamics				
Labor force participation (% of population ages 15+)	..	..	..	..
Women in the labor force (% of total labor force)	..		..	
Employment to population ratio (% ages 15+)	..	..	..	..
Vulnerable employment (% of employed ages 15+)	23	32	..	..
Employment in agriculture (% of employed ages 15+)	13	39	..	..
Employment in industry (% of employed ages 15+)	27	36	..	..
Employment in service (% of employed ages 15+)	55	29	..	..
Wage and salaried workers (% of employed ages 15+)	70	57	..	..
Self-employed workers (% of employed ages 15+)	25	38	..	..
Unpaid family workers (% of employed ages 15+)	3	3	..	..
Women in nonagricultural wage employment (%)	43		..	
Children in employment (% of children ages 7–14)	..	..	..	..
Unemployment (% of labor force ages 15+)	10	10	..	..
Long-term unemployment (% of total unemployment)	..	..	..	..
Youth unemployment (% of labor force ages 15–24)	29	14	..	..
Maternity leave (weeks)	9		12	
Maternal leave benefits (% of wages paid)	..		60	
Women's political participation				
Seats held by women in national parliament (%)	10		13	
Women in managerial positions (%)	..		..	

Dominican Republic

Latin America & Caribbean		Lower middle income

Population (millions)	9.7	Population living on less
GNI ($ billions)	34.6	than $1.25 a day (%) 5.0
GNI per capita ($)	3,560	

	1990		2007	
	Female	Male	Female	Male
Demography				
Sex ratio at birth (females per 1,000 males)	952		952	
Life expectancy at birth (years)	71	66	75	69
Child mortality rate (per 1,000)	20	18	4	6
Female-headed households (%)	25		35	
Education				
Gross primary enrollment (% of relevant age group)	..	..	103	110
Gross secondary enrollment (% of relevant age group)	..	..	86	72
Gross tertiary enrollment (% of relevant age group)	..	..	42	27
Primary completion rate (% of relevant age group)	..	..	91	87
Adult literacy rate (% of population ages 15+)	..	..	90	89
Family planning and maternal health				
Total fertility rate (births per woman)	3.3		2.4	
Adolescent fertility (births per 1,000 women ages 15–19)	..		108	
Women married by age 18 (% of women ages 20–24)	30		..	
Contraceptive prevalence (% of women ages 15–49)	56		73	
Unmet need for contraception (% of women ages 15–49)	17		11	
Pregnant women receiving prenatal care (%)	97		99	
Births attended by skilled health staff (% of total)	93		98	
Maternal mortality ratio (per 100,000 live births)	..		150	
Labor force and employment dynamics				
Labor force participation (% of population ages 15+)	26	82	57	73
Women in the labor force (% of total labor force)	24		44	
Employment to population ratio (% ages 15+)	16	71	41	65
Vulnerable employment (% of employed ages 15+)	30	42	30	49
Employment in agriculture (% of employed ages 15+)	3	27	3	21
Employment in industry (% of employed ages 15+)	24	23	15	26
Employment in service (% of employed ages 15+)	74	50	82	53
Wage and salaried workers (% of employed ages 15+)	69	53	67	46
Self-employed workers (% of employed ages 15+)	27	41	29	52
Unpaid family workers (% of employed ages 15+)	4	6	5	3
Women in nonagricultural wage employment (%)	36		39	
Children in employment (% of children ages 7–14)	..	..	3	9
Unemployment (% of labor force ages 15+)	33	13	29	11
Long-term unemployment (% of total unemployment)	..	..	..	..
Youth unemployment (% of labor force ages 15–24)	48	25	..	..
Maternity leave (weeks)	12		12	
Maternal leave benefits (% of wages paid)	100		100	
Women's political participation				
Seats held by women in national parliament (%)	8		20	
Women in managerial positions (%)	..		..	

Ecuador

Latin America & Caribbean		Lower middle income	

Population (millions)	13	Population living on less	
GNI ($ billions)	41.5	than $1.25 a day (%)	4.7
GNI per capita ($)	3,110		

	1990		2007	
	Female	Male	Female	Male
Demography				
Sex ratio at birth (females per 1,000 males)	952		952	
Life expectancy at birth (years)	72	67	78	72
Child mortality rate (per 1,000)	26	25	5	5
Female-headed households (%)	..		..	
Education				
Gross primary enrollment (% of relevant age group)	116	117	118	119
Gross secondary enrollment (% of relevant age group)	..	..	70	69
Gross tertiary enrollment (% of relevant age group)	..	..	..	..
Primary completion rate (% of relevant age group)	..	..	107	105
Adult literacy rate (% of population ages 15+)	86	90	82	87
Family planning and maternal health				
Total fertility rate (births per woman)	3.6		2.6	
Adolescent fertility (births per 1,000 women ages 15–19)	..		83	
Women married by age 18 (% of women ages 20–24)	26		..	
Contraceptive prevalence (% of women ages 15–49)	53		73	
Unmet need for contraception (% of women ages 15–49)	..		..	
Pregnant women receiving prenatal care (%)	76		84	
Births attended by skilled health staff (% of total)	61		75	
Maternal mortality ratio (per 100,000 live births)	..		210	
Labor force and employment dynamics				
Labor force participation (% of population ages 15+)	33	78	52	79
Women in the labor force (% of total labor force)	29		40	
Employment to population ratio (% ages 15+)	30	74	46	74
Vulnerable employment (% of employed ages 15+)	41	33	41	29
Employment in agriculture (% of employed ages 15+)	3	10	4	11
Employment in industry (% of employed ages 15+)	17	30	12	27
Employment in service (% of employed ages 15+)	81	60	84	62
Wage and salaried workers (% of employed ages 15+)	45	60	55	63
Self-employed workers (% of employed ages 15+)	32	36	34	33
Unpaid family workers (% of employed ages 15+)	11	4	11	4
Women in nonagricultural wage employment (%)	37		42	
Children in employment (% of children ages 7–14)	..	..	9	15
Unemployment (% of labor force ages 15+)	9	4	11	6
Long-term unemployment (% of total unemployment)	..	..	..	..
Youth unemployment (% of labor force ages 15–24)	17	11	21	12
Maternity leave (weeks)	12		12	
Maternal leave benefits (% of wages paid)	100		100	
Women's political participation				
Seats held by women in national parliament (%)	5		25	
Women in managerial positions (%)	..		..	

Egypt, Arab Rep.

Middle East & North Africa   **Lower middle income**

Population (millions)	75	Population living on less	
GNI ($ billions)	119.5	than $1.25 a day (%)	2.0
GNI per capita ($)	1,580		

	1990		2007	
	Female	**Male**	**Female**	**Male**
Demography				
Sex ratio at birth (females per 1,000 males)	952		952	
Life expectancy at birth (years)	64	61	74	69
Child mortality rate (per 1,000)	*36*	*25*	*10*	*10*
Female-headed households (%)	*12*		*12*	
Education				
Gross primary enrollment (% of relevant age group)	83	99	102	107
Gross secondary enrollment (% of relevant age group)	61	79	*85*	*91*
Gross tertiary enrollment (% of relevant age group)	..	..	..	..
Primary completion rate (% of relevant age group)	..	..	96	101
Adult literacy rate (% of population ages 15+)	..	..	58	75
Family planning and maternal health				
Total fertility rate (births per woman)	4.3		2.9	
Adolescent fertility (births per 1,000 women ages 15–19)	..		39	
Women married by age 18 (% of women ages 20-24)	*27*		..	
Contraceptive prevalence (% of women ages 15–49)	*47*		*59*	
Unmet need for contraception (% of women ages 15–49)	*20*		*10*	
Pregnant women receiving prenatal care (%)	*52*		*70*	
Births attended by skilled health staff (% of total)	*37*		*74*	
Maternal mortality ratio (per 100,000 live births)	..		*130*	
Labor force and employment dynamics				
Labor force participation (% of population ages 15+)	24	74	24	71
Women in the labor force (% of total labor force)	24		25	
Employment to population ratio (% ages 15+)	*17*	*69*	18	67
Vulnerable employment (% of employed ages 15+)	*46*	*24*	*44*	*20*
Employment in agriculture (% of employed ages 15+)	*52*	*35*	*39*	*28*
Employment in industry (% of employed ages 15+)	*10*	*24*	*6*	*23*
Employment in service (% of employed ages 15+)	*38*	*41*	*55*	*49*
Wage and salaried workers (% of employed ages 15+)	*50*	*57*	*54*	*64*
Self-employed workers (% of employed ages 15+)	*18*	*33*	*14*	*28*
Unpaid family workers (% of employed ages 15+)	*33*	*10*	*33*	*9*
Women in nonagricultural wage employment (%)	21		21	
Children in employment (% of children ages 7-14)	..	..	*4*	*12*
Unemployment (% of labor force ages 15+)	18	5	19	6
Long-term unemployment (% of total unemployment)	..	..	..	..
Youth unemployment (% of labor force ages 15–24)	..	..	..	..
Maternity leave (weeks)	7		*13*	
Maternal leave benefits (% of wages paid)	100		*100*	
Women's political participation				
Seats held by women in national parliament (%)	4		2	
Women in managerial positions (%)	..		..	

El Salvador

Latin America & Caribbean		Lower middle income	

Population (millions)	6.9	Population living on less	
GNI ($ billions)	19.6	than $1.25 a day (%)	11.0
GNI per capita ($)	2,850		

	1990		2007	
	Female	Male	Female	Male
Demography				
Sex ratio at birth (females per 1,000 males)	952		952	
Life expectancy at birth (years)	70	62	75	69
Child mortality rate (per 1,000)	..	..	..	..
Female-headed households (%)	..		..	
Education				
Gross primary enrollment (% of relevant age group)	97	98	118	118
Gross secondary enrollment (% of relevant age group)	39	34	66	63
Gross tertiary enrollment (% of relevant age group)	..	..	24	20
Primary completion rate (% of relevant age group)	62	60	93	89
Adult literacy rate (% of population ages 15+)	71	77	80	85
Family planning and maternal health				
Total fertility rate (births per woman)	3.7		2.7	
Adolescent fertility (births per 1,000 women ages 15–19)	..		81	
Women married by age 18 (% of women ages 20–24)	..		..	
Contraceptive prevalence (% of women ages 15–49)	53		67	
Unmet need for contraception (% of women ages 15–49)	..		..	
Pregnant women receiving prenatal care (%)	69		86	
Births attended by skilled health staff (% of total)	51		92	
Maternal mortality ratio (per 100,000 live births)	..		170	
Labor force and employment dynamics				
Labor force participation (% of population ages 15+)	51	80	47	79
Women in the labor force (% of total labor force)	41		39	
Employment to population ratio (% ages 15+)	47	71	45	73
Vulnerable employment (% of employed ages 15+)	46	27	44	29
Employment in agriculture (% of employed ages 15+)	3	11	3	30
Employment in industry (% of employed ages 15+)	22	35	22	25
Employment in service (% of employed ages 15+)	75	54	75	45
Wage and salaried workers (% of employed ages 15+)	50	62	43	64
Self-employed workers (% of employed ages 15+)	41	30	37	26
Unpaid family workers (% of employed ages 15+)	9	7	10	9
Women in nonagricultural wage employment (%)	46		49	
Children in employment (% of children ages 7–14)	..	..	8	17
Unemployment (% of labor force ages 15+)	10	10	4	8
Long-term unemployment (% of total unemployment)	..	..	..	..
Youth unemployment (% of labor force ages 15–24)	14	15	9	13
Maternity leave (weeks)	12		12	
Maternal leave benefits (% of wages paid)	75		75	
Women's political participation				
Seats held by women in national parliament (%)	12		17	
Women in managerial positions (%)	..		32	

Equatorial Guinea

Population (thousands)	508	Population living on less
GNI ($ billions)	6.5	than $1.25 a day (%) ..
GNI per capita ($)	12,860	

	1990		2007	
	Female	Male	Female	Male
Demography				
Sex ratio at birth (females per 1,000 males)	971		971	
Life expectancy at birth (years)	48	45	53	50
Child mortality rate (per 1,000)	..	..	..	..
Female-headed households (%)	..		..	
Education				
Gross primary enrollment (% of relevant age group)	*169*	*177*	121	128
Gross secondary enrollment (% of relevant age group)	..	..	..	..
Gross tertiary enrollment (% of relevant age group)	..	..	..	..
Primary completion rate (% of relevant age group)	..	..	65	68
Adult literacy rate (% of population ages 15+)	..	..	..	..
Family planning and maternal health				
Total fertility rate (births per woman)	5.9		5.4	
Adolescent fertility (births per 1,000 women ages 15-19)	..		123	
Women married by age 18 (% of women ages 20-24)	..		..	
Contraceptive prevalence (% of women ages 15-49)	..		..	
Unmet need for contraception (% of women ages 15-49)	..		..	
Pregnant women receiving prenatal care (%)	..		..	
Births attended by skilled health staff (% of total)	..		..	
Maternal mortality ratio (per 100,000 live births)	..		*680*	
Labor force and employment dynamics				
Labor force participation (% of population ages 15+)	42	91	43	92
Women in the labor force (% of total labor force)	33		33	
Employment to population ratio (% ages 15+)	*39*	*84*	40	85
Vulnerable employment (% of employed ages 15+)	..	..	..	..
Employment in agriculture (% of employed ages 15+)	..	..	..	..
Employment in industry (% of employed ages 15+)	..	..	..	..
Employment in service (% of employed ages 15+)	..	..	..	..
Wage and salaried workers (% of employed ages 15+)	..	..	..	..
Self-employed workers (% of employed ages 15+)	..	..	..	..
Unpaid family workers (% of employed ages 15+)	..	..	..	..
Women in nonagricultural wage employment (%)	11		..	
Children in employment (% of children ages 7-14)	..	..	..	..
Unemployment (% of labor force ages 15+)	..	..	..	..
Long-term unemployment (% of total unemployment)	..	..	..	..
Youth unemployment (% of labor force ages 15-24)	..	..	..	..
Maternity leave (weeks)	12		*12*	
Maternal leave benefits (% of wages paid)	75		75	
Women's political participation				
Seats held by women in national parliament (%)	13		18	
Women in managerial positions (%)	..		..	

Eritrea

Sub-Saharan Africa		Low income

Population (millions)	4.8	Population living on less
GNI ($ billions)	1.3	than $1.25 a day (%)
GNI per capita ($)	270	..

	1990		2007	
	Female	Male	Female	Male
Demography				
Sex ratio at birth (females per 1,000 males)	971		971	
Life expectancy at birth (years)	51	46	60	56
Child mortality rate (per 1,000)	..	..	..	..
Female-headed households (%)	..		..	
Education				
Gross primary enrollment (% of relevant age group)	20	21	50	60
Gross secondary enrollment (% of relevant age group)	..	..	24	34
Gross tertiary enrollment (% of relevant age group)	..	..	0	2
Primary completion rate (% of relevant age group)	..	..	41	52
Adult literacy rate (% of population ages 15+)	..	..	..	..
Family planning and maternal health				
Total fertility rate (births per woman)	6.2		5.0	
Adolescent fertility (births per 1,000 women ages 15–19)	..		72	
Women married by age 18 (% of women ages 20–24)	..		..	
Contraceptive prevalence (% of women ages 15–49)	..		..	
Unmet need for contraception (% of women ages 15–49)	..		..	
Pregnant women receiving prenatal care (%)	..		..	
Births attended by skilled health staff (% of total)	..		..	
Maternal mortality ratio (per 100,000 live births)	..		450	
Labor force and employment dynamics				
Labor force participation (% of population ages 15+)	55	88	55	86
Women in the labor force (% of total labor force)	40		41	
Employment to population ratio (% ages 15+)	51	80	52	79
Vulnerable employment (% of employed ages 15+)	..	..	..	..
Employment in agriculture (% of employed ages 15+)	..	..	..	..
Employment in industry (% of employed ages 15+)	..	..	..	..
Employment in service (% of employed ages 15+)	..	..	..	..
Wage and salaried workers (% of employed ages 15+)	..	..	..	..
Self-employed workers (% of employed ages 15+)	..	..	..	..
Unpaid family workers (% of employed ages 15+)	..	..	..	..
Women in nonagricultural wage employment (%)	..		..	
Children in employment (% of children ages 7–14)	..	..	..	..
Unemployment (% of labor force ages 15+)	..	..	..	..
Long-term unemployment (% of total unemployment)	..	..	..	..
Youth unemployment (% of labor force ages 15–24)	..	..	..	..
Maternity leave (weeks)	..		9	
Maternal leave benefits (% of wages paid)	..		..	
Women's political participation				
Seats held by women in national parliament (%)	..		22	
Women in managerial positions (%)	..		..	

Estonia

			High income
Population (millions)	1.3	Population living on less	
GNI ($ billions)	17.2	than $1.25 a day (%)	2.0
GNI per capita ($)	12,830		

	1990		2007	
	Female	**Male**	**Female**	**Male**
Demography				
Sex ratio at birth (females per 1,000 males)	947		947	
Life expectancy at birth (years)	75	65	79	67
Child mortality rate (per 1,000)	..	..	..	..
Female-headed households (%)	..		..	
Education				
Gross primary enrollment (% of relevant age group)	93	96	98	100
Gross secondary enrollment (% of relevant age group)	107	100	101	99
Gross tertiary enrollment (% of relevant age group)	..	..	82	49
Primary completion rate (% of relevant age group)	..	..	98	102
Adult literacy rate (% of population ages 15+)	100	100	100	100
Family planning and maternal health				
Total fertility rate (births per woman)	2.0		1.6	
Adolescent fertility (births per 1,000 women ages 15–19)	..		21	
Women married by age 18 (% of women ages 20–24)	..		..	
Contraceptive prevalence (% of women ages 15–49)	..		..	
Unmet need for contraception (% of women ages 15–49)	..		..	
Pregnant women receiving prenatal care (%)	..		..	
Births attended by skilled health staff (% of total)	..		100	
Maternal mortality ratio (per 100,000 live births)	..		25	
Labor force and employment dynamics				
Labor force participation (% of population ages 15+)	61	72	54	65
Women in the labor force (% of total labor force)	50		50	
Employment to population ratio (% ages 15+)	58	69	52	62
Vulnerable employment (% of employed ages 15+)	3	2	4	8
Employment in agriculture (% of employed ages 15+)	15	27	4	7
Employment in industry (% of employed ages 15+)	31	42	24	44
Employment in service (% of employed ages 15+)	53	31	72	49
Wage and salaried workers (% of employed ages 15+)	97	97	95	88
Self-employed workers (% of employed ages 15+)	1	2	5	12
Unpaid family workers (% of employed ages 15+)	2	1	0	0
Women in nonagricultural wage employment (%)	52		53	
Children in employment (% of children ages 7–14)	..	..	..	..
Unemployment (% of labor force ages 15+)	1	1	4	5
Long-term unemployment (% of total unemployment)	..	..	..	..
Youth unemployment (% of labor force ages 15–24)	..	..	15	16
Maternity leave (weeks)	..		20	
Maternal leave benefits (% of wages paid)	..		100	
Women's political participation				
Seats held by women in national parliament (%)	..		22	
Women in managerial positions (%)	..		35	

Ethiopia

Sub-Saharan Africa | **Low income**

Population (millions)	79	Population living on less	
GNI ($ billions)	17.6	than $1.25 a day (%)	39.0
GNI per capita ($)	220		

	1990		2007	
	Female	Male	Female	Male
Demography				
Sex ratio at birth (females per 1,000 males)	971		971	
Life expectancy at birth (years)	49	46	54	52
Child mortality rate (per 1,000)	..	..	56	56
Female-headed households (%)	..		23	
Education				
Gross primary enrollment (% of relevant age group)	26	40	85	97
Gross secondary enrollment (% of relevant age group)	11	16	24	36
Gross tertiary enrollment (% of relevant age group)	..	..	1	4
Primary completion rate (% of relevant age group)	..	..	41	51
Adult literacy rate (% of population ages 15+)	..	..	23	50
Family planning and maternal health				
Total fertility rate (births per woman)	6.8		5.3	
Adolescent fertility (births per 1,000 women ages 15–19)	..		94	
Women married by age 18 (% of women ages 20–24)	..		..	
Contraceptive prevalence (% of women ages 15–49)	4		15	
Unmet need for contraception (% of women ages 15–49)	..		34	
Pregnant women receiving prenatal care (%)	..		28	
Births attended by skilled health staff (% of total)	..		6	
Maternal mortality ratio (per 100,000 live births)	..		720	
Labor force and employment dynamics				
Labor force participation (% of population ages 15+)	63	89	80	91
Women in the labor force (% of total labor force)	42		47	
Employment to population ratio (% ages 15+)	58	86	73	89
Vulnerable employment (% of employed ages 15+)	..	..	56	48
Employment in agriculture (% of employed ages 15+)	..	..	76	84
Employment in industry (% of employed ages 15+)	..	..	8	5
Employment in service (% of employed ages 15+)	..	..	16	10
Wage and salaried workers (% of employed ages 15+)	..	..	43	49
Self-employed workers (% of employed ages 15+)	..	..	44	42
Unpaid family workers (% of employed ages 15+)	..	..	13	8
Women in nonagricultural wage employment (%)	..		47	
Children in employment (% of children ages 7–14)	..	..	47	64
Unemployment (% of labor force ages 15+)	..	..	8	3
Long-term unemployment (% of total unemployment)	..	..	..	..
Youth unemployment (% of labor force ages 15–24)	..	..	11	4
Maternity leave (weeks)	12		13	
Maternal leave benefits (% of wages paid)	100		100	
Women's political participation				
Seats held by women in national parliament (%)	..		22	
Women in managerial positions (%)	..		..	

Faeroe Islands

Population (thousands)	48
GNI ($ billions)	..
GNI per capita ($)	..

Population living on less than $1.25 a day (%)	..

	1990		2007	
	Female	Male	Female	Male
Demography				
Sex ratio at birth (females per 1,000 males)			..	
Life expectancy at birth (years)	..	..	81	77
Child mortality rate (per 1,000)	..	..	..	..
Female-headed households (%)	..		..	
Education				
Gross primary enrollment (% of relevant age group)	..	..	..	..
Gross secondary enrollment (% of relevant age group)	..	..	..	..
Gross tertiary enrollment (% of relevant age group)	..	..	..	..
Primary completion rate (% of relevant age group)	..	..	..	..
Adult literacy rate (% of population ages 15+)	..	..	..	..
Family planning and maternal health				
Total fertility rate (births per woman)	..		..	
Adolescent fertility (births per 1,000 women ages 15–19)	..		..	
Women married by age 18 (% of women ages 20–24)	..		..	
Contraceptive prevalence (% of women ages 15–49)	..		..	
Unmet need for contraception (% of women ages 15–49)	..		..	
Pregnant women receiving prenatal care (%)	..		..	
Births attended by skilled health staff (% of total)	..		..	
Maternal mortality ratio (per 100,000 live births)	..		..	
Labor force and employment dynamics				
Labor force participation (% of population ages 15+)	..	..	..	..
Women in the labor force (% of total labor force)	..		..	
Employment to population ratio (% ages 15+)	..	..	..	..
Vulnerable employment (% of employed ages 15+)	..	..	..	..
Employment in agriculture (% of employed ages 15+)	..	..	..	..
Employment in industry (% of employed ages 15+)	..	..	..	..
Employment in service (% of employed ages 15+)	..	..	..	..
Wage and salaried workers (% of employed ages 15+)	..	..	..	..
Self-employed workers (% of employed ages 15+)	..	..	..	..
Unpaid family workers (% of employed ages 15+)	..	..	..	..
Women in nonagricultural wage employment (%)	..		46	
Children in employment (% of children ages 7–14)	..	..	..	..
Unemployment (% of labor force ages 15+)	..	..	4	3
Long-term unemployment (% of total unemployment)	..	..	..	..
Youth unemployment (% of labor force ages 15–24)	..	..	..	..
Maternity leave (weeks)	..		..	
Maternal leave benefits (% of wages paid)	..		..	
Women's political participation				
Seats held by women in national parliament (%)	..		..	
Women in managerial positions (%)	..		..	

Fiji

East Asia & Pacific		Upper middle income

Population (thousands)	834	Population living on less
GNI ($ billions)	3.1	than $1.25 a day (%) ..
GNI per capita ($)	3,750	

	1990		2007	
	Female	Male	Female	Male
Demography				
Sex ratio at birth (females per 1,000 males)	943		943	
Life expectancy at birth (years)	69	65	71	67
Child mortality rate (per 1,000)	..	..	..	..
Female-headed households (%)	..		..	
Education				
Gross primary enrollment (% of relevant age group)	131	132	93	96
Gross secondary enrollment (% of relevant age group)	54	57	87	78
Gross tertiary enrollment (% of relevant age group)	..	..	17	14
Primary completion rate (% of relevant age group)	..	..	98	98
Adult literacy rate (% of population ages 15+)	..	..	..	..
Family planning and maternal health				
Total fertility rate (births per woman)	3.4		2.8	
Adolescent fertility (births per 1,000 women ages 15–19)	..		32	
Women married by age 18 (% of women ages 20–24)	..		..	
Contraceptive prevalence (% of women ages 15–49)	..		..	
Unmet need for contraception (% of women ages 15–49)	..		..	
Pregnant women receiving prenatal care (%)	..		..	
Births attended by skilled health staff (% of total)	..		..	
Maternal mortality ratio (per 100,000 live births)	..		210	
Labor force and employment dynamics				
Labor force participation (% of population ages 15+)	29	84	39	79
Women in the labor force (% of total labor force)	25		33	
Employment to population ratio (% ages 15+)	28	79	37	76
Vulnerable employment (% of employed ages 15+)	..	..	39	39
Employment in agriculture (% of employed ages 15+)	..	..	..	..
Employment in industry (% of employed ages 15+)	..	..	..	..
Employment in service (% of employed ages 15+)	..	..	..	..
Wage and salaried workers (% of employed ages 15+)	..	..	57	59
Self-employed workers (% of employed ages 15+)	..	..	21	28
Unpaid family workers (% of employed ages 15+)	..	..	20	12
Women in nonagricultural wage employment (%)	30		31	
Children in employment (% of children ages 7–14)	..	..	..	..
Unemployment (% of labor force ages 15+)	..	..	6	4
Long-term unemployment (% of total unemployment)	..	..	..	..
Youth unemployment (% of labor force ages 15–24)	..	..	..	..
Maternity leave (weeks)	12		12	
Maternal leave benefits (% of wages paid)	..		..	
Women's political participation				
Seats held by women in national parliament (%)	..		11	
Women in managerial positions (%)	..		..	

Finland

		High income
Population (millions)	5.3	Population living on less
GNI ($ billions)	234.3	than $1.25 a day (%) ..
GNI per capita ($)	44,300	

	1990		2007	
	Female	Male	Female	Male
Demography				
Sex ratio at birth (females per 1,000 males)	954		954	
Life expectancy at birth (years)	79	71	83	76
Child mortality rate (per 1,000)	..	..	..	..
Female-headed households (%)	..		..	
Education				
Gross primary enrollment (% of relevant age group)	99	100	98	98
Gross secondary enrollment (% of relevant age group)	123	104	114	109
Gross tertiary enrollment (% of relevant age group)	..	..	103	84
Primary completion rate (% of relevant age group)	102	102	97	97
Adult literacy rate (% of population ages 15+)	..	..	..	..
Family planning and maternal health				
Total fertility rate (births per woman)	1.8		1.8	
Adolescent fertility (births per 1,000 women ages 15–19)	..		9	
Women married by age 18 (% of women ages 20–24)	..		..	
Contraceptive prevalence (% of women ages 15–49)	77		..	
Unmet need for contraception (% of women ages 15–49)	..		..	
Pregnant women receiving prenatal care (%)	100		..	
Births attended by skilled health staff (% of total)	100		100	
Maternal mortality ratio (per 100,000 live births)	..		7	
Labor force and employment dynamics				
Labor force participation (% of population ages 15+)	59	71	58	65
Women in the labor force (% of total labor force)	48		48	
Employment to population ratio (% ages 15+)	55	64	53	61
Vulnerable employment (% of employed ages 15+)	..	..	..	..
Employment in agriculture (% of employed ages 15+)	7	11	3	7
Employment in industry (% of employed ages 15+)	17	42	12	38
Employment in service (% of employed ages 15+)	76	47	84	56
Wage and salaried workers (% of employed ages 15+)	89	80	92	82
Self-employed workers (% of employed ages 15+)	11	18	..	..
Unpaid family workers (% of employed ages 15+)	1	2	0	1
Women in nonagricultural wage employment (%)	51		51	
Children in employment (% of children ages 7–14)	..	..	..	..
Unemployment (% of labor force ages 15+)	3	3	7	6
Long-term unemployment (% of total unemployment)	8	10	20	27
Youth unemployment (% of labor force ages 15–24)	8	10	19	21
Maternity leave (weeks)	15		21	
Maternal leave benefits (% of wages paid)	80		70	
Women's political participation				
Seats held by women in national parliament (%)	32		42	
Women in managerial positions (%)	..		28	

France

Population (millions)	62	Population living on less	
GNI ($ billions)	2,466.6	than $1.25 a day (%)	..
GNI per capita ($)	38,810		

	1990		2007	
	Female	Male	Female	Male
Demography				
Sex ratio at birth (females per 1,000 males)	951		951	
Life expectancy at birth (years)	81	73	85	78
Child mortality rate (per 1,000)	..	..	..	..
Female-headed households (%)	..		..	
Education				
Gross primary enrollment (% of relevant age group)	108	110	109	110
Gross secondary enrollment (% of relevant age group)	98	92	114	114
Gross tertiary enrollment (% of relevant age group)	..	..	63	50
Primary completion rate (% of relevant age group)	..	..	..	..
Adult literacy rate (% of population ages 15+)	..	..	..	..
Family planning and maternal health				
Total fertility rate (births per woman)	1.8		2.0	
Adolescent fertility (births per 1,000 women ages 15–19)	..		7	
Women married by age 18 (% of women ages 20–24)	..		..	
Contraceptive prevalence (% of women ages 15–49)	81		..	
Unmet need for contraception (% of women ages 15–49)	..		..	
Pregnant women receiving prenatal care (%)	99		..	
Births attended by skilled health staff (% of total)	99		..	
Maternal mortality ratio (per 100,000 live births)	..		8	
Labor force and employment dynamics				
Labor force participation (% of population ages 15+)	46	65	50	62
Women in the labor force (% of total labor force)	43		46	
Employment to population ratio (% ages 15+)	40	60	46	57
Vulnerable employment (% of employed ages 15+)	..	..	5	8
Employment in agriculture (% of employed ages 15+)	..	..	2	5
Employment in industry (% of employed ages 15+)	..	..	12	35
Employment in service (% of employed ages 15+)	..	..	85	60
Wage and salaried workers (% of employed ages 15+)	89	85	93	86
Self-employed workers (% of employed ages 15+)	11	15	6	14
Unpaid family workers (% of employed ages 15+)	0	0	1	0
Women in nonagricultural wage employment (%)	44		48	
Children in employment (% of children ages 7–14)	..	..	..	..
Unemployment (% of labor force ages 15+)	12	7	9	7
Long-term unemployment (% of total unemployment)	40	36	40	41
Youth unemployment (% of labor force ages 15–24)	24	15	25	21
Maternity leave (weeks)	16		16	
Maternal leave benefits (% of wages paid)	84		100	
Women's political participation				
Seats held by women in national parliament (%)	7		19	
Women in managerial positions (%)	..		..	

French Polynesia

Population (thousands)	263	Population living on less	
GNI ($ billions)	..	than $1.25 a day (%)	..
GNI per capita ($)	..		

	1990		2007	
	Female	Male	Female	Male
Demography				
Sex ratio at birth (females per 1,000 males)	952		952	
Life expectancy at birth (years)	72	67	77	72
Child mortality rate (per 1,000)	..	..	..	..
Female-headed households (%)		..		..
Education				
Gross primary enrollment (% of relevant age group)	..	..	..	..
Gross secondary enrollment (% of relevant age group)	..	..	..	..
Gross tertiary enrollment (% of relevant age group)	..	..	..	..
Primary completion rate (% of relevant age group)	..	..	..	..
Adult literacy rate (% of population ages 15+)	..	..	..	..
Family planning and maternal health				
Total fertility rate (births per woman)	3.3		2.3	
Adolescent fertility (births per 1,000 women ages 15–19)	..		34	
Women married by age 18 (% of women ages 20–24)	..		..	
Contraceptive prevalence (% of women ages 15–49)	..		..	
Unmet need for contraception (% of women ages 15–49)	..		..	
Pregnant women receiving prenatal care (%)	..		..	
Births attended by skilled health staff (% of total)	..		..	
Maternal mortality ratio (per 100,000 live births)	..		..	
Labor force and employment dynamics				
Labor force participation (% of population ages 15+)	49	74	48	72
Women in the labor force (% of total labor force)	37		39	
Employment to population ratio (% ages 15+)	..	..	..	..
Vulnerable employment (% of employed ages 15+)	..	..	..	..
Employment in agriculture (% of employed ages 15+)	..	..	..	..
Employment in industry (% of employed ages 15+)	..	..	..	..
Employment in service (% of employed ages 15+)	..	..	..	..
Wage and salaried workers (% of employed ages 15+)	..	..	..	..
Self-employed workers (% of employed ages 15+)	..	..	..	..
Unpaid family workers (% of employed ages 15+)	..	..	..	..
Women in nonagricultural wage employment (%)	..		..	
Children in employment (% of children ages 7–14)	..	..	..	..
Unemployment (% of labor force ages 15+)	..	..	..	..
Long-term unemployment (% of total unemployment)	..	..	..	..
Youth unemployment (% of labor force ages 15–24)	..	..	..	..
Maternity leave (weeks)	..		..	
Maternal leave benefits (% of wages paid)	..		..	
Women's political participation				
Seats held by women in national parliament (%)	..		..	
Women in managerial positions (%)	..		..	

Gabon

Sub-Saharan Africa			Upper middle income	

Population (millions)	1.3	Population living on less	
GNI ($ billions)	9.3	than $1.25 a day (%)	4.8
GNI per capita ($)	7,020		

	1990		2007	
	Female	Male	Female	Male
Demography				
Sex ratio at birth (females per 1,000 males)	971		971	
Life expectancy at birth (years)	63	59	57	56
Child mortality rate (per 1,000)	..	..	..	..
Female-headed households (%)	..		..	
Education				
Gross primary enrollment (% of relevant age group)	153	156	152	153
Gross secondary enrollment (% of relevant age group)	36	42	..	..
Gross tertiary enrollment (% of relevant age group)	..	..	..	..
Primary completion rate (% of relevant age group)	..	..	76	73
Adult literacy rate (% of population ages 15+)	65	79	82	90
Family planning and maternal health				
Total fertility rate (births per woman)	4.7		3.1	
Adolescent fertility (births per 1,000 women ages 15–19)	..		82	
Women married by age 18 (% of women ages 20–24)	..		..	
Contraceptive prevalence (% of women ages 15–49)	..		..	
Unmet need for contraception (% of women ages 15–49)	..		..	
Pregnant women receiving prenatal care (%)	..		..	
Births attended by skilled health staff (% of total)	..		..	
Maternal mortality ratio (per 100,000 live births)	..		520	
Labor force and employment dynamics				
Labor force participation (% of population ages 15+)	63	83	62	80
Women in the labor force (% of total labor force)	44		44	
Employment to population ratio (% ages 15+)	51	66	53	65
Vulnerable employment (% of employed ages 15+)	63	37	..	..
Employment in agriculture (% of employed ages 15+)	61	26	..	..
Employment in industry (% of employed ages 15+)	3	19	..	..
Employment in service (% of employed ages 15+)	36	55	..	..
Wage and salaried workers (% of employed ages 15+)	29	59	..	..
Self-employed workers (% of employed ages 15+)	58	35	..	..
Unpaid family workers (% of employed ages 15+)	5	2	..	..
Women in nonagricultural wage employment (%)	29		..	
Children in employment (% of children ages 7–14)	..	..	..	..
Unemployment (% of labor force ages 15+)	16	19	..	..
Long-term unemployment (% of total unemployment)	..	..	..	..
Youth unemployment (% of labor force ages 15–24)	..	..	..	..
Maternity leave (weeks)	..		14	
Maternal leave benefits (% of wages paid)	..		100	
Women's political participation				
Seats held by women in national parliament (%)	13		13	
Women in managerial positions (%)	..		..	

Gambia, The

Population (millions)	1.7	Population living on less	
GNI ($ millions)	540.9	than $1.25 a day (%)	34.3
GNI per capita ($)	320		

	1990		2007	
	Female	Male	Female	Male
Demography				
Sex ratio at birth (females per 1,000 males)	971		971	
Life expectancy at birth (years)	52	50	60	59
Child mortality rate (per 1,000)	..	..	*39*	*46*
Female-headed households (%)	..		..	
Education				
Gross primary enrollment (% of relevant age group)	49	65	89	84
Gross secondary enrollment (% of relevant age group)	10	20	46	51
Gross tertiary enrollment (% of relevant age group)	..	..	0	2
Primary completion rate (% of relevant age group)	..	..	73	70
Adult literacy rate (% of population ages 15+)	..	..	..	..
Family planning and maternal health				
Total fertility rate (births per woman)	6.0		4.7	
Adolescent fertility (births per 1,000 women ages 15–19)	..		104	
Women married by age 18 (% of women ages 20–24)	..		..	
Contraceptive prevalence (% of women ages 15–49)	12		..	
Unmet need for contraception (% of women ages 15–49)	..		..	
Pregnant women receiving prenatal care (%)	..		98	
Births attended by skilled health staff (% of total)	44		57	
Maternal mortality ratio (per 100,000 live births)	..		690	
Labor force and employment dynamics				
Labor force participation (% of population ages 15+)	70	86	70	84
Women in the labor force (% of total labor force)	45		46	
Employment to population ratio (% ages 15+)	*66*	*80*	*66*	*78*
Vulnerable employment (% of employed ages 15+)	..	..	..	..
Employment in agriculture (% of employed ages 15+)	*77*	*54*	..	..
Employment in industry (% of employed ages 15+)	*1*	*11*	..	..
Employment in service (% of employed ages 15+)	*20*	*35*	..	..
Wage and salaried workers (% of employed ages 15+)	..	..	..	..
Self-employed workers (% of employed ages 15+)	..	..	..	..
Unpaid family workers (% of employed ages 15+)	..	..	..	..
Women in nonagricultural wage employment (%)	21		..	
Children in employment (% of children ages 7–14)	..	..	52	34
Unemployment (% of labor force ages 15+)	..	..	..	..
Long-term unemployment (% of total unemployment)	..	..	..	..
Youth unemployment (% of labor force ages 15–24)	..	..	..	..
Maternity leave (weeks)	..		*12*	
Maternal leave benefits (% of wages paid)	..		*100*	
Women's political participation				
Seats held by women in national parliament (%)	8		9	
Women in managerial positions (%)	..		..	

Georgia

Europe & Central Asia   **Lower middle income**

Population (millions)	4.4	Population living on less	
GNI ($ billions)	9.3	than $1.25 a day (%)	13.4
GNI per capita ($)	2,120		

	1990		2007	
	Female	Male	Female	Male
Demography				
Sex ratio at birth (females per 1,000 males)	929		901	
Life expectancy at birth (years)	74	67	75	67
Child mortality rate (per 1,000)	..	..	4	5
Female-headed households (%)	..		..	
Education				
Gross primary enrollment (% of relevant age group)	97	97	98	100
Gross secondary enrollment (% of relevant age group)	94	96	90	90
Gross tertiary enrollment (% of relevant age group)	..	..	39	35
Primary completion rate (% of relevant age group)	..	..	86	83
Adult literacy rate (% of population ages 15+)	..	..	..	..
Family planning and maternal health				
Total fertility rate (births per woman)	2.1		1.4	
Adolescent fertility (births per 1,000 women ages 15–19)	..		30	
Women married by age 18 (% of women ages 20–24)	..		..	
Contraceptive prevalence (% of women ages 15–49)	..		47	
Unmet need for contraception (% of women ages 15–49)	..		..	
Pregnant women receiving prenatal care (%)	..		94	
Births attended by skilled health staff (% of total)	..		98	
Maternal mortality ratio (per 100,000 live births)	..		66	
Labor force and employment dynamics				
Labor force participation (% of population ages 15+)	67	83	55	74
Women in the labor force (% of total labor force)	48		46	
Employment to population ratio (% ages 15+)	51	66	49	64
Vulnerable employment (% of employed ages 15+)	..	..	65	64
Employment in agriculture (% of employed ages 15+)	..	..	57	52
Employment in industry (% of employed ages 15+)	..	..	4	14
Employment in service (% of employed ages 15+)	..	..	38	34
Wage and salaried workers (% of employed ages 15+)	..	..	35	34
Self-employed workers (% of employed ages 15+)	..	..	26	46
Unpaid family workers (% of employed ages 15+)	..	..	39	19
Women in nonagricultural wage employment (%)	..		49	
Children in employment (% of children ages 7–14)	..	..	..	..
Unemployment (% of labor force ages 15+)	..	..	13	14
Long-term unemployment (% of total unemployment)	..	..	..	..
Youth unemployment (% of labor force ages 15–24)	..	..	31	27
Maternity leave (weeks)	..		..	
Maternal leave benefits (% of wages paid)	..		..	
Women's political participation				
Seats held by women in national parliament (%)	..		9	
Women in managerial positions (%)	..		28	

Germany

High income

Population (millions)	82	Population living on less
GNI ($ billions)	3,207.2	than $1.25 a day (%) ..
GNI per capita ($)	38,990	

	1990		2007	
	Female	Male	Female	Male
Demography				
Sex ratio at birth (females per 1,000 males)	948		948	
Life expectancy at birth (years)	79	72	82	77
Child mortality rate (per 1,000)	..	..	..	..
Female-headed households (%)	..		..	
Education				
Gross primary enrollment (% of relevant age group)	102	101	103	103
Gross secondary enrollment (% of relevant age group)	97	99	101	103
Gross tertiary enrollment (% of relevant age group)	..	..	..	..
Primary completion rate (% of relevant age group)	..	..	98	97
Adult literacy rate (% of population ages 15+)	..	..	..	..
Family planning and maternal health				
Total fertility rate (births per woman)	1.5		1.4	
Adolescent fertility (births per 1,000 women ages 15–19)	..		9	
Women married by age 18 (% of women ages 20–24)	..		..	
Contraceptive prevalence (% of women ages 15–49)	75		..	
Unmet need for contraception (% of women ages 15–49)	..		..	
Pregnant women receiving prenatal care (%)	..		..	
Births attended by skilled health staff (% of total)	..		100	
Maternal mortality ratio (per 100,000 live births)	..		4	
Labor force and employment dynamics				
Labor force participation (% of population ages 15+)	46	73	51	66
Women in the labor force (% of total labor force)	41		45	
Employment to population ratio (% ages 15+)	45	69	47	61
Vulnerable employment (% of employed ages 15+)	..	..	6	7
Employment in agriculture (% of employed ages 15+)	4	4	2	3
Employment in industry (% of employed ages 15+)	26	50	16	41
Employment in service (% of employed ages 15+)	70	45	82	56
Wage and salaried workers (% of employed ages 15+)	91	88	91	86
Self-employed workers (% of employed ages 15+)	9	12	8	14
Unpaid family workers (% of employed ages 15+)	3	0	2	0
Women in nonagricultural wage employment (%)	43		47	
Children in employment (% of children ages 7–14)	..	..	..	..
Unemployment (% of labor force ages 15+)	7	4	9	9
Long-term unemployment (% of total unemployment)	28	36	56	58
Youth unemployment (% of labor force ages 15–24)	6	5	14	16
Maternity leave (weeks)	14		14	
Maternal leave benefits (% of wages paid)	100		100	
Women's political participation				
Seats held by women in national parliament (%)	..		32	
Women in managerial positions (%)	..		36	

Ghana

Sub-Saharan Africa   **Low income**

Population (millions)	23	Population living on less	
GNI ($ billions)	13.8	than $1.25 a day (%)	30.0
GNI per capita ($)	590		

	1990		2007	
	Female	Male	Female	Male
Demography				
Sex ratio at birth (females per 1,000 males)	952		952	
Life expectancy at birth (years)	58	56	60	60
Child mortality rate (per 1,000)	62	63	35	51
Female-headed households (%)	37		34	
Education				
Gross primary enrollment (% of relevant age group)	65	77	97	98
Gross secondary enrollment (% of relevant age group)	29	44	46	52
Gross tertiary enrollment (% of relevant age group)	..	..	4	8
Primary completion rate (% of relevant age group)	54	69	68	73
Adult literacy rate (% of population ages 15+)	..	..	58	72
Family planning and maternal health				
Total fertility rate (births per woman)	5.7		3.8	
Adolescent fertility (births per 1,000 women ages 15–19)	..		55	
Women married by age 18 (% of women ages 20–24)	38		28	
Contraceptive prevalence (% of women ages 15–49)	20		17	
Unmet need for contraception (% of women ages 15–49)	37		34	
Pregnant women receiving prenatal care (%)	86		92	
Births attended by skilled health staff (% of total)	44		50	
Maternal mortality ratio (per 100,000 live births)	..		560	
Labor force and employment dynamics				
Labor force participation (% of population ages 15+)	73	74	72	73
Women in the labor force (% of total labor force)	49		49	
Employment to population ratio (% ages 15+)	67	70	64	66
Vulnerable employment (% of employed ages 15+)	..	..	..	..
Employment in agriculture (% of employed ages 15+)	59	66	..	..
Employment in industry (% of employed ages 15+)	10	10	..	..
Employment in service (% of employed ages 15+)	32	23	..	..
Wage and salaried workers (% of employed ages 15+)	..	..	..	..
Self-employed workers (% of employed ages 15+)	..	..	..	..
Unpaid family workers (% of employed ages 15+)	..	..	..	..
Women in nonagricultural wage employment (%)	..		..	
Children in employment (% of children ages 7–14)	..	..	6	6
Unemployment (% of labor force ages 15+)	6	4	..	..
Long-term unemployment (% of total unemployment)	..	..	..	..
Youth unemployment (% of labor force ages 15–24)	19	15	..	..
Maternity leave (weeks)	12		12	
Maternal leave benefits (% of wages paid)	50		100	
Women's political participation				
Seats held by women in national parliament (%)	..		11	
Women in managerial positions (%)	..		..	

Greece

High income

Population (millions)	11
GNI ($ billions)	288.1
GNI per capita ($)	25,740

Population living on less than $1.25 a day (%) ..

	1990		2007	
	Female	Male	Female	Male
Demography				
Sex ratio at birth (females per 1,000 males)	937		943	
Life expectancy at birth (years)	80	75	82	77
Child mortality rate (per 1,000)	..	..	..	..
Female-headed households (%)	..		..	
Education				
Gross primary enrollment (% of relevant age group)	99	100	102	102
Gross secondary enrollment (% of relevant age group)	92	94	102	104
Gross tertiary enrollment (% of relevant age group)	..	..	101	89
Primary completion rate (% of relevant age group)	..	..	103	104
Adult literacy rate (% of population ages 15+)	89	96	96	98
Family planning and maternal health				
Total fertility rate (births per woman)	1.4		1.4	
Adolescent fertility (births per 1,000 women ages 15–19)	..		9	
Women married by age 18 (% of women ages 20–24)	..		..	
Contraceptive prevalence (% of women ages 15–49)	..		..	
Unmet need for contraception (% of women ages 15–49)	..		..	
Pregnant women receiving prenatal care (%)	..		..	
Births attended by skilled health staff (% of total)	..		..	
Maternal mortality ratio (per 100,000 live births)	..		3	
Labor force and employment dynamics				
Labor force participation (% of population ages 15+)	36	67	43	65
Women in the labor force (% of total labor force)	36		40	
Employment to population ratio (% ages 15+)	30	63	38	62
Vulnerable employment (% of employed ages 15+)	42	38	27	28
Employment in agriculture (% of employed ages 15+)	30	20	14	12
Employment in industry (% of employed ages 15+)	17	33	10	30
Employment in service (% of employed ages 15+)	52	46	76	58
Wage and salaried workers (% of employed ages 15+)	52	53	69	61
Self-employed workers (% of employed ages 15+)	20	43	20	35
Unpaid family workers (% of employed ages 15+)	28	5	11	4
Women in nonagricultural wage employment (%)	35		42	
Children in employment (% of children ages 7–14)	..	..	..	..
Unemployment (% of labor force ages 15+)	12	4	13	5
Long-term unemployment (% of total unemployment)	56	40	55	42
Youth unemployment (% of labor force ages 15–24)	33	15	35	18
Maternity leave (weeks)	15		17	
Maternal leave benefits (% of wages paid)	100		100	
Women's political participation				
Seats held by women in national parliament (%)	7		16	
Women in managerial positions (%)	..		..	

Greenland

High income

Population (thousands)	57	Population living on less
GNI ($ billions)	..	than $1.25 a day (%) ..
GNI per capita ($)	..	

	1990		2007	
	Female	Male	Female	Male
Demography				
Sex ratio at birth (females per 1,000 males)	..		..	
Life expectancy at birth (years)	68	63	..	..
Child mortality rate (per 1,000)	..	..	..	..
Female-headed households (%)	..		..	
Education				
Gross primary enrollment (% of relevant age group)	..	..	..	..
Gross secondary enrollment (% of relevant age group)	..	..	..	..
Gross tertiary enrollment (% of relevant age group)	..	..	..	..
Primary completion rate (% of relevant age group)	..	..	..	..
Adult literacy rate (% of population ages 15+)	..	..	..	..
Family planning and maternal health				
Total fertility rate (births per woman)	2.4		2.4	
Adolescent fertility (births per 1,000 women ages 15–19)	..		..	
Women married by age 18 (% of women ages 20–24)	..		..	
Contraceptive prevalence (% of women ages 15–49)	..		..	
Unmet need for contraception (% of women ages 15–49)	..		..	
Pregnant women receiving prenatal care (%)	..		..	
Births attended by skilled health staff (% of total)	..		..	
Maternal mortality ratio (per 100,000 live births)	..		..	
Labor force and employment dynamics				
Labor force participation (% of population ages 15+)	..	..	..	..
Women in the labor force (% of total labor force)	..		..	
Employment to population ratio (% ages 15+)	..	..	..	..
Vulnerable employment (% of employed ages 15+)	..	..	..	..
Employment in agriculture (% of employed ages 15+)	..	..	..	..
Employment in industry (% of employed ages 15+)	..	..	..	..
Employment in service (% of employed ages 15+)	..	..	..	..
Wage and salaried workers (% of employed ages 15+)	..	..	..	..
Self-employed workers (% of employed ages 15+)	..	..	..	..
Unpaid family workers (% of employed ages 15+)	..	..	..	..
Women in nonagricultural wage employment (%)	..		49	
Children in employment (% of children ages 7–14)	..	..	..	..
Unemployment (% of labor force ages 15+)	..	..	7	10
Long-term unemployment (% of total unemployment)	..	..	..	..
Youth unemployment (% of labor force ages 15–24)	..	..	..	..
Maternity leave (weeks)	..		..	
Maternal leave benefits (% of wages paid)	..		..	
Women's political participation				
Seats held by women in national parliament (%)	..		..	
Women in managerial positions (%)	..		..	

Grenada

Latin America & Caribbean		Upper middle income

Population (thousands)	106	Population living on less	
GNI ($ millions)	413.8	than $1.25 a day (%)	..
GNI per capita ($)	3,920		

	1990		2007	
	Female	Male	Female	Male
Demography				
Sex ratio at birth (females per 1,000 males)	952		952	
Life expectancy at birth (years)	68	64	70	67
Child mortality rate (per 1,000)	..	..	..	..
Female-headed households (%)	..		..	
Education				
Gross primary enrollment (% of relevant age group)	114	117	81	82
Gross secondary enrollment (% of relevant age group)	99	89	98	99
Gross tertiary enrollment (% of relevant age group)	..	..	..	..
Primary completion rate (% of relevant age group)	..	..	81	81
Adult literacy rate (% of population ages 15+)	..	..	..	..
Family planning and maternal health				
Total fertility rate (births per woman)	3.6		2.3	
Adolescent fertility (births per 1,000 women ages 15–19)	..		42	
Women married by age 18 (% of women ages 20–24)	..		..	
Contraceptive prevalence (% of women ages 15–49)	54		54	
Unmet need for contraception (% of women ages 15–49)	..		..	
Pregnant women receiving prenatal care (%)	100		100	
Births attended by skilled health staff (% of total)	..		99	
Maternal mortality ratio (per 100,000 live births)			..	
Labor force and employment dynamics				
Labor force participation (% of population ages 15+)	..	..	..	..
Women in the labor force (% of total labor force)	..		..	
Employment to population ratio (% ages 15+)	..	..	..	..
Vulnerable employment (% of employed ages 15+)	..	..	..	..
Employment in agriculture (% of employed ages 15+)	10	18	..	..
Employment in industry (% of employed ages 15+)	12	29	..	..
Employment in service (% of employed ages 15+)	75	49	..	..
Wage and salaried workers (% of employed ages 15+)	84	74	..	..
Self-employed workers (% of employed ages 15+)	12	17	..	..
Unpaid family workers (% of employed ages 15+)	..	..	..	..
Women in nonagricultural wage employment (%)	40		..	
Children in employment (% of children ages 7–14)	..	..	..	..
Unemployment (% of labor force ages 15+)	..	..	..	..
Long-term unemployment (% of total unemployment)	..	..	..	..
Youth unemployment (% of labor force ages 15–24)	27	28	..	..
Maternity leave (weeks)	12		12	
Maternal leave benefits (% of wages paid)	60		100	
Women's political participation				
Seats held by women in national parliament (%)	..		27	
Women in managerial positions (%)	..		..	

Guam

Population (thousands)	173	Population living on less
GNI ($ billions)	..	than $1.25 a day (%) ..
GNI per capita ($)	..	

	1990		2007	
	Female	Male	Female	Male
Demography				
Sex ratio at birth (females per 1,000 males)	945		945	
Life expectancy at birth (years)	75	70	78	73
Child mortality rate (per 1,000)	..	..	..	..
Female-headed households (%)	..		..	
Education				
Gross primary enrollment (% of relevant age group)	..	..	..	..
Gross secondary enrollment (% of relevant age group)	..	..	..	..
Gross tertiary enrollment (% of relevant age group)	..	..	..	..
Primary completion rate (% of relevant age group)	..	..	..	..
Adult literacy rate (% of population ages 15+)	..	..	..	..
Family planning and maternal health				
Total fertility rate (births per woman)	3.1		2.5	
Adolescent fertility (births per 1,000 women ages 15–19)	..		52	
Women married by age 18 (% of women ages 20–24)	..		..	
Contraceptive prevalence (% of women ages 15–49)	..		..	
Unmet need for contraception (% of women ages 15–49)	..		..	
Pregnant women receiving prenatal care (%)	..		..	
Births attended by skilled health staff (% of total)	..		..	
Maternal mortality ratio (per 100,000 live births)	..		..	
Labor force and employment dynamics				
Labor force participation (% of population ages 15+)	50	81	56	78
Women in the labor force (% of total labor force)	34		41	
Employment to population ratio (% ages 15+)	..	..	..	..
Vulnerable employment (% of employed ages 15+)	..	..	..	..
Employment in agriculture (% of employed ages 15+)	..	..	..	..
Employment in industry (% of employed ages 15+)	..	..	..	..
Employment in service (% of employed ages 15+)	..	..	..	..
Wage and salaried workers (% of employed ages 15+)	..	..	..	..
Self-employed workers (% of employed ages 15+)	..	..	..	..
Unpaid family workers (% of employed ages 15+)	..	..	..	..
Women in nonagricultural wage employment (%)	..		45	
Children in employment (% of children ages 7–14)	..	..	..	..
Unemployment (% of labor force ages 15+)	5	4	..	..
Long-term unemployment (% of total unemployment)	..	..	..	..
Youth unemployment (% of labor force ages 15–24)	..	..	..	..
Maternity leave (weeks)	..		..	
Maternal leave benefits (% of wages paid)	..		..	
Women's political participation				
Seats held by women in national parliament (%)	..		..	
Women in managerial positions (%)	..		..	

Guatemala

Latin America & Caribbean		Lower middle income

			Population living on less	
Population (millions)	13	than $1.25 a day (%)		11.7
GNI ($ billions)	32.8			
GNI per capita ($)	2,450			

	1990		2007	
	Female	Male	Female	Male
Demography				
Sex ratio at birth (females per 1,000 males)	952		952	
Life expectancy at birth (years)	66	60	74	67
Child mortality rate (per 1,000)	*47*	*44*	..	..
Female-headed households (%)	..		..	
Education				
Gross primary enrollment (% of relevant age group)	72	82	110	117
Gross secondary enrollment (% of relevant age group)	..	..	53	58
Gross tertiary enrollment (% of relevant age group)	..	..	18	18
Primary completion rate (% of relevant age group)	..	..	74	80
Adult literacy rate (% of population ages 15+)	..	..	68	79
Family planning and maternal health				
Total fertility rate (births per woman)	5.6		4.2	
Adolescent fertility (births per 1,000 women ages 15–19)	..		107	
Women married by age 18 (% of women ages 20–24)	*41*		..	
Contraceptive prevalence (% of women ages 15–49)	23		..	
Unmet need for contraception (% of women ages 15–49)	..		..	
Pregnant women receiving prenatal care (%)	..		..	
Births attended by skilled health staff (% of total)	29		..	
Maternal mortality ratio (per 100,000 live births)	..		*290*	
Labor force and employment dynamics				
Labor force participation (% of population ages 15+)	28	89	45	85
Women in the labor force (% of total labor force)	24		37	
Employment to population ratio (% ages 15+)	*26*	*86*	44	84
Vulnerable employment (% of employed ages 15+)	..	..	..	..
Employment in agriculture (% of employed ages 15+)	*16*	*61*	..	..
Employment in industry (% of employed ages 15+)	*24*	*17*	..	..
Employment in service (% of employed ages 15+)	*60*	*22*	..	..
Wage and salaried workers (% of employed ages 15+)	..	..	..	..
Self-employed workers (% of employed ages 15+)	..	..	..	..
Unpaid family workers (% of employed ages 15+)	..	..	..	..
Women in nonagricultural wage employment (%)	37		38	
Children in employment (% of children ages 7–14)	..	..	11	23
Unemployment (% of labor force ages 15+)	3	2	4	3
Long-term unemployment (% of total unemployment)	..	..	..	..
Youth unemployment (% of labor force ages 15–24)	..	..	..	..
Maternity leave (weeks)	11		*12*	
Maternal leave benefits (% of wages paid)	100		*100*	
Women's political participation				
Seats held by women in national parliament (%)	7		12	
Women in managerial positions (%)	..		..	

Guinea

Sub-Saharan Africa			Low income

			Population living on less	
Population (millions)	9.4		than $1.25 a day (%)	70.1
GNI ($ billions)	3.7			
GNI per capita ($)	400			

	1990		2007	
	Female	Male	Female	Male
Demography				
Sex ratio at birth (females per 1,000 males)	942		942	
Life expectancy at birth (years)	49	46	58	54
Child mortality rate (per 1,000)	*112*	*122*	*86*	*89*
Female-headed households (%)	..		*17*	
Education				
Gross primary enrollment (% of relevant age group)	22	46	84	98
Gross secondary enrollment (% of relevant age group)	5	14	*24*	*45*
Gross tertiary enrollment (% of relevant age group)	..	..	*2*	*8*
Primary completion rate (% of relevant age group)	9	29	55	73
Adult literacy rate (% of population ages 15+)	..	..	*18*	*43*
Family planning and maternal health				
Total fertility rate (births per woman)	6.6		5.4	
Adolescent fertility (births per 1,000 women ages 15-19)	..		149	
Women married by age 18 (% of women ages 20-24)	..		..	
Contraceptive prevalence (% of women ages 15-49)	2		9	
Unmet need for contraception (% of women ages 15-49)	..		21	
Pregnant women receiving prenatal care (%)	58		82	
Births attended by skilled health staff (% of total)	31		38	
Maternal mortality ratio (per 100,000 live births)	..		910	
Labor force and employment dynamics				
Labor force participation (% of population ages 15+)	80	90	79	89
Women in the labor force (% of total labor force)	47		47	
Employment to population ratio (% ages 15+)	*78*	*87*	*78*	*85*
Vulnerable employment (% of employed ages 15+)	..	..	..	..
Employment in agriculture (% of employed ages 15+)	..	..	..	..
Employment in industry (% of employed ages 15+)	..	..	..	..
Employment in service (% of employed ages 15+)	..	..	..	..
Wage and salaried workers (% of employed ages 15+)	..	..	..	..
Self-employed workers (% of employed ages 15+)	..	..	..	..
Unpaid family workers (% of employed ages 15+)	..	..	..	..
Women in nonagricultural wage employment (%)	..		..	
Children in employment (% of children ages 7-14)	..	..	..	..
Unemployment (% of labor force ages 15+)	..	..	..	..
Long-term unemployment (% of total unemployment)	..	..	..	..
Youth unemployment (% of labor force ages 15-24)	..	..	..	..
Maternity leave (weeks)	14		*14*	
Maternal leave benefits (% of wages paid)	100		*100*	
Women's political participation				
Seats held by women in national parliament (%)	..		19	
Women in managerial positions (%)	..		..	

Guinea-Bissau

Sub-Saharan Africa   Low income

Population (millions)	1.7	Population living on less
GNI ($ millions)	331.0	than $1.25 a day (%) 48.8
GNI per capita ($)	200	

	1990		2007	
	Female	Male	Female	Male
Demography				
Sex ratio at birth (females per 1,000 males)	971		971	
Life expectancy at birth (years)	44	41	48	45
Child mortality rate (per 1,000)	..	..	88	110
Female-headed households (%)	..		..	
Education				
Gross primary enrollment (% of relevant age group)	35	64	..	..
Gross secondary enrollment (% of relevant age group)	4	8	..	..
Gross tertiary enrollment (% of relevant age group)	..	..	..	..
Primary completion rate (% of relevant age group)	..	..	..	..
Adult literacy rate (% of population ages 15+)	..	..	..	..
Family planning and maternal health				
Total fertility rate (births per woman)	7.1		7.1	
Adolescent fertility (births per 1,000 women ages 15–19)	..		188	
Women married by age 18 (% of women ages 20–24)	..		..	
Contraceptive prevalence (% of women ages 15–49)	..		10	
Unmet need for contraception (% of women ages 15–49)	..		..	
Pregnant women receiving prenatal care (%)	..		78	
Births attended by skilled health staff (% of total)	..		39	
Maternal mortality ratio (per 100,000 live births)	..		1,100	
Labor force and employment dynamics				
Labor force participation (% of population ages 15+)	56	87	54	90
Women in the labor force (% of total labor force)	40		38	
Employment to population ratio (% ages 15+)	52	80	50	83
Vulnerable employment (% of employed ages 15+)	..	..	..	..
Employment in agriculture (% of employed ages 15+)	..	..	..	..
Employment in industry (% of employed ages 15+)	..	..	..	..
Employment in service (% of employed ages 15+)	..	..	..	..
Wage and salaried workers (% of employed ages 15+)	..	..	..	..
Self-employed workers (% of employed ages 15+)	..	..	..	..
Unpaid family workers (% of employed ages 15+)	..	..	..	..
Women in nonagricultural wage employment (%)	11		..	
Children in employment (% of children ages 7–14)	..	..	..	..
Unemployment (% of labor force ages 15+)	..	..	..	..
Long-term unemployment (% of total unemployment)	..	..	..	..
Youth unemployment (% of labor force ages 15–24)	..	..	..	..
Maternity leave (weeks)	8		9	
Maternal leave benefits (% of wages paid)	100		100	
Women's political participation				
Seats held by women in national parliament (%)	20		14	
Women in managerial positions (%)	..		..	

Guyana

Latin America & Caribbean	Lower middle income

Population (thousands)	739	Population living on less
GNI ($ millions)	926.4	than $1.25 a day (%)
GNI per capita ($)	1,250	..

	1990		2007	
	Female	Male	Female	Male
Demography				
Sex ratio at birth (females per 1,000 males)	952		952	
Life expectancy at birth (years)	66	59	70	64
Child mortality rate (per 1,000)	..	..	..	..
Female-headed households (%)	..		..	
Education				
Gross primary enrollment (% of relevant age group)	93	94	111	113
Gross secondary enrollment (% of relevant age group)	82	78	103	111
Gross tertiary enrollment (% of relevant age group)	..	..	17	8
Primary completion rate (% of relevant age group)	..	..	116	116
Adult literacy rate (% of population ages 15+)	..	..	..	..
Family planning and maternal health				
Total fertility rate (births per woman)	2.6		2.3	
Adolescent fertility (births per 1,000 women ages 15–19)	..		63	
Women married by age 18 (% of women ages 20–24)	..		..	
Contraceptive prevalence (% of women ages 15–49)	31		34	
Unmet need for contraception (% of women ages 15–49)	..		..	
Pregnant women receiving prenatal care (%)	..		81	
Births attended by skilled health staff (% of total)	..		83	
Maternal mortality ratio (per 100,000 live births)	..		470	
Labor force and employment dynamics				
Labor force participation (% of population ages 15+)	36	82	48	82
Women in the labor force (% of total labor force)	33		35	
Employment to population ratio (% ages 15+)	31	75	42	74
Vulnerable employment (% of employed ages 15+)	..	..	..	..
Employment in agriculture (% of employed ages 15+)	17	36	..	..
Employment in industry (% of employed ages 15+)	13	24	..	..
Employment in service (% of employed ages 15+)	66	37	..	..
Wage and salaried workers (% of employed ages 15+)	53	52	..	..
Self-employed workers (% of employed ages 15+)	44	38	..	..
Unpaid family workers (% of employed ages 15+)	4	10	..	..
Women in nonagricultural wage employment (%)	..		..	
Children in employment (% of children ages 7–14)	..	..	..	..
Unemployment (% of labor force ages 15+)	18	8	..	..
Long-term unemployment (% of total unemployment)	..	..	..	..
Youth unemployment (% of labor force ages 15–24)	38	21	..	..
Maternity leave (weeks)	13		13	
Maternal leave benefits (% of wages paid)	..		70	
Women's political participation				
Seats held by women in national parliament (%)	37		29	
Women in managerial positions (%)	..		..	

Haiti

Latin America & Caribbean			Low income	

Population (millions)	9.6	Population living on less	
GNI ($ billions)	5.0	than $1.25 a day (%)	54.9
GNI per capita ($)	520		

	1990		2007	
	Female	Male	Female	Male
Demography				
Sex ratio at birth (females per 1,000 males)	952		952	
Life expectancy at birth (years)	56	53	63	59
Child mortality rate (per 1,000)	..	..	36	33
Female-headed households (%)		..	44	
Education				
Gross primary enrollment (% of relevant age group)	47	49	..	..
Gross secondary enrollment (% of relevant age group)	20	21	..	..
Gross tertiary enrollment (% of relevant age group)	..	..	..	..
Primary completion rate (% of relevant age group)	27	30	..	..
Adult literacy rate (% of population ages 15+)	..	..	..	..
Family planning and maternal health				
Total fertility rate (births per woman)	5.4		3.8	
Adolescent fertility (births per 1,000 women ages 15–19)	..		46	
Women married by age 18 (% of women ages 20–24)	..		..	
Contraceptive prevalence (% of women ages 15–49)	10		32	
Unmet need for contraception (% of women ages 15–49)	..		38	
Pregnant women receiving prenatal care (%)	71		85	
Births attended by skilled health staff (% of total)	23		26	
Maternal mortality ratio (per 100,000 live births)	..		670	
Labor force and employment dynamics				
Labor force participation (% of population ages 15+)	49	81	39	83
Women in the labor force (% of total labor force)	39		33	
Employment to population ratio (% ages 15+)	40	74	35	78
Vulnerable employment (% of employed ages 15+)	..	..	..	..
Employment in agriculture (% of employed ages 15+)	..	..	..	..
Employment in industry (% of employed ages 15+)	..	..	..	..
Employment in service (% of employed ages 15+)	..	..	..	..
Wage and salaried workers (% of employed ages 15+)	21	17	..	..
Self-employed workers (% of employed ages 15+)	66	69	..	..
Unpaid family workers (% of employed ages 15+)	11	12	..	..
Women in nonagricultural wage employment (%)	44		..	
Children in employment (% of children ages 7–14)	..	..	30	37
Unemployment (% of labor force ages 15+)	14	12	..	..
Long-term unemployment (% of total unemployment)	..	..	..	..
Youth unemployment (% of labor force ages 15–24)	24	23	..	..
Maternity leave (weeks)	12		12	
Maternal leave benefits (% of wages paid)	100		100	
Women's political participation				
Seats held by women in national parliament (%)	..		4	
Women in managerial positions (%)	..		..	

Honduras

| Latin America & Caribbean | | | Lower middle income | | |

Population (millions)	7.1	Population living on less	
GNI ($ billions)	11.3	than $1.25 a day (%)	18.2
GNI per capita ($)	1,590		

	1990		2007	
	Female	Male	Female	Male
Demography				
Sex ratio at birth (females per 1,000 males)	952		952	
Life expectancy at birth (years)	68	63	74	67
Child mortality rate (per 1,000)	..	..	9	8
Female-headed households (%)	..		26	
Education				
Gross primary enrollment (% of relevant age group)	110	106	116	117
Gross secondary enrollment (% of relevant age group)	37	30	68	55
Gross tertiary enrollment (% of relevant age group)	..	..	20	14
Primary completion rate (% of relevant age group)	61	67	90	85
Adult literacy rate (% of population ages 15+)	..	..	83	84
Family planning and maternal health				
Total fertility rate (births per woman)	5.1		3.3	
Adolescent fertility (births per 1,000 women ages 15–19)	..		93	
Women married by age 18 (% of women ages 20–24)	..		..	
Contraceptive prevalence (% of women ages 15–49)	47		65	
Unmet need for contraception (% of women ages 15–49)	..		17	
Pregnant women receiving prenatal care (%)	88		92	
Births attended by skilled health staff (% of total)	45		67	
Maternal mortality ratio (per 100,000 live births)	..		280	
Labor force and employment dynamics				
Labor force participation (% of population ages 15+)	37	87	37	82
Women in the labor force (% of total labor force)	30		32	
Employment to population ratio (% ages 15+)	36	83	34	79
Vulnerable employment (% of employed ages 15+)	50	48	51	48
Employment in agriculture (% of employed ages 15+)	6	65	13	51
Employment in industry (% of employed ages 15+)	23	15	23	20
Employment in service (% of employed ages 15+)	71	20	63	29
Wage and salaried workers (% of employed ages 15+)	49	50	53	49
Self-employed workers (% of employed ages 15+)	45	38	39	39
Unpaid family workers (% of employed ages 15+)	6	11	8	12
Women in nonagricultural wage employment (%)	48		45	
Children in employment (% of children ages 7–14)	..	..	3	10
Unemployment (% of labor force ages 15+)	6	4	6	3
Long-term unemployment (% of total unemployment)	..	..	..	..
Youth unemployment (% of labor force ages 15–24)	10	6	11	5
Maternity leave (weeks)	10		12	
Maternal leave benefits (% of wages paid)	100		100	
Women's political participation				
Seats held by women in national parliament (%)	10		23	
Women in managerial positions (%)	..		..	

Hong Kong, China

Population (millions)	6.9	Population living on less
GNI ($ billions)	218.6	than $1.25 a day (%) ..
GNI per capita ($)	31,560	

	1990		2007	
	Female	Male	Female	Male
Demography				
Sex ratio at birth (females per 1,000 males)	937		937	
Life expectancy at birth (years)	80	75	85	79
Child mortality rate (per 1,000)	..	..	..	..
Female-headed households (%)	..		..	
Education				
Gross primary enrollment (% of relevant age group)	103	102	95	100
Gross secondary enrollment (% of relevant age group)	82	78	86	86
Gross tertiary enrollment (% of relevant age group)	..	..	34	33
Primary completion rate (% of relevant age group)	..	..	99	104
Adult literacy rate (% of population ages 15+)	..	..	..	..
Family planning and maternal health				
Total fertility rate (births per woman)	1.3		1.0	
Adolescent fertility (births per 1,000 women ages 15–19)	..		5	
Women married by age 18 (% of women ages 20–24)	..		..	
Contraceptive prevalence (% of women ages 15–49)	86		..	
Unmet need for contraception (% of women ages 15–49)	..		..	
Pregnant women receiving prenatal care (%)	..		..	
Births attended by skilled health staff (% of total)	..		100	
Maternal mortality ratio (per 100,000 live births)	..		..	
Labor force and employment dynamics				
Labor force participation (% of population ages 15+)	47	80	53	70
Women in the labor force (% of total labor force)	36		45	
Employment to population ratio (% ages 15+)	47	78	52	67
Vulnerable employment (% of employed ages 15+)	4	7	4	10
Employment in agriculture (% of employed ages 15+)	1	1	0	0
Employment in industry (% of employed ages 15+)	33	39	7	22
Employment in service (% of employed ages 15+)	66	60	93	77
Wage and salaried workers (% of employed ages 15+)	95	85	94	84
Self-employed workers (% of employed ages 15+)	3	15	5	16
Unpaid family workers (% of employed ages 15+)	2	0	1	0
Women in nonagricultural wage employment (%)	41		48	
Children in employment (% of children ages 7–14)	..	..	..	..
Unemployment (% of labor force ages 15+)	1	1	3	5
Long-term unemployment (% of total unemployment)	..	..	..	..
Youth unemployment (% of labor force ages 15–24)	3	4	8	14
Maternity leave (weeks)	10		..	
Maternal leave benefits (% of wages paid)	67		..	
Women's political participation				
Seats held by women in national parliament (%)	..		..	
Women in managerial positions (%)	..		26	

Hungary

High income

Population (millions)	10	Population living on less	
GNI ($ billions)	117.5	than $1.25 a day (%)	2.0
GNI per capita ($)	11,680		

	1990		2007	
	Female	Male	Female	Male
Demography				
Sex ratio at birth (females per 1,000 males)	943		943	
Life expectancy at birth (years)	74	65	77	69
Child mortality rate (per 1,000)	..	..	..	..
Female-headed households (%)	..		..	
Education				
Gross primary enrollment (% of relevant age group)	95	96	96	98
Gross secondary enrollment (% of relevant age group)	87	86	95	96
Gross tertiary enrollment (% of relevant age group)	..	..	82	56
Primary completion rate (% of relevant age group)	95	93	96	96
Adult literacy rate (% of population ages 15+)	..	..	99	99
Family planning and maternal health				
Total fertility rate (births per woman)	1.8		1.3	
Adolescent fertility (births per 1,000 women ages 15–19)	..		19	
Women married by age 18 (% of women ages 20–24)	..		..	
Contraceptive prevalence (% of women ages 15–49)	77		..	
Unmet need for contraception (% of women ages 15–49)	..		..	
Pregnant women receiving prenatal care (%)	..		..	
Births attended by skilled health staff (% of total)	..		100	
Maternal mortality ratio (per 100,000 live births)	..		6	
Labor force and employment dynamics				
Labor force participation (% of population ages 15+)	47	66	44	59
Women in the labor force (% of total labor force)	45		45	
Employment to population ratio (% ages 15+)	43	57	40	55
Vulnerable employment (% of employed ages 15+)	7	8	6	8
Employment in agriculture (% of employed ages 15+)	..	..	3	7
Employment in industry (% of employed ages 15+)	..	..	21	42
Employment in service (% of employed ages 15+)	..	..	76	51
Wage and salaried workers (% of employed ages 15+)	89	81	91	85
Self-employed workers (% of employed ages 15+)	9	15	9	15
Unpaid family workers (% of employed ages 15+)	2	1	1	0
Women in nonagricultural wage employment (%)	..		48	
Children in employment (% of children ages 7–14)	..	..	..	..
Unemployment (% of labor force ages 15+)	9	11	8	7
Long-term unemployment (% of total unemployment)	20	21	48	47
Youth unemployment (% of labor force ages 15–24)	15	22	19	20
Maternity leave (weeks)	24		24	
Maternal leave benefits (% of wages paid)	100		70	
Women's political participation				
Seats held by women in national parliament (%)	21		10	
Women in managerial positions (%)	..		34	

Iceland

Population (thousands)	311
GNI ($ billions)	18.0
GNI per capita ($)	57,750

Population living on less than $1.25 a day (%) ..

	1990		2007	
	Female	Male	Female	Male
Demography				
Sex ratio at birth (females per 1,000 males)	943		943	
Life expectancy at birth (years)	78	75	83	79
Child mortality rate (per 1,000)	..	..	..	..
Female-headed households (%)	..		..	
Education				
Gross primary enrollment (% of relevant age group)	101	102	97	98
Gross secondary enrollment (% of relevant age group)	96	100	111	108
Gross tertiary enrollment (% of relevant age group)	..	..	96	51
Primary completion rate (% of relevant age group)	..	..	101	97
Adult literacy rate (% of population ages 15+)	..	..	..	..
Family planning and maternal health				
Total fertility rate (births per woman)	2.3		2.5	
Adolescent fertility (births per 1,000 women ages 15–19)	..		15	
Women married by age 18 (% of women ages 20–24)	..		..	
Contraceptive prevalence (% of women ages 15–49)	..		..	
Unmet need for contraception (% of women ages 15–49)	..		..	
Pregnant women receiving prenatal care (%)	..		..	
Births attended by skilled health staff (% of total)	..		..	
Maternal mortality ratio (per 100,000 live births)	..		4	
Labor force and employment dynamics				
Labor force participation (% of population ages 15+)	67	81	71	80
Women in the labor force (% of total labor force)	46		47	
Employment to population ratio (% ages 15+)	66	79	70	78
Vulnerable employment (% of employed ages 15+)	9	17	5	12
Employment in agriculture (% of employed ages 15+)	5	14	3	9
Employment in industry (% of employed ages 15+)	18	33	11	31
Employment in service (% of employed ages 15+)	77	52	86	59
Wage and salaried workers (% of employed ages 15+)	88	73	92	81
Self-employed workers (% of employed ages 15+)	9	25	7	19
Unpaid family workers (% of employed ages 15+)	3	2	0	0
Women in nonagricultural wage employment (%)	53		48	
Children in employment (% of children ages 7–14)	..	..	..	..
Unemployment (% of labor force ages 15+)	3	2	2	2
Long-term unemployment (% of total unemployment)	12	1	6	10
Youth unemployment (% of labor force ages 15–24)	4	6	6	9
Maternity leave (weeks)	8		12	
Maternal leave benefits (% of wages paid)	..		80	
Women's political participation				
Seats held by women in national parliament (%)	21		32	
Women in managerial positions (%)	..		..	

India

South Asia		**Lower middle income**	
Population (millions)	1,125	Population living on less	
GNI ($ billions)	1,071.0	than $1.25 a day (%)	41.6
GNI per capita ($)	950		

	1990		2007	
	Female	**Male**	**Female**	**Male**
Demography				
Sex ratio at birth (females per 1,000 males)	929		926	
Life expectancy at birth (years)	60	59	66	63
Child mortality rate (per 1,000)	42	29	12	9
Female-headed households (%)	9		14	
Education				
Gross primary enrollment (% of relevant age group)	79	107	109	114
Gross secondary enrollment (% of relevant age group)	30	52	49	59
Gross tertiary enrollment (% of relevant age group)	..	..	10	14
Primary completion rate (% of relevant age group)	52	75	83	88
Adult literacy rate (% of population ages 15+)	34	62	54	77
Family planning and maternal health				
Total fertility rate (births per woman)	4.0		2.7	
Adolescent fertility (births per 1,000 women ages 15–19)	..		62	
Women married by age 18 (% of women ages 20–24)	50		..	
Contraceptive prevalence (% of women ages 15–49)	41		56	
Unmet need for contraception (% of women ages 15–49)	17		13	
Pregnant women receiving prenatal care (%)	49		74	
Births attended by skilled health staff (% of total)	34		47	
Maternal mortality ratio (per 100,000 live births)	..		450	
Labor force and employment dynamics				
Labor force participation (% of population ages 15+)	35	85	34	82
Women in the labor force (% of total labor force)	28		28	
Employment to population ratio (% ages 15+)	34	82	32	77
Vulnerable employment (% of employed ages 15+)	..	..	..	..
Employment in agriculture (% of employed ages 15+)	..	..	..	..
Employment in industry (% of employed ages 15+)	..	..	..	..
Employment in service (% of employed ages 15+)	..	..	..	..
Wage and salaried workers (% of employed ages 15+)	..	..	..	..
Self-employed workers (% of employed ages 15+)	..	..	..	..
Unpaid family workers (% of employed ages 15+)	..	..	..	..
Women in nonagricultural wage employment (%)	13		18	
Children in employment (% of children ages 7–14)	..	..	4	4
Unemployment (% of labor force ages 15+)	..	..	5	5
Long-term unemployment (% of total unemployment)	..	..	..	..
Youth unemployment (% of labor force ages 15–24)	..	..	11	10
Maternity leave (weeks)	12		12	
Maternal leave benefits (% of wages paid)	100		100	
Women's political participation				
Seats held by women in national parliament (%)	5		8	
Women in managerial positions (%)	..		..	

Indonesia

East Asia & Pacific		Lower middle income	

		Population living on less	
Population (millions)	226	than $1.25 a day (%)	
GNI ($ billions)	372.6		..
GNI per capita ($)	1,650		

	1990		2007	
	Female	Male	Female	Male
Demography				
Sex ratio at birth (females per 1,000 males)	952		952	
Life expectancy at birth (years)	64	60	73	69
Child mortality rate (per 1,000)	35	36	11	13
Female-headed households (%)	13		12	
Education				
Gross primary enrollment (% of relevant age group)	113	117	112	116
Gross secondary enrollment (% of relevant age group)	42	51	66	66
Gross tertiary enrollment (% of relevant age group)	..	..	15	19
Primary completion rate (% of relevant age group)	..	..	99	99
Adult literacy rate (% of population ages 15+)	75	88	89	95
Family planning and maternal health				
Total fertility rate (births per woman)	3.1		2.2	
Adolescent fertility (births per 1,000 women ages 15–19)	..		40	
Women married by age 18 (% of women ages 20-24)	34		24	
Contraceptive prevalence (% of women ages 15-49)	50		61	
Unmet need for contraception (% of women ages 15-49)	14		9	
Pregnant women receiving prenatal care (%)	76		93	
Births attended by skilled health staff (% of total)	32		72	
Maternal mortality ratio (per 100,000 live births)	..		420	
Labor force and employment dynamics				
Labor force participation (% of population ages 15+)	50	81	50	86
Women in the labor force (% of total labor force)	38		37	
Employment to population ratio (% ages 15+)	48	79	44	79
Vulnerable employment (% of employed ages 15+)	..	..	68	60
Employment in agriculture (% of employed ages 15+)	56	56	41	41
Employment in industry (% of employed ages 15+)	12	15	15	21
Employment in service (% of employed ages 15+)	31	30	44	38
Wage and salaried workers (% of employed ages 15+)	..	..	31	36
Self-employed workers (% of employed ages 15+)	..	..	36	56
Unpaid family workers (% of employed ages 15+)	..	..	34	8
Women in nonagricultural wage employment (%)	29		29	
Children in employment (% of children ages 7-14)	..	..	..	..
Unemployment (% of labor force ages 15+)	3	3	11	8
Long-term unemployment (% of total unemployment)	..	..	..	..
Youth unemployment (% of labor force ages 15–24)	9	9	34	25
Maternity leave (weeks)	12		12	
Maternal leave benefits (% of wages paid)	100		100	
Women's political participation				
Seats held by women in national parliament (%)	12		11	
Women in managerial positions (%)	..		..	

Iran, Islamic Rep.

Middle East & North Africa		Lower middle income	

Population (millions)	71	Population living on less	
GNI ($ billions)	251.5	than $1.25 a day (%)	2.0
GNI per capita ($)	3,540		

	1990		2007	
	Female	Male	Female	Male
Demography				
Sex ratio at birth (females per 1,000 males)	952		952	
Life expectancy at birth (years)	66	64	73	69
Child mortality rate (per 1,000)	..	..	..	..
Female-headed households (%)	..		..	
Education				
Gross primary enrollment (% of relevant age group)	100	113	137	106
Gross secondary enrollment (% of relevant age group)	46	64	73	72
Gross tertiary enrollment (% of relevant age group)	..	..	34	29
Primary completion rate (% of relevant age group)	81	93	113	98
Adult literacy rate (% of population ages 15+)	56	74	77	87
Family planning and maternal health				
Total fertility rate (births per woman)	4.8		2.0	
Adolescent fertility (births per 1,000 women ages 15–19)	..		20	
Women married by age 18 (% of women ages 20–24)	..		..	
Contraceptive prevalence (% of women ages 15–49)	49		79	
Unmet need for contraception (% of women ages 15–49)	..		..	
Pregnant women receiving prenatal care (%)	..		..	
Births attended by skilled health staff (% of total)	..		97	
Maternal mortality ratio (per 100,000 live births)	..		140	
Labor force and employment dynamics				
Labor force participation (% of population ages 15+)	22	81	32	75
Women in the labor force (% of total labor force)	20		29	
Employment to population ratio (% ages 15+)	18	73	27	68
Vulnerable employment (% of employed ages 15+)	..	..	56	40
Employment in agriculture (% of employed ages 15+)	..	..	34	23
Employment in industry (% of employed ages 15+)	..	..	28	31
Employment in service (% of employed ages 15+)	..	..	37	46
Wage and salaried workers (% of employed ages 15+)	..	..	42	53
Self-employed workers (% of employed ages 15+)	..	..	24	41
Unpaid family workers (% of employed ages 15+)	..	..	33	5
Women in nonagricultural wage employment (%)	..		..	
Children in employment (% of children ages 7–14)	..	..	..	..
Unemployment (% of labor force ages 15+)	24	9	16	9
Long-term unemployment (% of total unemployment)	..	..	..	..
Youth unemployment (% of labor force ages 15–24)	..	..	32	20
Maternity leave (weeks)	12		13	
Maternal leave benefits (% of wages paid)	67		67	
Women's political participation				
Seats held by women in national parliament (%)	2		4	
Women in managerial positions (%)	..		..	

Iraq

Middle East & North Africa   **Lower middle income**

Population (millions)	..	Population living on less
GNI ($ billions)	..	than $1.25 a day (%) ..
GNI per capita ($)	..	

	1990		2007	
	Female	Male	Female	Male
Demography				
Sex ratio at birth (females per 1,000 males)	952		..	
Life expectancy at birth (years)	63	60	..	..
Child mortality rate (per 1,000)	..	..	..	..
Female-headed households (%)	..		..	
Education				
Gross primary enrollment (% of relevant age group)	95	114	..	..
Gross secondary enrollment (% of relevant age group)	35	54	..	..
Gross tertiary enrollment (% of relevant age group)	..	..	..	..
Primary completion rate (% of relevant age group)	..	..	..	..
Adult literacy rate (% of population ages 15+)	..	..	..	..
Family planning and maternal health				
Total fertility rate (births per woman)	5.9		..	
Adolescent fertility (births per 1,000 women ages 15–19)	..		..	
Women married by age 18 (% of women ages 20–24)	..		..	
Contraceptive prevalence (% of women ages 15–49)	*14*		..	
Unmet need for contraception (% of women ages 15–49)	..		..	
Pregnant women receiving prenatal care (%)	..		..	
Births attended by skilled health staff (% of total)	*54*		..	
Maternal mortality ratio (per 100,000 live births)	..		..	
Labor force and employment dynamics				
Labor force participation (% of population ages 15+)	12	74	..	..
Women in the labor force (% of total labor force)	13		..	
Employment to population ratio (% ages 15+)	*9*	*61*	..	..
Vulnerable employment (% of employed ages 15+)	..	..	..	..
Employment in agriculture (% of employed ages 15+)	..	..	..	..
Employment in industry (% of employed ages 15+)	..	..	..	..
Employment in service (% of employed ages 15+)	..	..	..	..
Wage and salaried workers (% of employed ages 15+)	..	..	..	..
Self-employed workers (% of employed ages 15+)	..	..	..	..
Unpaid family workers (% of employed ages 15+)	..	..	..	..
Women in nonagricultural wage employment (%)	..		..	
Children in employment (% of children ages 7–14)	..	..	..	..
Unemployment (% of labor force ages 15+)	..	..	..	..
Long-term unemployment (% of total unemployment)	..	..	..	..
Youth unemployment (% of labor force ages 15–24)	..	..	..	..
Maternity leave (weeks)	8		*9*	
Maternal leave benefits (% of wages paid)	100		*100*	
Women's political participation				
Seats held by women in national parliament (%)	11		26	
Women in managerial positions (%)	..		..	

Ireland

Population (millions)	4.4	Population living on less	
GNI ($ billions)	207.9	than $1.25 a day (%)	
GNI per capita ($)	47,610		..

	1990		2007	
	Female	Male	Female	Male
Demography				
Sex ratio at birth (females per 1,000 males)	935		935	
Life expectancy at birth (years)	77	72	82	77
Child mortality rate (per 1,000)	..	..	..	..
Female-headed households (%)	..		..	
Education				
Gross primary enrollment (% of relevant age group)	103	102	103	104
Gross secondary enrollment (% of relevant age group)	104	95	116	108
Gross tertiary enrollment (% of relevant age group)	..	..	66	52
Primary completion rate (% of relevant age group)	..	..	101	91
Adult literacy rate (% of population ages 15+)	..	..	..	..
Family planning and maternal health				
Total fertility rate (births per woman)	2.1		1.9	
Adolescent fertility (births per 1,000 women ages 15–19)	..		16	
Women married by age 18 (% of women ages 20–24)	..		..	
Contraceptive prevalence (% of women ages 15–49)	60		..	
Unmet need for contraception (% of women ages 15–49)	..		..	
Pregnant women receiving prenatal care (%)	..		..	
Births attended by skilled health staff (% of total)	..		100	
Maternal mortality ratio (per 100,000 live births)	..		1	
Labor force and employment dynamics				
Labor force participation (% of population ages 15+)	36	70	53	73
Women in the labor force (% of total labor force)	34		43	
Employment to population ratio (% ages 15+)	30	59	51	69
Vulnerable employment (% of employed ages 15+)	9	25	5	16
Employment in agriculture (% of employed ages 15+)	4	21	1	9
Employment in industry (% of employed ages 15+)	18	33	12	39
Employment in service (% of employed ages 15+)	77	46	86	51
Wage and salaried workers (% of employed ages 15+)	89	68	93	76
Self-employed workers (% of employed ages 15+)	8	30	6	24
Unpaid family workers (% of employed ages 15+)	3	2	1	0
Women in nonagricultural wage employment (%)	42		48	
Children in employment (% of children ages 7–14)	..	..	..	..
Unemployment (% of labor force ages 15+)	14	13	4	5
Long-term unemployment (% of total unemployment)	57	71	22	36
Youth unemployment (% of labor force ages 15–24)	16	19	7	9
Maternity leave (weeks)	14		18	
Maternal leave benefits (% of wages paid)	70		70	
Women's political participation				
Seats held by women in national parliament (%)	8		13	
Women in managerial positions (%)	..		29	

Isle of Man

Population (thousands)	77	Population living on less
GNI ($ billions)	3.5	than $1.25 a day (%) ‥
GNI per capita ($)	45,810	

	1990		2007	
	Female	Male	Female	Male
Demography				
Sex ratio at birth (females per 1,000 males)	‥		‥	
Life expectancy at birth (years)	‥	‥	‥	‥
Child mortality rate (per 1,000)	‥	‥	‥	‥
Female-headed households (%)	‥		‥	
Education				
Gross primary enrollment (% of relevant age group)	‥	‥	‥	‥
Gross secondary enrollment (% of relevant age group)	‥	‥	‥	‥
Gross tertiary enrollment (% of relevant age group)	‥	‥	‥	‥
Primary completion rate (% of relevant age group)	‥	‥	‥	‥
Adult literacy rate (% of population ages 15+)	‥	‥	‥	‥
Family planning and maternal health				
Total fertility rate (births per woman)	‥		‥	
Adolescent fertility (births per 1,000 women ages 15–19)	‥		‥	
Women married by age 18 (% of women ages 20–24)	‥		‥	
Contraceptive prevalence (% of women ages 15–49)	‥		‥	
Unmet need for contraception (% of women ages 15–49)	‥		‥	
Pregnant women receiving prenatal care (%)	‥		‥	
Births attended by skilled health staff (% of total)	‥		‥	
Maternal mortality ratio (per 100,000 live births)	‥		‥	
Labor force and employment dynamics				
Labor force participation (% of population ages 15+)	‥	‥	‥	‥
Women in the labor force (% of total labor force)	‥		‥	
Employment to population ratio (% ages 15+)	‥	‥	‥	‥
Vulnerable employment (% of employed ages 15+)	‥	‥	‥	‥
Employment in agriculture (% of employed ages 15+)	0	0	‥	‥
Employment in industry (% of employed ages 15+)	99	94	‥	‥
Employment in service (% of employed ages 15+)	0	0	‥	‥
Wage and salaried workers (% of employed ages 15+)	‥	‥	‥	‥
Self-employed workers (% of employed ages 15+)	‥	‥	‥	‥
Unpaid family workers (% of employed ages 15+)	‥	‥	‥	‥
Women in nonagricultural wage employment (%)	‥		‥	
Children in employment (% of children ages 7–14)	‥	‥	‥	‥
Unemployment (% of labor force ages 15+)	3	5	2	3
Long-term unemployment (% of total unemployment)	‥	‥	‥	‥
Youth unemployment (% of labor force ages 15–24)	‥	‥	‥	‥
Maternity leave (weeks)	‥		‥	
Maternal leave benefits (% of wages paid)	‥		‥	
Women's political participation				
Seats held by women in national parliament (%)	‥		‥	
Women in managerial positions (%)	‥		‥	

Israel

Population (millions)	7.2	Population living on less
GNI ($ billions)	159.2	than $1.25 a day (%)
GNI per capita ($)	22,170	..

	1990		2007	
	Female	Male	Female	Male
Demography				
Sex ratio at birth (females per 1,000 males)	943		943	
Life expectancy at birth (years)	78	75	83	79
Child mortality rate (per 1,000)	..	..	..	..
Female-headed households (%)	..		..	
Education				
Gross primary enrollment (% of relevant age group)	97	94	111	109
Gross secondary enrollment (% of relevant age group)	93	88	92	93
Gross tertiary enrollment (% of relevant age group)	..	..	65	51
Primary completion rate (% of relevant age group)	..	..	101	100
Adult literacy rate (% of population ages 15+)	..	..	..	..
Family planning and maternal health				
Total fertility rate (births per woman)	2.8		2.9	
Adolescent fertility (births per 1,000 women ages 15–19)	..		14	
Women married by age 18 (% of women ages 20–24)	..		..	
Contraceptive prevalence (% of women ages 15–49)	68		..	
Unmet need for contraception (% of women ages 15–49)	..		..	
Pregnant women receiving prenatal care (%)	..		..	
Births attended by skilled health staff (% of total)	99		..	
Maternal mortality ratio (per 100,000 live births)	..		4	
Labor force and employment dynamics				
Labor force participation (% of population ages 15+)	41	62	50	61
Women in the labor force (% of total labor force)	41		46	
Employment to population ratio (% ages 15+)	36	57	46	57
Vulnerable employment (% of employed ages 15+)	..	..	5	9
Employment in agriculture (% of employed ages 15+)	2	5	1	3
Employment in industry (% of employed ages 15+)	15	36	11	31
Employment in service (% of employed ages 15+)	82	58	88	65
Wage and salaried workers (% of employed ages 15+)	..	..	92	84
Self-employed workers (% of employed ages 15+)	..	..	8	17
Unpaid family workers (% of employed ages 15+)	..	..	0	0
Women in nonagricultural wage employment (%)	43		49	
Children in employment (% of children ages 7–14)	..	..	..	..
Unemployment (% of labor force ages 15+)	11	8	8	7
Long-term unemployment (% of total unemployment)	..	..	..	..
Youth unemployment (% of labor force ages 15–24)	23	21	19	17
Maternity leave (weeks)	12		12	
Maternal leave benefits (% of wages paid)	75		100	
Women's political participation				
Seats held by women in national parliament (%)	7		14	
Women in managerial positions (%)	..		29	

Italy

Population (millions)	59	Population living on less
GNI ($ billions)	1,988.2	than $1.25 a day (%) ..
GNI per capita ($)	33,490	

	1990		2007	
	Female	Male	Female	Male
Demography				
Sex ratio at birth (females per 1,000 males)	941		941	
Life expectancy at birth (years)	80	74	84	79
Child mortality rate (per 1,000)	..	..	..	..
Female-headed households (%)	..		..	
Education				
Gross primary enrollment (% of relevant age group)	102	102	103	104
Gross secondary enrollment (% of relevant age group)	82	82	100	101
Gross tertiary enrollment (% of relevant age group)	..	..	78	56
Primary completion rate (% of relevant age group)	105	105	99	100
Adult literacy rate (% of population ages 15+)	..	..	99	99
Family planning and maternal health				
Total fertility rate (births per woman)	1.3		1.3	
Adolescent fertility (births per 1,000 women ages 15–19)	..		6	
Women married by age 18 (% of women ages 20–24)	..		..	
Contraceptive prevalence (% of women ages 15–49)	..		..	
Unmet need for contraception (% of women ages 15–49)	..		..	
Pregnant women receiving prenatal care (%)	..		..	
Births attended by skilled health staff (% of total)	..		99	
Maternal mortality ratio (per 100,000 live births)	..		3	
Labor force and employment dynamics				
Labor force participation (% of population ages 15+)	36	66	39	61
Women in the labor force (% of total labor force)	37		40	
Employment to population ratio (% ages 15+)	30	61	36	58
Vulnerable employment (% of employed ages 15+)	16	15	16	27
Employment in agriculture (% of employed ages 15+)	9	9	3	5
Employment in industry (% of employed ages 15+)	23	37	18	39
Employment in service (% of employed ages 15+)	68	55	79	56
Wage and salaried workers (% of employed ages 15+)	76	69	80	70
Self-employed workers (% of employed ages 15+)	17	29	14	27
Unpaid family workers (% of employed ages 15+)	8	2	3	1
Women in nonagricultural wage employment (%)	36		43	
Children in employment (% of children ages 7–14)	..	..	..	..
Unemployment (% of labor force ages 15+)	18	8	8	5
Long-term unemployment (% of total unemployment)	71	69	52	47
Youth unemployment (% of labor force ages 15–24)	38	26	27	22
Maternity leave (weeks)	21		20	
Maternal leave benefits (% of wages paid)	80		80	
Women's political participation				
Seats held by women in national parliament (%)	13		17	
Women in managerial positions (%)	..		21	

Jamaica

Latin America & Caribbean   **Upper middle income**

Population (millions)	2.7	Population living on less
GNI ($ billions)	8.9	than $1.25 a day (%)
GNI per capita ($)	3,330	2.0

	1990		2007	
	Female	Male	Female	Male
Demography				
Sex ratio at birth (females per 1,000 males)	952		952	
Life expectancy at birth (years)	73	70	75	70
Child mortality rate (per 1,000)	..	..	6	5
Female-headed households (%)	..		..	
Education				
Gross primary enrollment (% of relevant age group)	101	101	95	95
Gross secondary enrollment (% of relevant age group)	66	62	88	86
Gross tertiary enrollment (% of relevant age group)	..	..	26	12
Primary completion rate (% of relevant age group)	94	88	84	81
Adult literacy rate (% of population ages 15+)	..	..	91	81
Family planning and maternal health				
Total fertility rate (births per woman)	2.9		2.4	
Adolescent fertility (births per 1,000 women ages 15-19)	..		78	
Women married by age 18 (% of women ages 20-24)	..		..	
Contraceptive prevalence (% of women ages 15-49)	62		..	
Unmet need for contraception (% of women ages 15-49)	..		..	
Pregnant women receiving prenatal care (%)	98		91	
Births attended by skilled health staff (% of total)	79		97	
Maternal mortality ratio (per 100,000 live births)	..		170	
Labor force and employment dynamics				
Labor force participation (% of population ages 15+)	66	80	55	74
Women in the labor force (% of total labor force)	47		44	
Employment to population ratio (% ages 15+)	51	72	48	70
Vulnerable employment (% of employed ages 15+)	37	46	31	38
Employment in agriculture (% of employed ages 15+)	16	36	9	25
Employment in industry (% of employed ages 15+)	12	25	5	27
Employment in service (% of employed ages 15+)	72	39	86	48
Wage and salaried workers (% of employed ages 15+)	61	52	66	58
Self-employed workers (% of employed ages 15+)	34	45	31	42
Unpaid family workers (% of employed ages 15+)	5	2	2	1
Women in nonagricultural wage employment (%)	50		48	
Children in employment (% of children ages 7-14)	..	..	..	..
Unemployment (% of labor force ages 15+)	23	9	14	5
Long-term unemployment (% of total unemployment)	28	21	..	..
Youth unemployment (% of labor force ages 15-24)	47	19	36	22
Maternity leave (weeks)	12		12	
Maternal leave benefits (% of wages paid)	100		100	
Women's political participation				
Seats held by women in national parliament (%)	5		13	
Women in managerial positions (%)	..		..	

Japan

Population (millions)	128	Population living on less
GNI ($ billions)	4,828.9	than $1.25 a day (%) ..
GNI per capita ($)	37,790	

	1990		2007	
	Female	Male	Female	Male
Demography				
Sex ratio at birth (females per 1,000 males)	947		947	
Life expectancy at birth (years)	82	76	86	79
Child mortality rate (per 1,000)	..	..	..	..
Female-headed households (%)	..		..	
Education				
Gross primary enrollment (% of relevant age group)	99	99	100	100
Gross secondary enrollment (% of relevant age group)	98	95	101	101
Gross tertiary enrollment (% of relevant age group)	..	..	54	61
Primary completion rate (% of relevant age group)	100	100	..	..
Adult literacy rate (% of population ages 15+)	..	..	..	..
Family planning and maternal health				
Total fertility rate (births per woman)	1.5		1.3	
Adolescent fertility (births per 1,000 women ages 15-19)	..		3	
Women married by age 18 (% of women ages 20-24)	..		..	
Contraceptive prevalence (% of women ages 15-49)	58		..	
Unmet need for contraception (% of women ages 15-49)	..		..	
Pregnant women receiving prenatal care (%)	..		..	
Births attended by skilled health staff (% of total)	100		100	
Maternal mortality ratio (per 100,000 live births)	..		6	
Labor force and employment dynamics				
Labor force participation (% of population ages 15+)	50	77	48	72
Women in the labor force (% of total labor force)	41		41	
Employment to population ratio (% ages 15+)	50	76	46	69
Vulnerable employment (% of employed ages 15+)	26	15	12	10
Employment in agriculture (% of employed ages 15+)	9	6	5	4
Employment in industry (% of employed ages 15+)	27	39	18	35
Employment in service (% of employed ages 15+)	64	55	77	59
Wage and salaried workers (% of employed ages 15+)	72	81	86	86
Self-employed workers (% of employed ages 15+)	11	16	6	13
Unpaid family workers (% of employed ages 15+)	17	3	7	1
Women in nonagricultural wage employment (%)	38		42	
Children in employment (% of children ages 7-14)	..	..	..	..
Unemployment (% of labor force ages 15+)	2	2	4	4
Long-term unemployment (% of total unemployment)	9	26	19	40
Youth unemployment (% of labor force ages 15-24)	4	5	7	10
Maternity leave (weeks)	14		14	
Maternal leave benefits (% of wages paid)	60		60	
Women's political participation				
Seats held by women in national parliament (%)	1		9	
Women in managerial positions (%)	..		10	

Jordan

Middle East & North Africa   **Lower middle income**

		Population living on less	
Population (millions)	5.7	than $1.25 a day (%)	2.0
GNI ($ billions)	16.3		
GNI per capita ($)	2,840		

	1990		2007	
	Female	Male	Female	Male
Demography				
Sex ratio at birth (females per 1,000 males)	952		952	
Life expectancy at birth (years)	69	65	74	71
Child mortality rate (per 1,000)	6	6	2	3
Female-headed households (%)	..		..	
Education				
Gross primary enrollment (% of relevant age group)	106	107	98	96
Gross secondary enrollment (% of relevant age group)	83	80	90	88
Gross tertiary enrollment (% of relevant age group)	..	..	41	37
Primary completion rate (% of relevant age group)	101	101	98	100
Adult literacy rate (% of population ages 15+)	..	..	87	95
Family planning and maternal health				
Total fertility rate (births per woman)	5.4		3.6	
Adolescent fertility (births per 1,000 women ages 15–19)	..		25	
Women married by age 18 (% of women ages 20–24)	16		..	
Contraceptive prevalence (% of women ages 15–49)	40		57	
Unmet need for contraception (% of women ages 15–49)	22		..	
Pregnant women receiving prenatal care (%)	80		99	
Births attended by skilled health staff (% of total)	87		99	
Maternal mortality ratio (per 100,000 live births)	..		62	
Labor force and employment dynamics				
Labor force participation (% of population ages 15+)	11	68	16	72
Women in the labor force (% of total labor force)	13		17	
Employment to population ratio (% ages 15+)	9	61	13	63
Vulnerable employment (% of employed ages 15+)	..	..	..	..
Employment in agriculture (% of employed ages 15+)	4	7	2	4
Employment in industry (% of employed ages 15+)	8	18	12	23
Employment in service (% of employed ages 15+)	87	75	84	73
Wage and salaried workers (% of employed ages 15+)	..	..	..	..
Self-employed workers (% of employed ages 15+)	..	..	..	..
Unpaid family workers (% of employed ages 15+)	..	..	..	..
Women in nonagricultural wage employment (%)	..		26	
Children in employment (% of children ages 7–14)	..	..	..	..
Unemployment (% of labor force ages 15+)	30	18	16	12
Long-term unemployment (% of total unemployment)	..	..	..	..
Youth unemployment (% of labor force ages 15–24)	..	..	..	..
Maternity leave (weeks)	6		10	
Maternal leave benefits (% of wages paid)	50		100	
Women's political participation				
Seats held by women in national parliament (%)	0		6	
Women in managerial positions (%)	..		..	

Kazakhstan

Europe & Central Asia			Upper middle income	

Population (millions)	15	Population living on less	
GNI ($ billions)	77.7	than $1.25 a day (%)	3.1
GNI per capita ($)	5,020		

	1990		2007	
	Female	Male	Female	Male
Demography				
Sex ratio at birth (females per 1,000 males)	944		944	
Life expectancy at birth (years)	73	64	72	61
Child mortality rate (per 1,000)	..	..	4	5
Female-headed households (%)	..		..	
Education				
Gross primary enrollment (% of relevant age group)	88	89	109	108
Gross secondary enrollment (% of relevant age group)	103	101	91	93
Gross tertiary enrollment (% of relevant age group)	..	..	56	39
Primary completion rate (% of relevant age group)	..	..	105	104
Adult literacy rate (% of population ages 15+)	96	99	99	100
Family planning and maternal health				
Total fertility rate (births per woman)	2.7		2.4	
Adolescent fertility (births per 1,000 women ages 15-19)	..		31	
Women married by age 18 (% of women ages 20-24)	..		..	
Contraceptive prevalence (% of women ages 15-49)	..		51	
Unmet need for contraception (% of women ages 15-49)	..		..	
Pregnant women receiving prenatal care (%)	..		100	
Births attended by skilled health staff (% of total)	..		100	
Maternal mortality ratio (per 100,000 live births)	..		140	
Labor force and employment dynamics				
Labor force participation (% of population ages 15+)	62	78	65	75
Women in the labor force (% of total labor force)	47		49	
Employment to population ratio (% ages 15+)	56	72	58	70
Vulnerable employment (% of employed ages 15+)	..	..	39	33
Employment in agriculture (% of employed ages 15+)	..	..	32	35
Employment in industry (% of employed ages 15+)	..	..	10	24
Employment in service (% of employed ages 15+)	..	..	58	41
Wage and salaried workers (% of employed ages 15+)	..	..	60	64
Self-employed workers (% of employed ages 15+)	..	..	38	35
Unpaid family workers (% of employed ages 15+)	..	..	1	1
Women in nonagricultural wage employment (%)	..		49	
Children in employment (% of children ages 7-14)	..	..	3	4
Unemployment (% of labor force ages 15+)	..	..	10	7
Long-term unemployment (% of total unemployment)	..	..	..	..
Youth unemployment (% of labor force ages 15-24)	..	..	16	13
Maternity leave (weeks)	..		18	
Maternal leave benefits (% of wages paid)	..		..	
Women's political participation				
Seats held by women in national parliament (%)	..		16	
Women in managerial positions (%)	..		34	

Kenya

Sub-Saharan Africa		Low income

			Population living on less	
Population (millions)	38		Population living on less	
GNI ($ billions)	24.0		than $1.25 a day (%)	19.7
GNI per capita ($)	640			

	1990		2007	
	Female	Male	Female	Male
Demography				
Sex ratio at birth (females per 1,000 males)	971		971	
Life expectancy at birth (years)	61	57	55	53
Child mortality rate (per 1,000)	*33*	*35*	*39*	*42*
Female-headed households (%)	*33*		*32*	
Education				
Gross primary enrollment (% of relevant age group)	99	102	*104*	*107*
Gross secondary enrollment (% of relevant age group)	44	52	*49*	*52*
Gross tertiary enrollment (% of relevant age group)	..	..	*2*	*3*
Primary completion rate (% of relevant age group)	..	..	*92*	*94*
Adult literacy rate (% of population ages 15+)	..	..	..	..
Family planning and maternal health				
Total fertility rate (births per woman)	5.8		5.0	
Adolescent fertility (births per 1,000 women ages 15-19)	..		104	
Women married by age 18 (% of women ages 20-24)	*28*		*25*	
Contraceptive prevalence (% of women ages 15-49)	*33*		*39*	
Unmet need for contraception (% of women ages 15-49)	*36*		*25*	
Pregnant women receiving prenatal care (%)	*95*		*88*	
Births attended by skilled health staff (% of total)	*45*		*42*	
Maternal mortality ratio (per 100,000 live births)	..		*560*	
Labor force and employment dynamics				
Labor force participation (% of population ages 15+)	75	90	74	87
Women in the labor force (% of total labor force)	46		46	
Employment to population ratio (% ages 15+)	*65*	*80*	*67*	*80*
Vulnerable employment (% of employed ages 15+)	..	..	..	..
Employment in agriculture (% of employed ages 15+)	21	19	..	..
Employment in industry (% of employed ages 15+)	10	23	..	..
Employment in service (% of employed ages 15+)	69	58	..	..
Wage and salaried workers (% of employed ages 15+)	..	..	..	..
Self-employed workers (% of employed ages 15+)	..	..	..	..
Unpaid family workers (% of employed ages 15+)	..	..	..	..
Women in nonagricultural wage employment (%)	21		..	
Children in employment (% of children ages 7-14)	..	..	..	..
Unemployment (% of labor force ages 15+)	..	..	..	..
Long-term unemployment (% of total unemployment)	..	..	..	..
Youth unemployment (% of labor force ages 15-24)	..	..	..	..
Maternity leave (weeks)	8		*8*	
Maternal leave benefits (% of wages paid)	..		*100*	
Women's political participation				
Seats held by women in national parliament (%)	1		7	
Women in managerial positions (%)	..		..	

Kiribati

East Asia & Pacific		Lower middle income	

		Population living on less	
Population (thousands)	95	than $1.25 a day (%)	
GNI ($ millions)	106.5		..
GNI per capita ($)	1,120		

	1990		2007	
	Female	Male	Female	Male
Demography				
Sex ratio at birth (females per 1,000 males)	..		..	
Life expectancy at birth (years)	59	55	63	59
Child mortality rate (per 1,000)	..	..	..	..
Female-headed households (%)	..		..	
Education				
Gross primary enrollment (% of relevant age group)	..	..	114	112
Gross secondary enrollment (% of relevant age group)	..	..	94	82
Gross tertiary enrollment (% of relevant age group)	..	..	..	..
Primary completion rate (% of relevant age group)	..	..	126	124
Adult literacy rate (% of population ages 15+)	..	..	..	..
Family planning and maternal health				
Total fertility rate (births per woman)	4.0		3.4	
Adolescent fertility (births per 1,000 women ages 15–19)	..		..	
Women married by age 18 (% of women ages 20–24)	..		..	
Contraceptive prevalence (% of women ages 15–49)	..		..	
Unmet need for contraception (% of women ages 15–49)	..		..	
Pregnant women receiving prenatal care (%)	..		..	
Births attended by skilled health staff (% of total)	..		..	
Maternal mortality ratio (per 100,000 live births)	..		..	
Labor force and employment dynamics				
Labor force participation (% of population ages 15+)	..	..	..	..
Women in the labor force (% of total labor force)	..		..	
Employment to population ratio (% ages 15+)	..	..	..	..
Vulnerable employment (% of employed ages 15+)	..	..	..	..
Employment in agriculture (% of employed ages 15+)	..	..	..	..
Employment in industry (% of employed ages 15+)	..	..	..	..
Employment in service (% of employed ages 15+)	..	..	..	..
Wage and salaried workers (% of employed ages 15+)	..	..	..	..
Self-employed workers (% of employed ages 15+)	..	..	..	..
Unpaid family workers (% of employed ages 15+)	..	..	..	..
Women in nonagricultural wage employment (%)	..		..	
Children in employment (% of children ages 7–14)	..	..	..	..
Unemployment (% of labor force ages 15+)	..	..	..	..
Long-term unemployment (% of total unemployment)	..	..	..	..
Youth unemployment (% of labor force ages 15–24)	..	..	..	..
Maternity leave (weeks)	..		12	
Maternal leave benefits (% of wages paid)	..		25	
Women's political participation				
Seats held by women in national parliament (%)	0		4	
Women in managerial positions (%)	..		..	

Korea, Dem. Rep.

East Asia & Pacific   **Low income**

Population (millions)	24	Population living on less	
GNI ($ billions)	..	than $1.25 a day (%)	..
GNI per capita ($)	..		

	1990 Female	1990 Male	2007 Female	2007 Male
Demography				
Sex ratio at birth (females per 1,000 males)	952		952	
Life expectancy at birth (years)	74	66	69	65
Child mortality rate (per 1,000)	..	..	..	..
Female-headed households (%)	..		..	
Education				
Gross primary enrollment (% of relevant age group)	..	..	..	..
Gross secondary enrollment (% of relevant age group)	..	..	..	..
Gross tertiary enrollment (% of relevant age group)	..	..	..	..
Primary completion rate (% of relevant age group)	..	..	..	..
Adult literacy rate (% of population ages 15+)	..	..	..	..
Family planning and maternal health				
Total fertility rate (births per woman)	2.4		1.9	
Adolescent fertility (births per 1,000 women ages 15–19)	..		1	
Women married by age 18 (% of women ages 20–24)	..		..	
Contraceptive prevalence (% of women ages 15–49)	62		..	
Unmet need for contraception (% of women ages 15–49)	..		..	
Pregnant women receiving prenatal care (%)	..		..	
Births attended by skilled health staff (% of total)	..		97	
Maternal mortality ratio (per 100,000 live births)	..		370	
Labor force and employment dynamics				
Labor force participation (% of population ages 15+)	51	79	58	78
Women in the labor force (% of total labor force)	41		44	
Employment to population ratio (% ages 15+)	49	76	56	74
Vulnerable employment (% of employed ages 15+)	..	..	..	..
Employment in agriculture (% of employed ages 15+)	..	..	..	..
Employment in industry (% of employed ages 15+)	..	..	..	..
Employment in service (% of employed ages 15+)	..	..	..	..
Wage and salaried workers (% of employed ages 15+)	..	..	..	..
Self-employed workers (% of employed ages 15+)	..	..	..	..
Unpaid family workers (% of employed ages 15+)	..	..	..	..
Women in nonagricultural wage employment (%)	41		..	
Children in employment (% of children ages 7–14)	..	..	..	..
Unemployment (% of labor force ages 15+)	..	..	..	..
Long-term unemployment (% of total unemployment)	..	..	..	..
Youth unemployment (% of labor force ages 15–24)	..	..	..	..
Maternity leave (weeks)	..		..	
Maternal leave benefits (% of wages paid)	..		..	
Women's political participation				
Seats held by women in national parliament (%)	21		20	
Women in managerial positions (%)	..		..	

Korea, Rep.

High income

Population (millions)	48	Population living on less		
GNI ($ billions)	955.8	than $1.25 a day (%)		..
GNI per capita ($)	19,730			

	1990		2007	
	Female	Male	Female	Male
Demography				
Sex ratio at birth (females per 1,000 males)	952		909	
Life expectancy at birth (years)	76	67	82	76
Child mortality rate (per 1,000)	..	..	..	..
Female-headed households (%)	..		..	
Education				
Gross primary enrollment (% of relevant age group)	104	103	103	107
Gross secondary enrollment (% of relevant age group)	90	93	94	100
Gross tertiary enrollment (% of relevant age group)	..	..	72	111
Primary completion rate (% of relevant age group)	97	96	95	106
Adult literacy rate (% of population ages 15+)	..	..	..	..
Family planning and maternal health				
Total fertility rate (births per woman)	1.6		1.3	
Adolescent fertility (births per 1,000 women ages 15–19)	..		4	
Women married by age 18 (% of women ages 20–24)	..		..	
Contraceptive prevalence (% of women ages 15–49)	79		..	
Unmet need for contraception (% of women ages 15–49)	..		..	
Pregnant women receiving prenatal care (%)	..		..	
Births attended by skilled health staff (% of total)	98		100	
Maternal mortality ratio (per 100,000 live births)	..		14	
Labor force and employment dynamics				
Labor force participation (% of population ages 15+)	47	73	49	73
Women in the labor force (% of total labor force)	39		41	
Employment to population ratio (% ages 15+)	46	72	48	70
Vulnerable employment (% of employed ages 15+)	..	..	28	23
Employment in agriculture (% of employed ages 15+)	20	16	9	7
Employment in industry (% of employed ages 15+)	30	39	17	34
Employment in service (% of employed ages 15+)	50	45	74	59
Wage and salaried workers (% of employed ages 15+)	57	63	69	68
Self-employed workers (% of employed ages 15+)	19	34	19	31
Unpaid family workers (% of employed ages 15+)	25	3	13	1
Women in nonagricultural wage employment (%)	38		42	
Children in employment (% of children ages 7–14)	..	..	..	..
Unemployment (% of labor force ages 15+)	2	3	3	4
Long-term unemployment (% of total unemployment)	1	3	0	1
Youth unemployment (% of labor force ages 15–24)	6	10	9	12
Maternity leave (weeks)	..		13	
Maternal leave benefits (% of wages paid)	..		100	
Women's political participation				
Seats held by women in national parliament (%)	2		13	
Women in managerial positions (%)	..		6	

Kuwait

High income

Population (millions)	2.7	Population living on less
GNI ($ billions)	99.9	than $1.25 a day (%)
GNI per capita ($)	38,420	..

	1990		2007	
	Female	Male	Female	Male
Demography				
Sex ratio at birth (females per 1,000 males)	971		971	
Life expectancy at birth (years)	77	73	80	76
Child mortality rate (per 1,000)	..	..	..	..
Female-headed households (%)	..		..	
Education				
Gross primary enrollment (% of relevant age group)	91	92	97	100
Gross secondary enrollment (% of relevant age group)	81	85	92	90
Gross tertiary enrollment (% of relevant age group)	..	..	26	11
Primary completion rate (% of relevant age group)	..	..	98	98
Adult literacy rate (% of population ages 15+)	..	..	93	95
Family planning and maternal health				
Total fertility rate (births per woman)	3.5		2.2	
Adolescent fertility (births per 1,000 women ages 15–19)	..		13	
Women married by age 18 (% of women ages 20–24)	..		..	
Contraceptive prevalence (% of women ages 15–49)	35		..	
Unmet need for contraception (% of women ages 15–49)	..		..	
Pregnant women receiving prenatal care (%)	..		..	
Births attended by skilled health staff (% of total)	..		..	
Maternal mortality ratio (per 100,000 live births)	..		4	
Labor force and employment dynamics				
Labor force participation (% of population ages 15+)	34	81	43	81
Women in the labor force (% of total labor force)	22		24	
Employment to population ratio (% ages 15+)	34	80	42	80
Vulnerable employment (% of employed ages 15+)	..	..	..	..
Employment in agriculture (% of employed ages 15+)	..	..	..	..
Employment in industry (% of employed ages 15+)	..	..	..	..
Employment in service (% of employed ages 15+)	..	..	..	..
Wage and salaried workers (% of employed ages 15+)	..	..	..	..
Self-employed workers (% of employed ages 15+)	..	..	..	..
Unpaid family workers (% of employed ages 15+)	..	..	..	..
Women in nonagricultural wage employment (%)	..		..	
Children in employment (% of children ages 7–14)	..	..	..	..
Unemployment (% of labor force ages 15+)	3	2	..	..
Long-term unemployment (% of total unemployment)	..	..	..	..
Youth unemployment (% of labor force ages 15–24)	..	..	..	..
Maternity leave (weeks)	10		10	
Maternal leave benefits (% of wages paid)	100		100	
Women's political participation				
Seats held by women in national parliament (%)	..		2	
Women in managerial positions (%)	..		..	

Kyrgyz Republic

Europe & Central Asia		Low income

Population (millions)	5.2	Population living on less	
GNI ($ billions)	3.2	than $1.25 a day (%)	21.8
GNI per capita ($)	610		

	1990		2007	
	Female	Male	Female	Male
Demography				
Sex ratio at birth (females per 1,000 males)	948		948	
Life expectancy at birth (years)	73	64	72	64
Child mortality rate (per 1,000)	..	..	4	8
Female-headed households (%)	..		..	
Education				
Gross primary enrollment (% of relevant age group)	111	109	95	96
Gross secondary enrollment (% of relevant age group)	102	103	87	86
Gross tertiary enrollment (% of relevant age group)	..	..	48	37
Primary completion rate (% of relevant age group)	..	..	94	95
Adult literacy rate (% of population ages 15+)	..	..	99	100
Family planning and maternal health				
Total fertility rate (births per woman)	3.7		2.7	
Adolescent fertility (births per 1,000 women ages 15–19)	..		31	
Women married by age 18 (% of women ages 20–24)	..		..	
Contraceptive prevalence (% of women ages 15–49)	..		48	
Unmet need for contraception (% of women ages 15–49)	..		1	
Pregnant women receiving prenatal care (%)	..		97	
Births attended by skilled health staff (% of total)	..		98	
Maternal mortality ratio (per 100,000 live births)	..		150	
Labor force and employment dynamics				
Labor force participation (% of population ages 15+)	58	74	53	75
Women in the labor force (% of total labor force)	46		43	
Employment to population ratio (% ages 15+)	52	68	49	70
Vulnerable employment (% of employed ages 15+)	..	..	47	47
Employment in agriculture (% of employed ages 15+)	..	..	39	39
Employment in industry (% of employed ages 15+)	..	..	11	23
Employment in service (% of employed ages 15+)	..	..	50	38
Wage and salaried workers (% of employed ages 15+)	..	..	52	50
Self-employed workers (% of employed ages 15+)	..	..	29	41
Unpaid family workers (% of employed ages 15+)	..	..	19	9
Women in nonagricultural wage employment (%)	..		52	
Children in employment (% of children ages 7–14)	..	..	5	6
Unemployment (% of labor force ages 15+)	..	..	9	8
Long-term unemployment (% of total unemployment)	..	..	..	..
Youth unemployment (% of labor force ages 15–24)	..	..	18	14
Maternity leave (weeks)	..		18	
Maternal leave benefits (% of wages paid)	..		100	
Women's political participation				
Seats held by women in national parliament (%)	..		0	
Women in managerial positions (%)	..		..	

Lao PDR

East Asia & Pacific   **Low income**

Population (millions)	5.9	Population living on less
GNI ($ billions)	3.7	than $1.25 a day (%) 44.0
GNI per capita ($)	630	

	1990 Female	1990 Male	2007 Female	2007 Male
Demography				
Sex ratio at birth (females per 1,000 males)	952		952	
Life expectancy at birth (years)	56	53	66	63
Child mortality rate (per 1,000)	..	..	..	..
Female-headed households (%)	..		..	
Education				
Gross primary enrollment (% of relevant age group)	91	115	111	124
Gross secondary enrollment (% of relevant age group)	19	28	39	49
Gross tertiary enrollment (% of relevant age group)	..	..	7	11
Primary completion rate (% of relevant age group)	..	..	72	81
Adult literacy rate (% of population ages 15+)	..	..	63	82
Family planning and maternal health				
Total fertility rate (births per woman)	6.1		3.2	
Adolescent fertility (births per 1,000 women ages 15–19)	..		72	
Women married by age 18 (% of women ages 20–24)	..		..	
Contraceptive prevalence (% of women ages 15–49)	19		38	
Unmet need for contraception (% of women ages 15–49)	..		..	
Pregnant women receiving prenatal care (%)	..		..	
Births attended by skilled health staff (% of total)	..		..	
Maternal mortality ratio (per 100,000 live births)	..		660	
Labor force and employment dynamics				
Labor force participation (% of population ages 15+)	80	83	79	80
Women in the labor force (% of total labor force)	50		51	
Employment to population ratio (% ages 15+)	79	82	78	78
Vulnerable employment (% of employed ages 15+)	..	..	..	..
Employment in agriculture (% of employed ages 15+)	..	..	..	..
Employment in industry (% of employed ages 15+)	..	..	..	..
Employment in service (% of employed ages 15+)	..	..	..	..
Wage and salaried workers (% of employed ages 15+)	..	..	..	..
Self-employed workers (% of employed ages 15+)	..	..	..	..
Unpaid family workers (% of employed ages 15+)	..	..	..	..
Women in nonagricultural wage employment (%)	..		50	
Children in employment (% of children ages 7–14)	..	..	..	..
Unemployment (% of labor force ages 15+)	..	..	1	1
Long-term unemployment (% of total unemployment)	..	..	..	..
Youth unemployment (% of labor force ages 15–24)	..	..	..	..
Maternity leave (weeks)	12		12	
Maternal leave benefits (% of wages paid)	100		70	
Women's political participation				
Seats held by women in national parliament (%)	6		25	
Women in managerial positions (%)	..		..	

Latvia

Europe & Central Asia		Upper middle income

Population (millions)	2.3	Population living on less	
GNI ($ billions)	22.6	than $1.25 a day (%)	2.0
GNI per capita ($)	9,920		

	1990		2007	
	Female	Male	Female	Male
Demography				
Sex ratio at birth (females per 1,000 males)	946		946	
Life expectancy at birth (years)	75	64	77	66
Child mortality rate (per 1,000)	..	..	..	..
Female-headed households (%)	..		..	
Education				
Gross primary enrollment (% of relevant age group)	98	91	93	96
Gross secondary enrollment (% of relevant age group)	93	92	99	98
Gross tertiary enrollment (% of relevant age group)	..	..	95	53
Primary completion rate (% of relevant age group)	..	..	91	93
Adult literacy rate (% of population ages 15+)	99	100	100	100
Family planning and maternal health				
Total fertility rate (births per woman)	2.0		1.4	
Adolescent fertility (births per 1,000 women ages 15–19)	..		14	
Women married by age 18 (% of women ages 20–24)	..		..	
Contraceptive prevalence (% of women ages 15–49)	..		..	
Unmet need for contraception (% of women ages 15–49)	..		..	
Pregnant women receiving prenatal care (%)	..		..	
Births attended by skilled health staff (% of total)	..		100	
Maternal mortality ratio (per 100,000 live births)	..		10	
Labor force and employment dynamics				
Labor force participation (% of population ages 15+)	63	77	54	69
Women in the labor force (% of total labor force)	50		48	
Employment to population ratio (% ages 15+)	54	65	51	64
Vulnerable employment (% of employed ages 15+)	..	..	6	9
Employment in agriculture (% of employed ages 15+)	..	..	8	15
Employment in industry (% of employed ages 15+)	..	..	16	35
Employment in service (% of employed ages 15+)	..	..	75	49
Wage and salaried workers (% of employed ages 15+)	..	..	92	87
Self-employed workers (% of employed ages 15+)	..	..	7	11
Unpaid family workers (% of employed ages 15+)	..	..	2	2
Women in nonagricultural wage employment (%)	52		53	
Children in employment (% of children ages 7–14)	..	..	..	..
Unemployment (% of labor force ages 15+)	..	..	5	6
Long-term unemployment (% of total unemployment)	..	..	..	..
Youth unemployment (% of labor force ages 15–24)	..	..	14	12
Maternity leave (weeks)	..		16	
Maternal leave benefits (% of wages paid)	..		100	
Women's political participation				
Seats held by women in national parliament (%)	..		19	
Women in managerial positions (%)	..		40	

Lebanon

Middle East & North Africa	Upper middle income

Population (millions)	4.1	Population living on less
GNI ($ billions)	23.8	than $1.25 a day (%) ..
GNI per capita ($)	5,800	

	1990		2007	
	Female	Male	Female	Male
Demography				
Sex ratio at birth (females per 1,000 males)	952		952	
Life expectancy at birth (years)	71	67	74	70
Child mortality rate (per 1,000)	..	..	..	..
Female-headed households (%)	..		..	
Education				
Gross primary enrollment (% of relevant age group)	95	98	94	97
Gross secondary enrollment (% of relevant age group)	..	..	86	77
Gross tertiary enrollment (% of relevant age group)	..	..	56	47
Primary completion rate (% of relevant age group)	..	..	83	80
Adult literacy rate (% of population ages 15+)	..	..	86	93
Family planning and maternal health				
Total fertility rate (births per woman)	3.1		2.2	
Adolescent fertility (births per 1,000 women ages 15–19)	..		25	
Women married by age 18 (% of women ages 20–24)	..		..	
Contraceptive prevalence (% of women ages 15–49)	..		58	
Unmet need for contraception (% of women ages 15–49)	..		..	
Pregnant women receiving prenatal care (%)	..		..	
Births attended by skilled health staff (% of total)	..		98	
Maternal mortality ratio (per 100,000 live births)	..		150	
Labor force and employment dynamics				
Labor force participation (% of population ages 15+)	22	83	25	77
Women in the labor force (% of total labor force)	23		26	
Employment to population ratio (% ages 15+)	20	75	22	71
Vulnerable employment (% of employed ages 15+)	..	..	..	..
Employment in agriculture (% of employed ages 15+)	..	..	..	..
Employment in industry (% of employed ages 15+)	..	..	..	..
Employment in service (% of employed ages 15+)	..	..	..	..
Wage and salaried workers (% of employed ages 15+)	..	..	..	..
Self-employed workers (% of employed ages 15+)	..	..	..	..
Unpaid family workers (% of employed ages 15+)	..	..	..	..
Women in nonagricultural wage employment (%)	..		..	
Children in employment (% of children ages 7–14)	..	..	..	..
Unemployment (% of labor force ages 15+)	..	..	..	..
Long-term unemployment (% of total unemployment)	..	..	..	..
Youth unemployment (% of labor force ages 15–24)	..	..	..	..
Maternity leave (weeks)	5		7	
Maternal leave benefits (% of wages paid)	100		100	
Women's political participation				
Seats held by women in national parliament (%)	0		5	
Women in managerial positions (%)	..		..	

Lesotho

Population (millions)	2.0	Population living on less
GNI ($ billions)	2.1	than $1.25 a day (%) 43.4
GNI per capita ($)	1,030	

	1990		2007	
	Female	Male	Female	Male
Demography				
Sex ratio at birth (females per 1,000 males)	971		971	
Life expectancy at birth (years)	60	57	42	43
Child mortality rate (per 1,000)	..	..	19	22
Female-headed households (%)		..	37	
Education				
Gross primary enrollment (% of relevant age group)	119	98	114	115
Gross secondary enrollment (% of relevant age group)	29	20	41	33
Gross tertiary enrollment (% of relevant age group)	..	..	4	3
Primary completion rate (% of relevant age group)	76	41	92	65
Adult literacy rate (% of population ages 15+)	..	..	..	..
Family planning and maternal health				
Total fertility rate (births per woman)	4.9		3.4	
Adolescent fertility (births per 1,000 women ages 15–19)	..		73	
Women married by age 18 (% of women ages 20–24)	..		..	
Contraceptive prevalence (% of women ages 15–49)	23		37	
Unmet need for contraception (% of women ages 15–49)	..		31	
Pregnant women receiving prenatal care (%)	91		90	
Births attended by skilled health staff (% of total)	50		55	
Maternal mortality ratio (per 100,000 live births)	..		960	
Labor force and employment dynamics				
Labor force participation (% of population ages 15+)	68	85	68	75
Women in the labor force (% of total labor force)	51		52	
Employment to population ratio (% ages 15+)	41	63	50	64
Vulnerable employment (% of employed ages 15+)	48	33	..	..
Employment in agriculture (% of employed ages 15+)	..	..	..	..
Employment in industry (% of employed ages 15+)	..	..	..	..
Employment in service (% of employed ages 15+)	..	..	..	..
Wage and salaried workers (% of employed ages 15+)	38	62	..	..
Self-employed workers (% of employed ages 15+)	23	18	..	..
Unpaid family workers (% of employed ages 15+)	26	15	..	..
Women in nonagricultural wage employment (%)		..		
Children in employment (% of children ages 7–14)	..	..	..	..
Unemployment (% of labor force ages 15+)	..	..	..	..
Long-term unemployment (% of total unemployment)	..	..	..	..
Youth unemployment (% of labor force ages 15–24)	..	..	..	..
Maternity leave (weeks)		..	12	
Maternal leave benefits (% of wages paid)		..	0	
Women's political participation				
Seats held by women in national parliament (%)		..	24	
Women in managerial positions (%)		..	..	

Liberia

Sub-Saharan Africa		Low income

Population (millions)	3.7	Population living on less	
GNI ($ millions)	530.6	than $1.25 a day (%)	83.7
GNI per capita ($)	140		

	1990		2007	
	Female	Male	Female	Male
Demography				
Sex ratio at birth (females per 1,000 males)	971		971	
Life expectancy at birth (years)	44	42	47	45
Child mortality rate (per 1,000)	..	..	51	57
Female-headed households (%)	..		31	
Education				
Gross primary enrollment (% of relevant age group)	..	..	79	88
Gross secondary enrollment (% of relevant age group)	..	..	..	..
Gross tertiary enrollment (% of relevant age group)	..	..	..	..
Primary completion rate (% of relevant age group)	..	..	50	60
Adult literacy rate (% of population ages 15+)	..	..	51	60
Family planning and maternal health				
Total fertility rate (births per woman)	6.9		5.2	
Adolescent fertility (births per 1,000 women ages 15–19)	..		219	
Women married by age 18 (% of women ages 20–24)	..		..	
Contraceptive prevalence (% of women ages 15–49)	..		11	
Unmet need for contraception (% of women ages 15–49)	..		36	
Pregnant women receiving prenatal care (%)	..		..	
Births attended by skilled health staff (% of total)	..		46	
Maternal mortality ratio (per 100,000 live births)	..		*1,200*	
Labor force and employment dynamics				
Labor force participation (% of population ages 15+)	54	85	55	85
Women in the labor force (% of total labor force)	39		40	
Employment to population ratio (% ages 15+)	*52*	*79*	53	79
Vulnerable employment (% of employed ages 15+)	..	..	..	..
Employment in agriculture (% of employed ages 15+)	..	..	..	..
Employment in industry (% of employed ages 15+)	..	..	..	..
Employment in service (% of employed ages 15+)	..	..	..	..
Wage and salaried workers (% of employed ages 15+)	..	..	..	..
Self-employed workers (% of employed ages 15+)	..	..	..	..
Unpaid family workers (% of employed ages 15+)	..	..	..	..
Women in nonagricultural wage employment (%)	..		..	
Children in employment (% of children ages 7–14)	..	..	37	38
Unemployment (% of labor force ages 15+)	..	..	4	7
Long-term unemployment (% of total unemployment)	..	..	..	..
Youth unemployment (% of labor force ages 15–24)	..	..	..	..
Maternity leave (weeks)	..		..	
Maternal leave benefits (% of wages paid)	..		..	
Women's political participation				
Seats held by women in national parliament (%)	..		13	
Women in managerial positions (%)	..		..	

Libya

Middle East & North Africa			**Upper middle income**	

Population (millions)	6.2	Population living on less
GNI ($ billions)	55.5	than $1.25 a day (%)
GNI per capita ($)	9,010	..

	1990		2007	
	Female	Male	Female	Male
Demography				
Sex ratio at birth (females per 1,000 males)	952		952	
Life expectancy at birth (years)	71	66	77	72
Child mortality rate (per 1,000)	..	..	..	..
Female-headed households (%)	..		..	
Education				
Gross primary enrollment (% of relevant age group)	..	..	108	113
Gross secondary enrollment (% of relevant age group)	..	..	101	86
Gross tertiary enrollment (% of relevant age group)	..	..	58	53
Primary completion rate (% of relevant age group)	..	..	..	..
Adult literacy rate (% of population ages 15+)	..	..	78	94
Family planning and maternal health				
Total fertility rate (births per woman)	4.7		2.7	
Adolescent fertility (births per 1,000 women ages 15–19)	..		3	
Women married by age 18 (% of women ages 20–24)	..		..	
Contraceptive prevalence (% of women ages 15–49)	..		..	
Unmet need for contraception (% of women ages 15–49)	..		..	
Pregnant women receiving prenatal care (%)	..		..	
Births attended by skilled health staff (% of total)	..		..	
Maternal mortality ratio (per 100,000 live births)	..		97	
Labor force and employment dynamics				
Labor force participation (% of population ages 15+)	17	78	26	78
Women in the labor force (% of total labor force)	16		24	
Employment to population ratio (% ages 15+)	15	72	23	72
Vulnerable employment (% of employed ages 15+)	..	..	..	..
Employment in agriculture (% of employed ages 15+)	..	..	..	..
Employment in industry (% of employed ages 15+)	..	..	..	..
Employment in service (% of employed ages 15+)	..	..	..	..
Wage and salaried workers (% of employed ages 15+)	..	..	..	..
Self-employed workers (% of employed ages 15+)	..	..	..	..
Unpaid family workers (% of employed ages 15+)	..	..	..	..
Women in nonagricultural wage employment (%)	..		..	
Children in employment (% of children ages 7–14)	..	..	..	..
Unemployment (% of labor force ages 15+)	..	..	..	..
Long-term unemployment (% of total unemployment)	..	..	..	..
Youth unemployment (% of labor force ages 15–24)	..	..	..	..
Maternity leave (weeks)	7		7	
Maternal leave benefits (% of wages paid)	50		50	
Women's political participation				
Seats held by women in national parliament (%)	..		8	
Women in managerial positions (%)	..		..	

Liechtenstein

Population (thousands)	35	Population living on less
GNI ($ billions)	..	than $1.25 a day (%) ..
GNI per capita ($)	..	

	1990		2007	
	Female	Male	Female	Male
Demography				
Sex ratio at birth (females per 1,000 males)		..		..
Life expectancy at birth (years)	..	..	..	..
Child mortality rate (per 1,000)	..	..	..	..
Female-headed households (%)		..		..
Education				
Gross primary enrollment (% of relevant age group)	..	..	106	108
Gross secondary enrollment (% of relevant age group)	..	..	101	115
Gross tertiary enrollment (% of relevant age group)	..	..	18	42
Primary completion rate (% of relevant age group)	..	..	98	98
Adult literacy rate (% of population ages 15+)	..	..	..	..
Family planning and maternal health				
Total fertility rate (births per woman)		..		..
Adolescent fertility (births per 1,000 women ages 15–19)		..		..
Women married by age 18 (% of women ages 20–24)		..		..
Contraceptive prevalence (% of women ages 15–49)		..		..
Unmet need for contraception (% of women ages 15–49)		..		..
Pregnant women receiving prenatal care (%)		..		..
Births attended by skilled health staff (% of total)		..		..
Maternal mortality ratio (per 100,000 live births)		..		..
Labor force and employment dynamics				
Labor force participation (% of population ages 15+)	..	..	..	..
Women in the labor force (% of total labor force)		..		..
Employment to population ratio (% ages 15+)	..	..	..	..
Vulnerable employment (% of employed ages 15+)	..	..	..	..
Employment in agriculture (% of employed ages 15+)	..	..	..	..
Employment in industry (% of employed ages 15+)	..	..	..	..
Employment in service (% of employed ages 15+)	..	..	..	..
Wage and salaried workers (% of employed ages 15+)	..	..	..	..
Self-employed workers (% of employed ages 15+)	..	..	..	..
Unpaid family workers (% of employed ages 15+)	..	..	..	..
Women in nonagricultural wage employment (%)		..	39	
Children in employment (% of children ages 7–14)	..	..	..	..
Unemployment (% of labor force ages 15+)	..	..	..	..
Long-term unemployment (% of total unemployment)	..	..	..	..
Youth unemployment (% of labor force ages 15–24)	..	..	..	..
Maternity leave (weeks)		8		..
Maternal leave benefits (% of wages paid)		80		..
Women's political participation				
Seats held by women in national parliament (%)		4		24
Women in managerial positions (%)		..		..

Lithuania

Europe & Central Asia		Upper middle income	

Population (millions)	3.4	Population living on less
GNI ($ billions)	33.0	than $1.25 a day (%) 2.0
GNI per capita ($)	9,770	

	1990		2007	
	Female	Male	Female	Male
Demography				
Sex ratio at birth (females per 1,000 males)	945		945	
Life expectancy at birth (years)	76	66	77	65
Child mortality rate (per 1,000)	..	..	..	..
Female-headed households (%)		..		..
Education				
Gross primary enrollment (% of relevant age group)	90	94	94	95
Gross secondary enrollment (% of relevant age group)	..	..	99	99
Gross tertiary enrollment (% of relevant age group)	..	..	93	60
Primary completion rate (% of relevant age group)	..	..	93	92
Adult literacy rate (% of population ages 15+)	98	99	100	100
Family planning and maternal health				
Total fertility rate (births per woman)	2.0		1.4	
Adolescent fertility (births per 1,000 women ages 15–19)	..		18	
Women married by age 18 (% of women ages 20–24)	..		..	
Contraceptive prevalence (% of women ages 15–49)	..		..	
Unmet need for contraception (% of women ages 15–49)	..		..	
Pregnant women receiving prenatal care (%)	..		..	
Births attended by skilled health staff (% of total)	..		100	
Maternal mortality ratio (per 100,000 live births)	..		11	
Labor force and employment dynamics				
Labor force participation (% of population ages 15+)	59	74	51	61
Women in the labor force (% of total labor force)	48		50	
Employment to population ratio (% ages 15+)	49	62	49	58
Vulnerable employment (% of employed ages 15+)	..	..	..	..
Employment in agriculture (% of employed ages 15+)	13	26	11	17
Employment in industry (% of employed ages 15+)	32	52	21	37
Employment in service (% of employed ages 15+)	54	22	68	46
Wage and salaried workers (% of employed ages 15+)	..	..	89	84
Self-employed workers (% of employed ages 15+)	..	..	9	15
Unpaid family workers (% of employed ages 15+)	..	..	2	1
Women in nonagricultural wage employment (%)	55		54	
Children in employment (% of children ages 7–14)	..	..	..	..
Unemployment (% of labor force ages 15+)	..	..	4	4
Long-term unemployment (% of total unemployment)	..	..	..	..
Youth unemployment (% of labor force ages 15–24)	..	..	15	16
Maternity leave (weeks)	..		18	
Maternal leave benefits (% of wages paid)	..		100	
Women's political participation				
Seats held by women in national parliament (%)	..		25	
Women in managerial positions (%)	..		39	

Luxembourg

High income

Population (thousands)	480	Population living on less	
GNI ($ billions)	34.2	than $1.25 a day (%)	..
GNI per capita ($)	72,430		

	1990		2007	
	Female	Male	Female	Male
Demography				
Sex ratio at birth (females per 1,000 males)	941		941	
Life expectancy at birth (years)	79	72	82	76
Child mortality rate (per 1,000)	..	..	..	..
Female-headed households (%)	..		..	
Education				
Gross primary enrollment (% of relevant age group)	94	87	102	101
Gross secondary enrollment (% of relevant age group)	..	..	98	94
Gross tertiary enrollment (% of relevant age group)	..	..	11	10
Primary completion rate (% of relevant age group)	..	..	88	84
Adult literacy rate (% of population ages 15+)	..	..	..	..
Family planning and maternal health				
Total fertility rate (births per woman)	1.6		1.6	
Adolescent fertility (births per 1,000 women ages 15–19)	..		10	
Women married by age 18 (% of women ages 20–24)	..		..	
Contraceptive prevalence (% of women ages 15–49)	..		..	
Unmet need for contraception (% of women ages 15–49)	..		..	
Pregnant women receiving prenatal care (%)	..		..	
Births attended by skilled health staff (% of total)	..		100	
Maternal mortality ratio (per 100,000 live births)	..		12	
Labor force and employment dynamics				
Labor force participation (% of population ages 15+)	34	68	48	64
Women in the labor force (% of total labor force)	35		43	
Employment to population ratio (% ages 15+)	35	68	46	62
Vulnerable employment (% of employed ages 15+)	..	..	..	..
Employment in agriculture (% of employed ages 15+)	3	3	..	..
Employment in industry (% of employed ages 15+)	8	42	..	..
Employment in service (% of employed ages 15+)	89	55	..	..
Wage and salaried workers (% of employed ages 15+)	..	..	..	..
Self-employed workers (% of employed ages 15+)	..	..	..	..
Unpaid family workers (% of employed ages 15+)	..	..	..	..
Women in nonagricultural wage employment (%)	..		42	
Children in employment (% of children ages 7–14)	..	..	..	..
Unemployment (% of labor force ages 15+)	2	1	4	4
Long-term unemployment (% of total unemployment)	33	60	25	39
Youth unemployment (% of labor force ages 15–24)	5	3	16	12
Maternity leave (weeks)	14		16	
Maternal leave benefits (% of wages paid)	100		100	
Women's political participation				
Seats held by women in national parliament (%)	13		23	
Women in managerial positions (%)	..		..	

Macao, China

Population (thousands)	480	Population living on less
GNI ($ billions)	..	than $1.25 a day (%) ..
GNI per capita ($)	..	

	1990		2007	
	Female	Male	Female	Male
Demography				
Sex ratio at birth (females per 1,000 males)	952		952	
Life expectancy at birth (years)	79	75	83	79
Child mortality rate (per 1,000)	..	..	..	..
Female-headed households (%)	..		..	
Education				
Gross primary enrollment (% of relevant age group)	98	104	103	112
Gross secondary enrollment (% of relevant age group)	64	58	99	99
Gross tertiary enrollment (% of relevant age group)	..	..	55	59
Primary completion rate (% of relevant age group)	97	97	100	105
Adult literacy rate (% of population ages 15+)	..	..	*91*	*96*
Family planning and maternal health				
Total fertility rate (births per woman)	1.8		0.9	
Adolescent fertility (births per 1,000 women ages 15–19)	..		5	
Women married by age 18 (% of women ages 20–24)	..		..	
Contraceptive prevalence (% of women ages 15–49)	..		..	
Unmet need for contraception (% of women ages 15–49)	..		..	
Pregnant women receiving prenatal care (%)	..		..	
Births attended by skilled health staff (% of total)	..		*100*	
Maternal mortality ratio (per 100,000 live births)	..		..	
Labor force and employment dynamics				
Labor force participation (% of population ages 15+)	45	73	59	73
Women in the labor force (% of total labor force)	41		47	
Employment to population ratio (% ages 15+)	*44*	*71*	*58*	*71*
Vulnerable employment (% of employed ages 15+)	..	..	4	6
Employment in agriculture (% of employed ages 15+)	0	0	*0*	*0*
Employment in industry (% of employed ages 15+)	50	37	*23*	*27*
Employment in service (% of employed ages 15+)	49	63	77	73
Wage and salaried workers (% of employed ages 15+)	..	..	95	89
Self-employed workers (% of employed ages 15+)	..	..	4	11
Unpaid family workers (% of employed ages 15+)	..	..	1	0
Women in nonagricultural wage employment (%)	43		48	
Children in employment (% of children ages 7–14)	..	..	..	..
Unemployment (% of labor force ages 15+)	4	3	3	3
Long-term unemployment (% of total unemployment)	..	..	..	..
Youth unemployment (% of labor force ages 15–24)	*3*	*4*	6	*11*
Maternity leave (weeks)	..		..	
Maternal leave benefits (% of wages paid)	..		..	
Women's political participation				
Seats held by women in national parliament (%)	..		..	
Women in managerial positions (%)	..		*22*	

Macedonia, FYR

| Europe & Central Asia | | | Lower middle income | |

Population (millions)	2.0	Population living on less	
GNI ($ billions)	7.1	than $1.25 a day (%)	2.0
GNI per capita ($)	3,470		

	1990		2007	
	Female	Male	Female	Male
Demography				
Sex ratio at birth (females per 1,000 males)	926		926	
Life expectancy at birth (years)	74	69	77	72
Child mortality rate (per 1,000)	..	..	1	2
Female-headed households (%)		..	8	
Education				
Gross primary enrollment (% of relevant age group)	..	..	98	98
Gross secondary enrollment (% of relevant age group)	..	..	83	85
Gross tertiary enrollment (% of relevant age group)	..	..	35	25
Primary completion rate (% of relevant age group)	..	..	98	96
Adult literacy rate (% of population ages 15+)	..	..	95	99
Family planning and maternal health				
Total fertility rate (births per woman)	2.0		1.4	
Adolescent fertility (births per 1,000 women ages 15–19)	..		21	
Women married by age 18 (% of women ages 20–24)	..		..	
Contraceptive prevalence (% of women ages 15–49)	..		14	
Unmet need for contraception (% of women ages 15–49)	..		34	
Pregnant women receiving prenatal care (%)	..		98	
Births attended by skilled health staff (% of total)	..		98	
Maternal mortality ratio (per 100,000 live births)	..		10	
Labor force and employment dynamics				
Labor force participation (% of population ages 15+)	54	73	42	66
Women in the labor force (% of total labor force)	43		39	
Employment to population ratio (% ages 15+)	30	46	27	43
Vulnerable employment (% of employed ages 15+)	..	..	20	24
Employment in agriculture (% of employed ages 15+)	..	..	19	20
Employment in industry (% of employed ages 15+)	..	..	30	34
Employment in service (% of employed ages 15+)	..	..	51	46
Wage and salaried workers (% of employed ages 15+)	..	..	77	69
Self-employed workers (% of employed ages 15+)	..	..	8	24
Unpaid family workers (% of employed ages 15+)	..	..	15	7
Women in nonagricultural wage employment (%)	38		40	
Children in employment (% of children ages 7–14)	..	..	9	15
Unemployment (% of labor force ages 15+)	..	..	36	35
Long-term unemployment (% of total unemployment)	..	..	..	..
Youth unemployment (% of labor force ages 15–24)	..	..	62	63
Maternity leave (weeks)	..		..	
Maternal leave benefits (% of wages paid)	..		..	
Women's political participation				
Seats held by women in national parliament (%)	..		28	
Women in managerial positions (%)	..		27	

Madagascar

Sub-Saharan Africa   **Low income**

Population (millions)	20	Population living on less	
GNI ($ billions)	6.4	than $1.25 a day (%)	67.8
GNI per capita ($)	320		

	1990		2007	
	Female	Male	Female	Male
Demography				
Sex ratio at birth (females per 1,000 males)	984		976	
Life expectancy at birth (years)	52	50	61	58
Child mortality rate (per 1,000)	82	85	45	45
Female-headed households (%)	22		22	
Education				
Gross primary enrollment (% of relevant age group)	90	94	139	144
Gross secondary enrollment (% of relevant age group)	18	19	26	27
Gross tertiary enrollment (% of relevant age group)	..	..	3	3
Primary completion rate (% of relevant age group)	36	34	61	62
Adult literacy rate (% of population ages 15+)	..	..	..	..
Family planning and maternal health				
Total fertility rate (births per woman)	6.2		4.8	
Adolescent fertility (births per 1,000 women ages 15–19)	..		133	
Women married by age 18 (% of women ages 20–24)	37		39	
Contraceptive prevalence (% of women ages 15–49)	17		27	
Unmet need for contraception (% of women ages 15–49)	32		24	
Pregnant women receiving prenatal care (%)	78		80	
Births attended by skilled health staff (% of total)	57		51	
Maternal mortality ratio (per 100,000 live births)	..		510	
Labor force and employment dynamics				
Labor force participation (% of population ages 15+)	80	85	82	88
Women in the labor force (% of total labor force)	49		49	
Employment to population ratio (% ages 15+)	75	83	79	87
Vulnerable employment (% of employed ages 15+)	87	83	89	84
Employment in agriculture (% of employed ages 15+)	..	..	79	77
Employment in industry (% of employed ages 15+)	..	..	6	7
Employment in service (% of employed ages 15+)	..	..	15	16
Wage and salaried workers (% of employed ages 15+)	11	15	11	16
Self-employed workers (% of employed ages 15+)	46	59	35	52
Unpaid family workers (% of employed ages 15+)	42	24	73	32
Women in nonagricultural wage employment (%)	..		38	
Children in employment (% of children ages 7–14)	..	..	..	..
Unemployment (% of labor force ages 15+)	..	..	3	2
Long-term unemployment (% of total unemployment)	..	..	..	..
Youth unemployment (% of labor force ages 15–24)	..	..	7	7
Maternity leave (weeks)	14		14	
Maternal leave benefits (% of wages paid)	50		100	
Women's political participation				
Seats held by women in national parliament (%)	7		8	
Women in managerial positions (%)	..		..	

Malawi

Sub-Saharan Africa		Low income

Population (millions)	14	Population living on less		
GNI ($ billions)	3.5	than $1.25 a day (%)		73.9
GNI per capita ($)	250			

	1990		2007	
	Female	Male	Female	Male
Demography				
Sex ratio at birth (females per 1,000 males)	971		971	
Life expectancy at birth (years)	50	47	48	48
Child mortality rate (per 1,000)	114	126	54	52
Female-headed households (%)	25		25	
Education				
Gross primary enrollment (% of relevant age group)	58	71	119	114
Gross secondary enrollment (% of relevant age group)	4	9	26	31
Gross tertiary enrollment (% of relevant age group)	..	..	0	1
Primary completion rate (% of relevant age group)	19	35	56	55
Adult literacy rate (% of population ages 15+)	34	65	65	79
Family planning and maternal health				
Total fertility rate (births per woman)	6.9		5.6	
Adolescent fertility (births per 1,000 women ages 15–19)	..		135	
Women married by age 18 (% of women ages 20–24)	55		..	
Contraceptive prevalence (% of women ages 15–49)	13		42	
Unmet need for contraception (% of women ages 15–49)	36		28	
Pregnant women receiving prenatal care (%)	90		92	
Births attended by skilled health staff (% of total)	55		54	
Maternal mortality ratio (per 100,000 live births)	..		1,100	
Labor force and employment dynamics				
Labor force participation (% of population ages 15+)	76	80	76	80
Women in the labor force (% of total labor force)	51		50	
Employment to population ratio (% ages 15+)	69	75	69	75
Vulnerable employment (% of employed ages 15+)	..	..	..	..
Employment in agriculture (% of employed ages 15+)	..	..	..	..
Employment in industry (% of employed ages 15+)	..	..	..	..
Employment in service (% of employed ages 15+)	..	..	..	..
Wage and salaried workers (% of employed ages 15+)	4	29	..	..
Self-employed workers (% of employed ages 15+)	96	71	..	..
Unpaid family workers (% of employed ages 15+)	..	..	..	..
Women in nonagricultural wage employment (%)	11		..	
Children in employment (% of children ages 7–14)	..	..	39	41
Unemployment (% of labor force ages 15+)	..	..	10	5
Long-term unemployment (% of total unemployment)	..	..	..	..
Youth unemployment (% of labor force ages 15–24)	0	2	..	..
Maternity leave (weeks)	..		8	
Maternal leave benefits (% of wages paid)	..		100	
Women's political participation				
Seats held by women in national parliament (%)	10		14	
Women in managerial positions (%)	..		..	

Malaysia

East Asia & Pacific				Upper middle income	

Population (millions)	27	Population living on less			
GNI ($ billions)	170.5	than $1.25 a day (%)			2.0
GNI per capita ($)	6,420				

	1990		2007	
	Female	**Male**	**Female**	**Male**
Demography				
Sex ratio at birth (females per 1,000 males)	943		943	
Life expectancy at birth (years)	72	68	77	72
Child mortality rate (per 1,000)	..	..	..	..
Female-headed households (%)	..		..	
Education				
Gross primary enrollment (% of relevant age group)	92	93	100	101
Gross secondary enrollment (% of relevant age group)	58	54	72	66
Gross tertiary enrollment (% of relevant age group)	..	..	32	25
Primary completion rate (% of relevant age group)	90	90	98	98
Adult literacy rate (% of population ages 15+)	77	89	90	94
Family planning and maternal health				
Total fertility rate (births per woman)	3.7		2.6	
Adolescent fertility (births per 1,000 women ages 15–19)	..		13	
Women married by age 18 (% of women ages 20–24)	..		..	
Contraceptive prevalence (% of women ages 15–49)	50		..	
Unmet need for contraception (% of women ages 15–49)	..		..	
Pregnant women receiving prenatal care (%)	..		79	
Births attended by skilled health staff (% of total)	..		98	
Maternal mortality ratio (per 100,000 live births)	..		62	
Labor force and employment dynamics				
Labor force participation (% of population ages 15+)	43	81	45	80
Women in the labor force (% of total labor force)	34		35	
Employment to population ratio (% ages 15+)	41	78	43	78
Vulnerable employment (% of employed ages 15+)	25	31	21	23
Employment in agriculture (% of employed ages 15+)	25	26	11	16
Employment in industry (% of employed ages 15+)	28	27	27	35
Employment in service (% of employed ages 15+)	47	46	62	49
Wage and salaried workers (% of employed ages 15+)	71	64	77	73
Self-employed workers (% of employed ages 15+)	19	32	14	25
Unpaid family workers (% of employed ages 15+)	8	2	9	3
Women in nonagricultural wage employment (%)	38		38	
Children in employment (% of children ages 7–14)	..	..	..	..
Unemployment (% of labor force ages 15+)	..	..	3	3
Long-term unemployment (% of total unemployment)	..	..	..	..
Youth unemployment (% of labor force ages 15–24)	..	..	..	..
Maternity leave (weeks)	8		9	
Maternal leave benefits (% of wages paid)	100		100	
Women's political participation				
Seats held by women in national parliament (%)	5		9	
Women in managerial positions (%)	..		23	

Maldives

South Asia	Lower middle income

Population (thousands)	305	Population living on less
GNI ($ billions)	1.0	than $1.25 a day (%)
GNI per capita ($)	3,190	..

	1990		2007	
	Female	Male	Female	Male
Demography				
Sex ratio at birth (females per 1,000 males)	966		966	
Life expectancy at birth (years)	59	62	69	68
Child mortality rate (per 1,000)	..	..	..	..
Female-headed households (%)	..		..	
Education				
Gross primary enrollment (% of relevant age group)	132	136	109	112
Gross secondary enrollment (% of relevant age group)	44	44	86	80
Gross tertiary enrollment (% of relevant age group)	..	..	0	0
Primary completion rate (% of relevant age group)	..	..	111	117
Adult literacy rate (% of population ages 15+)	96	96	97	97
Family planning and maternal health				
Total fertility rate (births per woman)	6.0		2.6	
Adolescent fertility (births per 1,000 women ages 15–19)	..		23	
Women married by age 18 (% of women ages 20–24)	..		..	
Contraceptive prevalence (% of women ages 15–49)	..		39	
Unmet need for contraception (% of women ages 15–49)	..		..	
Pregnant women receiving prenatal care (%)	..		..	
Births attended by skilled health staff (% of total)	..		84	
Maternal mortality ratio (per 100,000 live births)	..		120	
Labor force and employment dynamics				
Labor force participation (% of population ages 15+)	20	78	54	76
Women in the labor force (% of total labor force)	20		40	
Employment to population ratio (% ages 15+)	21	76	42	71
Vulnerable employment (% of employed ages 15+)	56	44	..	..
Employment in agriculture (% of employed ages 15+)	..	..	9	22
Employment in industry (% of employed ages 15+)	..	..	34	18
Employment in service (% of employed ages 15+)	..	..	56	57
Wage and salaried workers (% of employed ages 15+)	37	49	..	..
Self-employed workers (% of employed ages 15+)	51	43	..	..
Unpaid family workers (% of employed ages 15+)	7	4	..	..
Women in nonagricultural wage employment (%)	..		39	
Children in employment (% of children ages 7–14)	..	..	..	..
Unemployment (% of labor force ages 15+)	..	..	24	8
Long-term unemployment (% of total unemployment)	..	..	..	..
Youth unemployment (% of labor force ages 15–24)	..	..	..	..
Maternity leave (weeks)	..		..	
Maternal leave benefits (% of wages paid)	..		..	
Women's political participation				
Seats held by women in national parliament (%)	6		12	
Women in managerial positions (%)	..		..	

Mali

Sub-Saharan Africa				**Low income**

Population (millions)	12	Population living on less	
GNI ($ billions)	6.1	than $1.25 a day (%)	51.4
GNI per capita ($)	500		

	1990		2007	
	Female	**Male**	**Female**	**Male**
Demography				
Sex ratio at birth (females per 1,000 males)	972		972	
Life expectancy at birth (years)	50	46	57	52
Child mortality rate (per 1,000)	*174*	*166*	*114*	*117*
Female-headed households (%)	..		*12*	
Education				
Gross primary enrollment (% of relevant age group)	22	38	74	92
Gross secondary enrollment (% of relevant age group)	5	10	27	37
Gross tertiary enrollment (% of relevant age group)	..	..	2	4
Primary completion rate (% of relevant age group)	9	16	*40*	*59*
Adult literacy rate (% of population ages 15+)	..	..	*18*	*35*
Family planning and maternal health				
Total fertility rate (births per woman)	7.4		6.5	
Adolescent fertility (births per 1,000 women ages 15–19)	..		179	
Women married by age 18 (% of women ages 20–24)	78		..	
Contraceptive prevalence (% of women ages 15–49)	5		8	
Unmet need for contraception (% of women ages 15–49)	..		31	
Pregnant women receiving prenatal care (%)	31		70	
Births attended by skilled health staff (% of total)	..		45	
Maternal mortality ratio (per 100,000 live births)	..		970	
Labor force and employment dynamics				
Labor force participation (% of population ages 15+)	34	69	37	65
Women in the labor force (% of total labor force)	35		38	
Employment to population ratio (% ages 15+)	*32*	*64*	*34*	*58*
Vulnerable employment (% of employed ages 15+)	..	..	..	..
Employment in agriculture (% of employed ages 15+)	..	..	30	50
Employment in industry (% of employed ages 15+)	..	..	15	18
Employment in service (% of employed ages 15+)	..	..	55	32
Wage and salaried workers (% of employed ages 15+)	..	..	11	15
Self-employed workers (% of employed ages 15+)	..	..	78	66
Unpaid family workers (% of employed ages 15+)	..	..	10	18
Women in nonagricultural wage employment (%)	..		35	
Children in employment (% of children ages 7–14)	..	..	44	55
Unemployment (% of labor force ages 15+)	..	..	*11*	*7*
Long-term unemployment (% of total unemployment)	..	..	..	..
Youth unemployment (% of labor force ages 15–24)	..	..	..	..
Maternity leave (weeks)	14		*14*	
Maternal leave benefits (% of wages paid)	100		*100*	
Women's political participation				
Seats held by women in national parliament (%)	..		10	
Women in managerial positions (%)	..		..	

Malta

Population (thousands)	409	Population living on less
GNI ($ billions)	6.8	than $1.25 a day (%)
GNI per capita ($)	16,680	..

	1990		2007	
	Female	Male	Female	Male
Demography				
Sex ratio at birth (females per 1,000 males)	943		943	
Life expectancy at birth (years)	78	73	82	77
Child mortality rate (per 1,000)	..	..	..	..
Female-headed households (%)		..		..
Education				
Gross primary enrollment (% of relevant age group)	106	110	99	101
Gross secondary enrollment (% of relevant age group)	80	85	100	99
Gross tertiary enrollment (% of relevant age group)	..	..	36	27
Primary completion rate (% of relevant age group)	101	103	98	98
Adult literacy rate (% of population ages 15+)	..	..	94	91
Family planning and maternal health				
Total fertility rate (births per woman)	2.1		1.3	
Adolescent fertility (births per 1,000 women ages 15–19)	..		12	
Women married by age 18 (% of women ages 20–24)	..		..	
Contraceptive prevalence (% of women ages 15–49)	..		..	
Unmet need for contraception (% of women ages 15–49)	..		..	
Pregnant women receiving prenatal care (%)	..		..	
Births attended by skilled health staff (% of total)	98		100	
Maternal mortality ratio (per 100,000 live births)	..		8	
Labor force and employment dynamics				
Labor force participation (% of population ages 15+)	22	74	33	68
Women in the labor force (% of total labor force)	24		33	
Employment to population ratio (% ages 15+)	20	69	30	64
Vulnerable employment (% of employed ages 15+)	..	..	6	11
Employment in agriculture (% of employed ages 15+)	1	3	1	3
Employment in industry (% of employed ages 15+)	34	35	17	35
Employment in service (% of employed ages 15+)	64	62	82	61
Wage and salaried workers (% of employed ages 15+)	..	..	93	83
Self-employed workers (% of employed ages 15+)	..	..	7	17
Unpaid family workers (% of employed ages 15+)	..	..	0	0
Women in nonagricultural wage employment (%)	..		34	
Children in employment (% of children ages 7–14)	..	..	..	..
Unemployment (% of labor force ages 15+)	..	..	7	5
Long-term unemployment (% of total unemployment)	..	..	..	..
Youth unemployment (% of labor force ages 15–24)	..	..	17	16
Maternity leave (weeks)	13		14	
Maternal leave benefits (% of wages paid)	100		100	
Women's political participation				
Seats held by women in national parliament (%)	3		9	
Women in managerial positions (%)	..		18	

Marshall Islands

              Lower middle income

Population (thousands)	58	Population living on less	
GNI ($ millions)	189.0	than $1.25 a day (%)	..
GNI per capita ($)	3,240		

	1990		2007	
	Female	**Male**	**Female**	**Male**
Demography				
Sex ratio at birth (females per 1,000 males)	..		..	
Life expectancy at birth (years)	73	69	..	..
Child mortality rate (per 1,000)	..	..	..	..
Female-headed households (%)	..		..	
Education				
Gross primary enrollment (% of relevant age group)	..	..	101	105
Gross secondary enrollment (% of relevant age group)	..	..	78	75
Gross tertiary enrollment (% of relevant age group)	..	..	19	15
Primary completion rate (% of relevant age group)	..	..	128	123
Adult literacy rate (% of population ages 15+)	..	..	..	..
Family planning and maternal health				
Total fertility rate (births per woman)	5.9		..	
Adolescent fertility (births per 1,000 women ages 15–19)	..		..	
Women married by age 18 (% of women ages 20–24)	..		..	
Contraceptive prevalence (% of women ages 15–49)	..		..	
Unmet need for contraception (% of women ages 15–49)	..		..	
Pregnant women receiving prenatal care (%)	..		..	
Births attended by skilled health staff (% of total)	..		..	
Maternal mortality ratio (per 100,000 live births)	..		..	
Labor force and employment dynamics				
Labor force participation (% of population ages 15+)	..	..	..	..
Women in the labor force (% of total labor force)	..		..	
Employment to population ratio (% ages 15+)	..	..	..	..
Vulnerable employment (% of employed ages 15+)	..	..	..	..
Employment in agriculture (% of employed ages 15+)	..	..	..	..
Employment in industry (% of employed ages 15+)	..	..	..	..
Employment in service (% of employed ages 15+)	..	..	..	..
Wage and salaried workers (% of employed ages 15+)	..	..	..	..
Self-employed workers (% of employed ages 15+)	..	..	..	..
Unpaid family workers (% of employed ages 15+)	..	..	..	..
Women in nonagricultural wage employment (%)	..		33	
Children in employment (% of children ages 7–14)	..	..	..	..
Unemployment (% of labor force ages 15+)	13	12	..	..
Long-term unemployment (% of total unemployment)	..	..	..	..
Youth unemployment (% of labor force ages 15–24)	..	..	..	..
Maternity leave (weeks)	..		..	
Maternal leave benefits (% of wages paid)	..		..	
Women's political participation				
Seats held by women in national parliament (%)	..		3	
Women in managerial positions (%)	..		..	

Mauritania

Sub-Saharan Africa		Low income

Population (millions)	3.1	Population living on less	
GNI ($ billions)	2.6	than $1.25 a day (%)	21.2
GNI per capita ($)	840		

	1990		2007	
	Female	Male	Female	Male
Demography				
Sex ratio at birth (females per 1,000 males)	928		928	
Life expectancy at birth (years)	60	56	66	62
Child mortality rate (per 1,000)	..	..	48	50
Female-headed households (%)	..		..	
Education				
Gross primary enrollment (% of relevant age group)	42	56	106	100
Gross secondary enrollment (% of relevant age group)	9	19	23	27
Gross tertiary enrollment (% of relevant age group)	..	..	2	5
Primary completion rate (% of relevant age group)	23	37	60	59
Adult literacy rate (% of population ages 15+)	..	..	48	63
Family planning and maternal health				
Total fertility rate (births per woman)	5.8		4.4	
Adolescent fertility (births per 1,000 women ages 15–19)	..		85	
Women married by age 18 (% of women ages 20–24)	..		..	
Contraceptive prevalence (% of women ages 15–49)	3		..	
Unmet need for contraception (% of women ages 15–49)	..		..	
Pregnant women receiving prenatal care (%)	48		..	
Births attended by skilled health staff (% of total)	40		..	
Maternal mortality ratio (per 100,000 live births)	..		820	
Labor force and employment dynamics				
Labor force participation (% of population ages 15+)	58	84	60	80
Women in the labor force (% of total labor force)	42		43	
Employment to population ratio (% ages 15+)	49	60	45	49
Vulnerable employment (% of employed ages 15+)	..	..	..	..
Employment in agriculture (% of employed ages 15+)	..	..	..	..
Employment in industry (% of employed ages 15+)	..	..	..	..
Employment in service (% of employed ages 15+)	..	..	..	..
Wage and salaried workers (% of employed ages 15+)	..	..	..	..
Self-employed workers (% of employed ages 15+)	..	..	..	..
Unpaid family workers (% of employed ages 15+)	..	..	..	..
Women in nonagricultural wage employment (%)	..		..	
Children in employment (% of children ages 7–14)	..	..	..	..
Unemployment (% of labor force ages 15+)	36	22	..	25
Long-term unemployment (% of total unemployment)	..	..	..	..
Youth unemployment (% of labor force ages 15–24)	..	..	..	..
Maternity leave (weeks)	14		14	
Maternal leave benefits (% of wages paid)	100		100	
Women's political participation				
Seats held by women in national parliament (%)	..		18	
Women in managerial positions (%)	..		..	

Mauritius

Sub-Saharan Africa		Upper middle income	

Population (millions)	1.3	Population living on less
GNI ($ billions)	7.0	than $1.25 a day (%) ..
GNI per capita ($)	5,580	

	1990		2007	
	Female	Male	Female	Male
Demography				
Sex ratio at birth (females per 1,000 males)	960		960	
Life expectancy at birth (years)	73	66	76	69
Child mortality rate (per 1,000)	..	..	..	..
Female-headed households (%)	..		..	
Education				
Gross primary enrollment (% of relevant age group)	109	109	101	101
Gross secondary enrollment (% of relevant age group)	53	53	90	86
Gross tertiary enrollment (% of relevant age group)	..	..	18	16
Primary completion rate (% of relevant age group)	105	106	95	92
Adult literacy rate (% of population ages 15+)	75	85	85	90
Family planning and maternal health				
Total fertility rate (births per woman)	2.3		1.7	
Adolescent fertility (births per 1,000 women ages 15–19)	..		41	
Women married by age 18 (% of women ages 20–24)	..		..	
Contraceptive prevalence (% of women ages 15–49)	75		..	
Unmet need for contraception (% of women ages 15–49)	..		..	
Pregnant women receiving prenatal care (%)	..		..	
Births attended by skilled health staff (% of total)	91		99	
Maternal mortality ratio (per 100,000 live births)	..		15	
Labor force and employment dynamics				
Labor force participation (% of population ages 15+)	40	82	42	77
Women in the labor force (% of total labor force)	33		36	
Employment to population ratio (% ages 15+)	35	78	36	73
Vulnerable employment (% of employed ages 15+)	7	13	15	18
Employment in agriculture (% of employed ages 15+)	14	16	9	11
Employment in industry (% of employed ages 15+)	50	35	29	34
Employment in service (% of employed ages 15+)	35	53	62	55
Wage and salaried workers (% of employed ages 15+)	91	82	83	77
Self-employed workers (% of employed ages 15+)	6	16	12	21
Unpaid family workers (% of employed ages 15+)	3	2	5	1
Women in nonagricultural wage employment (%)	37		38	
Children in employment (% of children ages 7–14)	..	..	..	..
Unemployment (% of labor force ages 15+)	..	..	14	5
Long-term unemployment (% of total unemployment)	..	..	..	..
Youth unemployment (% of labor force ages 15–24)	..	..	34	21
Maternity leave (weeks)	..		12	
Maternal leave benefits (% of wages paid)	..		100	
Women's political participation				
Seats held by women in national parliament (%)	7		17	
Women in managerial positions (%)	..		..	

Mayotte

Sub-Saharan Africa		Upper middle income

Population (thousands)	186	Population living on less	
GNI ($ billions)	..	than $1.25 a day (%)	
GNI per capita ($)	..		..

	1990		2007	
	Female	Male	Female	Male
Demography				
Sex ratio at birth (females per 1,000 males)	..		..	
Life expectancy at birth (years)	..	..	..	..
Child mortality rate (per 1,000)	..	..	..	..
Female-headed households (%)	..		..	
Education				
Gross primary enrollment (% of relevant age group)	..	..	..	..
Gross secondary enrollment (% of relevant age group)	..	..	..	..
Gross tertiary enrollment (% of relevant age group)	..	..	..	..
Primary completion rate (% of relevant age group)	..	..	..	..
Adult literacy rate (% of population ages 15+)	..	..	..	..
Family planning and maternal health				
Total fertility rate (births per woman)	..		..	
Adolescent fertility (births per 1,000 women ages 15–19)	..		..	
Women married by age 18 (% of women ages 20–24)	..		..	
Contraceptive prevalence (% of women ages 15–49)	..		..	
Unmet need for contraception (% of women ages 15–49)	..		..	
Pregnant women receiving prenatal care (%)	..		..	
Births attended by skilled health staff (% of total)	..		..	
Maternal mortality ratio (per 100,000 live births)	..		..	
Labor force and employment dynamics				
Labor force participation (% of population ages 15+)	..	..	..	..
Women in the labor force (% of total labor force)	..		..	
Employment to population ratio (% ages 15+)	..	..	..	..
Vulnerable employment (% of employed ages 15+)	..	..	..	..
Employment in agriculture (% of employed ages 15+)	..	..	..	..
Employment in industry (% of employed ages 15+)	..	..	..	..
Employment in service (% of employed ages 15+)	..	..	..	..
Wage and salaried workers (% of employed ages 15+)	..	..	..	..
Self-employed workers (% of employed ages 15+)	..	..	..	..
Unpaid family workers (% of employed ages 15+)	..	..	..	..
Women in nonagricultural wage employment (%)	..		..	
Children in employment (% of children ages 7–14)	..	..	..	..
Unemployment (% of labor force ages 15+)	..	..	..	..
Long-term unemployment (% of total unemployment)	..	..	..	..
Youth unemployment (% of labor force ages 15–24)	..	..	..	..
Maternity leave (weeks)	..		..	
Maternal leave benefits (% of wages paid)	..		..	
Women's political participation				
Seats held by women in national parliament (%)	..		..	
Women in managerial positions (%)	..		..	

Mexico

Latin America & Caribbean		Upper middle income	

Population (millions)	105	Population living on less	
GNI ($ billions)	989.4	than $1.25 a day (%)	2.0
GNI per capita ($)	9,400		

	1990		2007	
	Female	Male	Female	Male
Demography				
Sex ratio at birth (females per 1,000 males)	952		952	
Life expectancy at birth (years)	74	68	77	73
Child mortality rate (per 1,000)	17	15	..	..
Female-headed households (%)	..		..	
Education				
Gross primary enrollment (% of relevant age group)	110	115	111	114
Gross secondary enrollment (% of relevant age group)	54	55	88	86
Gross tertiary enrollment (% of relevant age group)	..	..	25	27
Primary completion rate (% of relevant age group)	..	..	104	104
Adult literacy rate (% of population ages 15+)	85	90	91	94
Family planning and maternal health				
Total fertility rate (births per woman)	3.4		2.1	
Adolescent fertility (births per 1,000 women ages 15–19)	..		65	
Women married by age 18 (% of women ages 20–24)	28		..	
Contraceptive prevalence (% of women ages 15–49)	53		71	
Unmet need for contraception (% of women ages 15–49)	..		..	
Pregnant women receiving prenatal care (%)	78		..	
Births attended by skilled health staff (% of total)	69		93	
Maternal mortality ratio (per 100,000 live births)	..		60	
Labor force and employment dynamics				
Labor force participation (% of population ages 15+)	34	84	41	80
Women in the labor force (% of total labor force)	30		36	
Employment to population ratio (% ages 15+)	33	82	40	78
Vulnerable employment (% of employed ages 15+)	15	29	32	28
Employment in agriculture (% of employed ages 15+)	3	29	5	21
Employment in industry (% of employed ages 15+)	21	30	19	30
Employment in service (% of employed ages 15+)	67	31	76	49
Wage and salaried workers (% of employed ages 15+)	80	65	65	66
Self-employed workers (% of employed ages 15+)	15	29	25	29
Unpaid family workers (% of employed ages 15+)	1	3	10	5
Women in nonagricultural wage employment (%)	37		39	
Children in employment (% of children ages 7–14)	..	..	6	12
Unemployment (% of labor force ages 15+)	4	3	4	3
Long-term unemployment (% of total unemployment)	..	..	2	3
Youth unemployment (% of labor force ages 15–24)	6	5	7	6
Maternity leave (weeks)	12		12	
Maternal leave benefits (% of wages paid)	100		100	
Women's political participation				
Seats held by women in national parliament (%)	12		23	
Women in managerial positions (%)	..		..	

Micronesia, Fed. Sts.

East Asia & Pacific **Lower middle income**

Population (thousands)	111	Population living on less
GNI ($ millions)	253.5	than $1.25 a day (%)
GNI per capita ($)	2,280	..

	1990		2007	
	Female	Male	Female	Male
Demography				
Sex ratio at birth (females per 1,000 males)	935		935	
Life expectancy at birth (years)	67	66	69	68
Child mortality rate (per 1,000)	..	..	..	..
Female-headed households (%)	..		..	
Education				
Gross primary enrollment (% of relevant age group)	..	..	110	109
Gross secondary enrollment (% of relevant age group)	..	..	86	80
Gross tertiary enrollment (% of relevant age group)	..	..	..	..
Primary completion rate (% of relevant age group)	..	..	..	..
Adult literacy rate (% of population ages 15+)	..	..	..	..
Family planning and maternal health				
Total fertility rate (births per woman)	5.0		3.7	
Adolescent fertility (births per 1,000 women ages 15–19)	..		26	
Women married by age 18 (% of women ages 20–24)	..		..	
Contraceptive prevalence (% of women ages 15–49)	..		..	
Unmet need for contraception (% of women ages 15–49)	..		..	
Pregnant women receiving prenatal care (%)	..		..	
Births attended by skilled health staff (% of total)	..		..	
Maternal mortality ratio (per 100,000 live births)	..		..	
Labor force and employment dynamics				
Labor force participation (% of population ages 15+)	..	..	..	..
Women in the labor force (% of total labor force)	..		..	
Employment to population ratio (% ages 15+)	..	..	..	..
Vulnerable employment (% of employed ages 15+)	..	..	..	..
Employment in agriculture (% of employed ages 15+)	..	..	..	..
Employment in industry (% of employed ages 15+)	..	..	..	..
Employment in service (% of employed ages 15+)	..	..	..	..
Wage and salaried workers (% of employed ages 15+)	..	..	..	..
Self-employed workers (% of employed ages 15+)	..	..	..	..
Unpaid family workers (% of employed ages 15+)	..	..	..	..
Women in nonagricultural wage employment (%)	..		..	
Children in employment (% of children ages 7–14)	..	..	..	..
Unemployment (% of labor force ages 15+)	..	..	..	..
Long-term unemployment (% of total unemployment)	..	..	..	..
Youth unemployment (% of labor force ages 15–24)	..	..	..	..
Maternity leave (weeks)	..		..	
Maternal leave benefits (% of wages paid)	..		..	
Women's political participation				
Seats held by women in national parliament (%)	..		0	
Women in managerial positions (%)	..		..	

Moldova

Population (millions)	3.8	Population living on less
GNI ($ billions)	4.1	than $1.25 a day (%) 8.1
GNI per capita ($)	1,210	

	1990		2007	
	Female	Male	Female	Male
Demography				
Sex ratio at birth (females per 1,000 males)	943		943	
Life expectancy at birth (years)	71	64	72	65
Child mortality rate (per 1,000)	..	..	4	7
Female-headed households (%)	..		34	
Education				
Gross primary enrollment (% of relevant age group)	87	87	94	95
Gross secondary enrollment (% of relevant age group)	85	78	90	87
Gross tertiary enrollment (% of relevant age group)	..	..	48	35
Primary completion rate (% of relevant age group)	..	..	93	93
Adult literacy rate (% of population ages 15+)	94	99	99	100
Family planning and maternal health				
Total fertility rate (births per woman)	2.3		1.7	
Adolescent fertility (births per 1,000 women ages 15–19)	..		32	
Women married by age 18 (% of women ages 20–24)	..		..	
Contraceptive prevalence (% of women ages 15–49)	..		68	
Unmet need for contraception (% of women ages 15–49)	..		7	
Pregnant women receiving prenatal care (%)	..		98	
Births attended by skilled health staff (% of total)	..		100	
Maternal mortality ratio (per 100,000 live births)	..		22	
Labor force and employment dynamics				
Labor force participation (% of population ages 15+)	61	74	45	48
Women in the labor force (% of total labor force)	49		51	
Employment to population ratio (% ages 15+)	54	63	44	45
Vulnerable employment (% of employed ages 15+)	..	..	30	35
Employment in agriculture (% of employed ages 15+)	..	..	40	41
Employment in industry (% of employed ages 15+)	..	..	12	21
Employment in service (% of employed ages 15+)	..	..	48	38
Wage and salaried workers (% of employed ages 15+)	..	..	70	64
Self-employed workers (% of employed ages 15+)	..	..	27	35
Unpaid family workers (% of employed ages 15+)	..	..	3	1
Women in nonagricultural wage employment (%)	..		54	
Children in employment (% of children ages 7–14)	..	..	..	..
Unemployment (% of labor force ages 15+)	..	..	4	6
Long-term unemployment (% of total unemployment)	..	..	..	..
Youth unemployment (% of labor force ages 15–24)	..	..	18	19
Maternity leave (weeks)	..		18	
Maternal leave benefits (% of wages paid)	..		100	
Women's political participation				
Seats held by women in national parliament (%)	..		22	
Women in managerial positions (%)	..		40	

Monaco

Population (thousands)	33	Population living on less	
GNI ($ billions)	..	than $1.25 a day (%)	..
GNI per capita ($)	..		

	1990		2007	
	Female	**Male**	**Female**	**Male**
Demography				
Sex ratio at birth (females per 1,000 males)	..		..	
Life expectancy at birth (years)	..	..	..	..
Child mortality rate (per 1,000)	..	..	..	..
Female-headed households (%)	..		..	
Education				
Gross primary enrollment (% of relevant age group)	..	..	..	..
Gross secondary enrollment (% of relevant age group)	..	..	..	..
Gross tertiary enrollment (% of relevant age group)	..	..	..	..
Primary completion rate (% of relevant age group)	..	..	..	..
Adult literacy rate (% of population ages 15+)	..	..	..	..
Family planning and maternal health				
Total fertility rate (births per woman)	..		..	
Adolescent fertility (births per 1,000 women ages 15–19)	..		..	
Women married by age 18 (% of women ages 20–24)	..		..	
Contraceptive prevalence (% of women ages 15–49)	..		..	
Unmet need for contraception (% of women ages 15–49)	..		..	
Pregnant women receiving prenatal care (%)	..		..	
Births attended by skilled health staff (% of total)	..		..	
Maternal mortality ratio (per 100,000 live births)	..		..	
Labor force and employment dynamics				
Labor force participation (% of population ages 15+)	..	..	..	..
Women in the labor force (% of total labor force)	..		..	
Employment to population ratio (% ages 15+)	..	..	..	..
Vulnerable employment (% of employed ages 15+)	..	..	..	..
Employment in agriculture (% of employed ages 15+)	..	..	..	..
Employment in industry (% of employed ages 15+)	..	..	..	..
Employment in service (% of employed ages 15+)	..	..	..	..
Wage and salaried workers (% of employed ages 15+)	..	..	..	..
Self-employed workers (% of employed ages 15+)	..	..	..	..
Unpaid family workers (% of employed ages 15+)	..	..	..	..
Women in nonagricultural wage employment (%)	..		..	
Children in employment (% of children ages 7–14)	..	..	..	..
Unemployment (% of labor force ages 15+)	..	..	..	..
Long-term unemployment (% of total unemployment)	..	..	..	..
Youth unemployment (% of labor force ages 15–24)	..	..	..	..
Maternity leave (weeks)	..		..	
Maternal leave benefits (% of wages paid)	..		..	
Women's political participation				
Seats held by women in national parliament (%)	11		21	
Women in managerial positions (%)	..		..	

Mongolia

East Asia & Pacific **Lower middle income**

Population (millions)	2.6	Population living on less	
GNI ($ billions)	3.4	than $1.25 a day (%)	22.4
GNI per capita ($)	1,290		

	1990		2007	
	Female	Male	Female	Male
Demography				
Sex ratio at birth (females per 1,000 males)	952		952	
Life expectancy at birth (years)	63	59	70	64
Child mortality rate (per 1,000)	..	..	10	11
Female-headed households (%)	..		..	
Education				
Gross primary enrollment (% of relevant age group)	98	96	101	99
Gross secondary enrollment (% of relevant age group)	91	84	97	87
Gross tertiary enrollment (% of relevant age group)	..	..	58	37
Primary completion rate (% of relevant age group)	..	..	113	108
Adult literacy rate (% of population ages 15+)	..	..	98	97
Family planning and maternal health				
Total fertility rate (births per woman)	4.0		1.9	
Adolescent fertility (births per 1,000 women ages 15–19)	..		45	
Women married by age 18 (% of women ages 20–24)	..		..	
Contraceptive prevalence (% of women ages 15–49)	..		66	
Unmet need for contraception (% of women ages 15–49)	..		14	
Pregnant women receiving prenatal care (%)	..		99	
Births attended by skilled health staff (% of total)	..		99	
Maternal mortality ratio (per 100,000 live births)	..		46	
Labor force and employment dynamics				
Labor force participation (% of population ages 15+)	55	65	58	61
Women in the labor force (% of total labor force)	46		49	
Employment to population ratio (% ages 15+)	47	56	51	53
Vulnerable employment (% of employed ages 15+)	..	..	57	62
Employment in agriculture (% of employed ages 15+)	37	42	37	43
Employment in industry (% of employed ages 15+)	20	22	15	19
Employment in service (% of employed ages 15+)	44	37	48	38
Wage and salaried workers (% of employed ages 15+)	..	..	42	37
Self-employed workers (% of employed ages 15+)	..	..	26	44
Unpaid family workers (% of employed ages 15+)	..	..	32	18
Women in nonagricultural wage employment (%)	50		53	
Children in employment (% of children ages 7–14)	..	..	11	14
Unemployment (% of labor force ages 15+)	..	..	14	14
Long-term unemployment (% of total unemployment)	..	..	..	..
Youth unemployment (% of labor force ages 15–24)	..	..	21	20
Maternity leave (weeks)	14		17	
Maternal leave benefits (% of wages paid)	..		70	
Women's political participation				
Seats held by women in national parliament (%)	25		3	
Women in managerial positions (%)	..		..	

Montenegro

Population (thousands)	599	Population living on less
GNI ($ billions)	3.2	than $1.25 a day (%) ..
GNI per capita ($)	5,270	

	1990		2007	
	Female	Male	Female	Male
Demography				
Sex ratio at birth (females per 1,000 males)	926		926	
Life expectancy at birth (years)	78	73	77	72
Child mortality rate (per 1,000)	..	..	..	..
Female-headed households (%)		..		..
Education				
Gross primary enrollment (% of relevant age group)	..	..	..	..
Gross secondary enrollment (% of relevant age group)	..	..	..	..
Gross tertiary enrollment (% of relevant age group)	..	..	..	..
Primary completion rate (% of relevant age group)	..	..	..	..
Adult literacy rate (% of population ages 15+)	..	..	..	..
Family planning and maternal health				
Total fertility rate (births per woman)	2.0		1.7	
Adolescent fertility (births per 1,000 women ages 15–19)	..		16	
Women married by age 18 (% of women ages 20–24)	..		..	
Contraceptive prevalence (% of women ages 15–49)	..		39	
Unmet need for contraception (% of women ages 15–49)	..		..	
Pregnant women receiving prenatal care (%)	..		97	
Births attended by skilled health staff (% of total)	..		99	
Maternal mortality ratio (per 100,000 live births)	..		..	
Labor force and employment dynamics				
Labor force participation (% of population ages 15+)	..	..	..	..
Women in the labor force (% of total labor force)	..		..	
Employment to population ratio (% ages 15+)	..	..	..	..
Vulnerable employment (% of employed ages 15+)	..	..	..	..
Employment in agriculture (% of employed ages 15+)	..	..	..	..
Employment in industry (% of employed ages 15+)	..	..	..	..
Employment in service (% of employed ages 15+)	..	..	..	..
Wage and salaried workers (% of employed ages 15+)	..	..	85	77
Self-employed workers (% of employed ages 15+)	..	..	12	21
Unpaid family workers (% of employed ages 15+)	..	..	3	2
Women in nonagricultural wage employment (%)	..		41	
Children in employment (% of children ages 7–14)	..	..	..	..
Unemployment (% of labor force ages 15+)	..	..	36	26
Long-term unemployment (% of total unemployment)	..	..	..	..
Youth unemployment (% of labor force ages 15–24)	..	..	..	..
Maternity leave (weeks)	..		..	
Maternal leave benefits (% of wages paid)	..		..	
Women's political participation				
Seats held by women in national parliament (%)	..		9	
Women in managerial positions (%)	..		..	

Morocco

Middle East & North Africa   **Lower middle income**

Population (millions)	31	Population living on less	
GNI ($ billions)	70.6	than $1.25 a day (%)	2.5
GNI per capita ($)	2,290		

	1990		2007	
	Female	Male	Female	Male
Demography				
Sex ratio at birth (females per 1,000 males)	952		952	
Life expectancy at birth (years)	66	62	73	69
Child mortality rate (per 1,000)	24	21	11	9
Female-headed households (%)	16		17	
Education				
Gross primary enrollment (% of relevant age group)	54	81	101	113
Gross secondary enrollment (% of relevant age group)	31	44	45	53
Gross tertiary enrollment (% of relevant age group)	..	..	11	12
Primary completion rate (% of relevant age group)	42	61	79	87
Adult literacy rate (% of population ages 15+)	..	..	43	69
Family planning and maternal health				
Total fertility rate (births per woman)	4.0		2.4	
Adolescent fertility (births per 1,000 women ages 15–19)	..		19	
Women married by age 18 (% of women ages 20–24)	18		16	
Contraceptive prevalence (% of women ages 15–49)	42		63	
Unmet need for contraception (% of women ages 15–49)	20		10	
Pregnant women receiving prenatal care (%)	32		68	
Births attended by skilled health staff (% of total)	31		63	
Maternal mortality ratio (per 100,000 live births)	..		240	
Labor force and employment dynamics				
Labor force participation (% of population ages 15+)	24	82	25	80
Women in the labor force (% of total labor force)	23		25	
Employment to population ratio (% ages 15+)	22	72	22	72
Vulnerable employment (% of employed ages 15+)	..	..	65	47
Employment in agriculture (% of employed ages 15+)	..	..	61	40
Employment in industry (% of employed ages 15+)	..	..	16	21
Employment in service (% of employed ages 15+)	..	..	23	39
Wage and salaried workers (% of employed ages 15+)	..	..	33	47
Self-employed workers (% of employed ages 15+)	..	..	11	36
Unpaid family workers (% of employed ages 15+)	..	..	55	17
Women in nonagricultural wage employment (%)	29		28	
Children in employment (% of children ages 7–14)	..	..	..	..
Unemployment (% of labor force ages 15+)	20	14	10	10
Long-term unemployment (% of total unemployment)	..	..	..	..
Youth unemployment (% of labor force ages 15–24)	32	31	14	16
Maternity leave (weeks)	12		14	
Maternal leave benefits (% of wages paid)	100		100	
Women's political participation				
Seats held by women in national parliament (%)	0		11	
Women in managerial positions (%)	..		..	

Mozambique

Sub-Saharan Africa **Low income**

Population (millions)	21	Population living on less
GNI ($ billions)	7.1	than $1.25 a day (%) 74.7
GNI per capita ($)	330	

	1990		2007	
	Female	Male	Female	Male
Demography				
Sex ratio at birth (females per 1,000 males)	971		971	
Life expectancy at birth (years)	45	42	42	42
Child mortality rate (per 1,000)	..	..	64	61
Female-headed households (%)	..		26	
Education				
Gross primary enrollment (% of relevant age group)	54	72	103	119
Gross secondary enrollment (% of relevant age group)	5	9	15	21
Gross tertiary enrollment (% of relevant age group)	..	..	1	2
Primary completion rate (% of relevant age group)	21	32	39	53
Adult literacy rate (% of population ages 15+)	..	..	33	57
Family planning and maternal health				
Total fertility rate (births per woman)	6.2		5.1	
Adolescent fertility (births per 1,000 women ages 15–19)	..		149	
Women married by age 18 (% of women ages 20–24)	..		56	
Contraceptive prevalence (% of women ages 15–49)	..		17	
Unmet need for contraception (% of women ages 15–49)	..		18	
Pregnant women receiving prenatal care (%)	..		85	
Births attended by skilled health staff (% of total)	..		48	
Maternal mortality ratio (per 100,000 live births)	..		520	
Labor force and employment dynamics				
Labor force participation (% of population ages 15+)	86	84	88	77
Women in the labor force (% of total labor force)	55		56	
Employment to population ratio (% ages 15+)	81	77	82	71
Vulnerable employment (% of employed ages 15+)	..	..	..	..
Employment in agriculture (% of employed ages 15+)	..	..	..	..
Employment in industry (% of employed ages 15+)	..	..	..	..
Employment in service (% of employed ages 15+)	..	..	..	..
Wage and salaried workers (% of employed ages 15+)	..	..	..	..
Self-employed workers (% of employed ages 15+)	..	..	..	..
Unpaid family workers (% of employed ages 15+)	..	..	..	..
Women in nonagricultural wage employment (%)	11		..	
Children in employment (% of children ages 7–14)	..	..	..	..
Unemployment (% of labor force ages 15+)	..	..	..	..
Long-term unemployment (% of total unemployment)	..	..	..	..
Youth unemployment (% of labor force ages 15–24)	..	..	..	..
Maternity leave (weeks)	8		9	
Maternal leave benefits (% of wages paid)	100		100	
Women's political participation				
Seats held by women in national parliament (%)	16		35	
Women in managerial positions (%)	..		..	

Myanmar

East Asia & Pacific   **Low income**

		Population living on less
Population (millions)	49	than $1.25 a day (%) ..
GNI ($ billions)	..	
GNI per capita ($)	..	

	1990		2007	
	Female	Male	Female	Male
Demography				
Sex ratio at birth (females per 1,000 males)	952		952	
Life expectancy at birth (years)	61	57	65	59
Child mortality rate (per 1,000)	..	..	..	..
Female-headed households (%)	..		..	
Education				
Gross primary enrollment (% of relevant age group)	101	105	*114*	*111*
Gross secondary enrollment (% of relevant age group)	20	21	..	..
Gross tertiary enrollment (% of relevant age group)	..	..	..	..
Primary completion rate (% of relevant age group)	..	..	..	..
Adult literacy rate (% of population ages 15+)	..	..	..	..
Family planning and maternal health				
Total fertility rate (births per woman)	3.4		2.1	
Adolescent fertility (births per 1,000 women ages 15–19)	..		16	
Women married by age 18 (% of women ages 20–24)	..		..	
Contraceptive prevalence (% of women ages 15–49)	*17*		*34*	
Unmet need for contraception (% of women ages 15–49)	..		..	
Pregnant women receiving prenatal care (%)	..		..	
Births attended by skilled health staff (% of total)	..		*68*	
Maternal mortality ratio (per 100,000 live births)	..		*380*	
Labor force and employment dynamics				
Labor force participation (% of population ages 15+)	69	88	69	86
Women in the labor force (% of total labor force)	45		45	
Employment to population ratio (% ages 15+)	66	*84*	67	83
Vulnerable employment (% of employed ages 15+)	..	..	..	..
Employment in agriculture (% of employed ages 15+)	..	..	..	..
Employment in industry (% of employed ages 15+)	..	..	..	..
Employment in service (% of employed ages 15+)	..	..	..	..
Wage and salaried workers (% of employed ages 15+)	..	..	..	..
Self-employed workers (% of employed ages 15+)	..	..	..	..
Unpaid family workers (% of employed ages 15+)	..	..	..	..
Women in nonagricultural wage employment (%)	41		..	
Children in employment (% of children ages 7–14)	..	..	..	..
Unemployment (% of labor force ages 15+)	9	5	..	..
Long-term unemployment (% of total unemployment)	..	..	..	..
Youth unemployment (% of labor force ages 15–24)	..	..	..	..
Maternity leave (weeks)	..		*12*	
Maternal leave benefits (% of wages paid)	..		*67*	
Women's political participation				
Seats held by women in national parliament (%)	..		..	
Women in managerial positions (%)	..		..	

Namibia

Sub-Saharan Africa			Lower middle income	

Population (millions)	2.1	Population living on less	
GNI ($ billions)	7.2	than $1.25 a day (%)	..
GNI per capita ($)	3,450		

	1990		2007	
	Female	Male	Female	Male
Demography				
Sex ratio at birth (females per 1,000 males)	976		976	
Life expectancy at birth (years)	64	59	53	52
Child mortality rate (per 1,000)	34	30	19	24
Female-headed households (%)	31		..	
Education				
Gross primary enrollment (% of relevant age group)	126	116	109	110
Gross secondary enrollment (% of relevant age group)	44	35	64	54
Gross tertiary enrollment (% of relevant age group)	..	..	6	7
Primary completion rate (% of relevant age group)	..	..	81	73
Adult literacy rate (% of population ages 15+)	74	78	87	89
Family planning and maternal health				
Total fertility rate (births per woman)	5.7		3.6	
Adolescent fertility (births per 1,000 women ages 15–19)	..		59	
Women married by age 18 (% of women ages 20–24)	11		..	
Contraceptive prevalence (% of women ages 15–49)	29		55	
Unmet need for contraception (% of women ages 15–49)	22		..	
Pregnant women receiving prenatal care (%)	87		95	
Births attended by skilled health staff (% of total)	68		81	
Maternal mortality ratio (per 100,000 live births)	..		210	
Labor force and employment dynamics				
Labor force participation (% of population ages 15+)	49	65	49	59
Women in the labor force (% of total labor force)	45		46	
Employment to population ratio (% ages 15+)	39	53	37	47
Vulnerable employment (% of employed ages 15+)	..	..	28	17
Employment in agriculture (% of employed ages 15+)	52	45	..	..
Employment in industry (% of employed ages 15+)	8	21	..	..
Employment in service (% of employed ages 15+)	40	34	..	..
Wage and salaried workers (% of employed ages 15+)	..	..	69	76
Self-employed workers (% of employed ages 15+)	..	..	27	20
Unpaid family workers (% of employed ages 15+)	..	..	6	3
Women in nonagricultural wage employment (%)	..		47	
Children in employment (% of children ages 7–14)	..	..	..	..
Unemployment (% of labor force ages 15+)	19	20	25	19
Long-term unemployment (% of total unemployment)	..	..	..	..
Youth unemployment (% of labor force ages 15–24)	40	36	..	..
Maternity leave (weeks)	12		12	
Maternal leave benefits (% of wages paid)	..		80	
Women's political participation				
Seats held by women in national parliament (%)	7		27	
Women in managerial positions (%)	..		..	

Nepal

South Asia			Low income	

Population (millions)	28	Population living on less		
GNI ($ billions)	9.8	than $1.25 a day (%)		55.1
GNI per capita ($)	350			

	1990		2007	
	Female	Male	Female	Male
Demography				
Sex ratio at birth (females per 1,000 males)	952		952	
Life expectancy at birth (years)	54	55	64	63
Child mortality rate (per 1,000)	..	..	18	21
Female-headed households (%)		..		23
Education				
Gross primary enrollment (% of relevant age group)	81	135	125	123
Gross secondary enrollment (% of relevant age group)	19	44	47	50
Gross tertiary enrollment (% of relevant age group)	..	..	3	8
Primary completion rate (% of relevant age group)	..	..	78	79
Adult literacy rate (% of population ages 15+)	17	49	44	70
Family planning and maternal health				
Total fertility rate (births per woman)	5.1		3.0	
Adolescent fertility (births per 1,000 women ages 15–19)	..		115	
Women married by age 18 (% of women ages 20–24)	..		..	
Contraceptive prevalence (% of women ages 15–49)	23		48	
Unmet need for contraception (% of women ages 15–49)	..		25	
Pregnant women receiving prenatal care (%)	15		44	
Births attended by skilled health staff (% of total)	7		19	
Maternal mortality ratio (per 100,000 live births)	..		830	
Labor force and employment dynamics				
Labor force participation (% of population ages 15+)	48	80	59	76
Women in the labor force (% of total labor force)	38		45	
Employment to population ratio (% ages 15+)	47	76	55	69
Vulnerable employment (% of employed ages 15+)	..	..	..	..
Employment in agriculture (% of employed ages 15+)	91	75	..	..
Employment in industry (% of employed ages 15+)	1	4	..	..
Employment in service (% of employed ages 15+)	8	20	..	..
Wage and salaried workers (% of employed ages 15+)	..	..	..	..
Self-employed workers (% of employed ages 15+)	..	..	..	..
Unpaid family workers (% of employed ages 15+)	..	..	..	..
Women in nonagricultural wage employment (%)	..		..	
Children in employment (% of children ages 7–14)	..	..	..	..
Unemployment (% of labor force ages 15+)	..	..	..	..
Long-term unemployment (% of total unemployment)	..	..	..	..
Youth unemployment (% of labor force ages 15–24)	..	..	..	..
Maternity leave (weeks)	7		7	
Maternal leave benefits (% of wages paid)	100		100	
Women's political participation				
Seats held by women in national parliament (%)	6		17	
Women in managerial positions (%)	..		..	

Netherlands

Population (millions)	16	Population living on less
GNI ($ billions)	747.8	than $1.25 a day (%) ..
GNI per capita ($)	45,650	

	1990		2007	
	Female	Male	Female	Male
Demography				
Sex ratio at birth (females per 1,000 males)	951		951	
Life expectancy at birth (years)	80	74	82	78
Child mortality rate (per 1,000)	..	..	..	..
Female-headed households (%)	..		..	
Education				
Gross primary enrollment (% of relevant age group)	104	101	105	108
Gross secondary enrollment (% of relevant age group)	114	123	117	119
Gross tertiary enrollment (% of relevant age group)	..	..	62	58
Primary completion rate (% of relevant age group)	..	..	99	101
Adult literacy rate (% of population ages 15+)	..	..	..	..
Family planning and maternal health				
Total fertility rate (births per woman)	1.6		1.7	
Adolescent fertility (births per 1,000 women ages 15–19)	..		5	
Women married by age 18 (% of women ages 20–24)	..		..	
Contraceptive prevalence (% of women ages 15–49)	79		..	
Unmet need for contraception (% of women ages 15–49)	..		..	
Pregnant women receiving prenatal care (%)	..		..	
Births attended by skilled health staff (% of total)	..		100	
Maternal mortality ratio (per 100,000 live births)	..		6	
Labor force and employment dynamics				
Labor force participation (% of population ages 15+)	43	70	57	71
Women in the labor force (% of total labor force)	39		45	
Employment to population ratio (% ages 15+)	40	67	54	69
Vulnerable employment (% of employed ages 15+)	..	..	..	..
Employment in agriculture (% of employed ages 15+)	3	5	2	4
Employment in industry (% of employed ages 15+)	11	35	8	30
Employment in service (% of employed ages 15+)	84	59	86	62
Wage and salaried workers (% of employed ages 15+)	..	..	90	84
Self-employed workers (% of employed ages 15+)	..	..	9	16
Unpaid family workers (% of employed ages 15+)	..	..	1	0
Women in nonagricultural wage employment (%)	38		47	
Children in employment (% of children ages 7–14)	..	..	..	..
Unemployment (% of labor force ages 15+)	11	5	4	3
Long-term unemployment (% of total unemployment)	45	55	40	44
Youth unemployment (% of labor force ages 15–24)	12	10	10	10
Maternity leave (weeks)	16		16	
Maternal leave benefits (% of wages paid)	100		100	
Women's political participation				
Seats held by women in national parliament (%)	21		37	
Women in managerial positions (%)	..		..	

Netherlands Antilles

Population (thousands)	191	Population living on less
GNI ($ billions)	..	than $1.25 a day (%) ..
GNI per capita ($)	..	

	1990		2007	
	Female	Male	Female	Male
Demography				
Sex ratio at birth (females per 1,000 males)	952		952	
Life expectancy at birth (years)	78	71	79	71
Child mortality rate (per 1,000)	..	..	..	..
Female-headed households (%)	..		..	
Education				
Gross primary enrollment (% of relevant age group)	..	..	123	125
Gross secondary enrollment (% of relevant age group)	101	85	95	87
Gross tertiary enrollment (% of relevant age group)	..	..	..	..
Primary completion rate (% of relevant age group)	..	..	110	96
Adult literacy rate (% of population ages 15+)	95	95	96	96
Family planning and maternal health				
Total fertility rate (births per woman)	2.3		1.9	
Adolescent fertility (births per 1,000 women ages 15–19)	..		30	
Women married by age 18 (% of women ages 20–24)	..		..	
Contraceptive prevalence (% of women ages 15–49)	..		..	
Unmet need for contraception (% of women ages 15–49)	..		..	
Pregnant women receiving prenatal care (%)	..		..	
Births attended by skilled health staff (% of total)	..		..	
Maternal mortality ratio (per 100,000 live births)	..		..	
Labor force and employment dynamics				
Labor force participation (% of population ages 15+)	46	69	55	68
Women in the labor force (% of total labor force)	43		49	
Employment to population ratio (% ages 15+)	39	61	47	61
Vulnerable employment (% of employed ages 15+)	7	9	..	..
Employment in agriculture (% of employed ages 15+)	0	1	..	..
Employment in industry (% of employed ages 15+)	6	34	..	..
Employment in service (% of employed ages 15+)	93	65	..	..
Wage and salaried workers (% of employed ages 15+)	91	85	..	..
Self-employed workers (% of employed ages 15+)	5	12	..	..
Unpaid family workers (% of employed ages 15+)	2	1	..	..
Women in nonagricultural wage employment (%)	41		..	
Children in employment (% of children ages 7–14)	..	..	..	..
Unemployment (% of labor force ages 15+)	18	12	14	10
Long-term unemployment (% of total unemployment)	49	53	..	..
Youth unemployment (% of labor force ages 15–24)	31	28	..	..
Maternity leave (weeks)	..		..	
Maternal leave benefits (% of wages paid)	..		..	
Women's political participation				
Seats held by women in national parliament (%)	..		..	
Women in managerial positions (%)	..		..	

New Caledonia

High income

Population (thousands)	242	Population living on less
GNI ($ billions)	..	than $1.25 a day (%) ..
GNI per capita ($)	..	

	1990		2007	
	Female	Male	Female	Male
Demography				
Sex ratio at birth (females per 1,000 males)	952		952	
Life expectancy at birth (years)	73	68	80	72
Child mortality rate (per 1,000)	..	..	..	..
Female-headed households (%)	..		..	
Education				
Gross primary enrollment (% of relevant age group)				
Gross secondary enrollment (% of relevant age group)	..	..	..	..
Gross tertiary enrollment (% of relevant age group)	..	..	..	..
Primary completion rate (% of relevant age group)	..	..	..	..
Adult literacy rate (% of population ages 15+)	92	94	95	96
Family planning and maternal health				
Total fertility rate (births per woman)	3.2		2.2	
Adolescent fertility (births per 1,000 women ages 15-19)	..		26	
Women married by age 18 (% of women ages 20-24)	..		..	
Contraceptive prevalence (% of women ages 15-49)	..		..	
Unmet need for contraception (% of women ages 15-49)	..		..	
Pregnant women receiving prenatal care (%)	..		..	
Births attended by skilled health staff (% of total)	..		..	
Maternal mortality ratio (per 100,000 live births)	..		..	
Labor force and employment dynamics				
Labor force participation (% of population ages 15+)	47	74	44	71
Women in the labor force (% of total labor force)	38		38	
Employment to population ratio (% ages 15+)	..	..	..	..
Vulnerable employment (% of employed ages 15+)	..	..	..	..
Employment in agriculture (% of employed ages 15+)	..	..	..	..
Employment in industry (% of employed ages 15+)	..	..	..	..
Employment in service (% of employed ages 15+)	..	..	..	..
Wage and salaried workers (% of employed ages 15+)	..	..	..	..
Self-employed workers (% of employed ages 15+)	..	..	..	..
Unpaid family workers (% of employed ages 15+)	..	..	..	..
Women in nonagricultural wage employment (%)	..		..	
Children in employment (% of children ages 7-14)	..	..	..	..
Unemployment (% of labor force ages 15+)	..	..	..	..
Long-term unemployment (% of total unemployment)	..	..	..	..
Youth unemployment (% of labor force ages 15-24)	..	..	..	..
Maternity leave (weeks)	..		..	
Maternal leave benefits (% of wages paid)	..		..	
Women's political participation				
Seats held by women in national parliament (%)	..		..	
Women in managerial positions (%)	..		..	

New Zealand

Population (millions)	4.2	Population living on less	
GNI ($ billions)	114.5	than $1.25 a day (%)	..
GNI per capita ($)	27,080		

	1990		2007	
	Female	**Male**	**Female**	**Male**
Demography				
Sex ratio at birth (females per 1,000 males)	943		943	
Life expectancy at birth (years)	78	73	82	78
Child mortality rate (per 1,000)	..	..	..	..
Female-headed households (%)	..		..	
Education				
Gross primary enrollment (% of relevant age group)	103	105	102	102
Gross secondary enrollment (% of relevant age group)	89	87	123	117
Gross tertiary enrollment (% of relevant age group)	..	..	96	64
Primary completion rate (% of relevant age group)	99	100	..	..
Adult literacy rate (% of population ages 15+)	..	..	..	..
Family planning and maternal health				
Total fertility rate (births per woman)	2.2		2.2	
Adolescent fertility (births per 1,000 women ages 15–19)	..		22	
Women married by age 18 (% of women ages 20–24)	..		..	
Contraceptive prevalence (% of women ages 15–49)	..		..	
Unmet need for contraception (% of women ages 15–49)	..		..	
Pregnant women receiving prenatal care (%)	..		..	
Births attended by skilled health staff (% of total)	..		..	
Maternal mortality ratio (per 100,000 live births)	..		9	
Labor force and employment dynamics				
Labor force participation (% of population ages 15+)	54	74	61	75
Women in the labor force (% of total labor force)	43		46	
Employment to population ratio (% ages 15+)	49	66	58	72
Vulnerable employment (% of employed ages 15+)	10	15	10	14
Employment in agriculture (% of employed ages 15+)	8	13	5	9
Employment in industry (% of employed ages 15+)	14	33	11	32
Employment in service (% of employed ages 15+)	78	54	84	59
Wage and salaried workers (% of employed ages 15+)	87	75	87	79
Self-employed workers (% of employed ages 15+)	11	24	11	20
Unpaid family workers (% of employed ages 15+)	2	1	2	1
Women in nonagricultural wage employment (%)	45		47	
Children in employment (% of children ages 7–14)	..	..	..	..
Unemployment (% of labor force ages 15+)	7	8	4	3
Long-term unemployment (% of total unemployment)	16	26	5	6
Youth unemployment (% of labor force ages 15–24)	13	15	10	9
Maternity leave (weeks)	14		14	
Maternal leave benefits (% of wages paid)	0		100	
Women's political participation				
Seats held by women in national parliament (%)	14		32	
Women in managerial positions (%)	..		36	

Nicaragua

Latin America & Caribbean			Lower middle income	

Population (millions)	5.6	Population living on less	
GNI ($ billions)	5.5	than $1.25 a day (%)	15.8
GNI per capita ($)	990		

	1990		2007	
	Female	Male	Female	Male
Demography				
Sex ratio at birth (females per 1,000 males)	952		952	
Life expectancy at birth (years)	67	62	76	70
Child mortality rate (per 1,000)	..	..	..	..
Female-headed households (%)	..		..	
Education				
Gross primary enrollment (% of relevant age group)	90	84	114	117
Gross secondary enrollment (% of relevant age group)	42	31	70	62
Gross tertiary enrollment (% of relevant age group)	..	..	19	17
Primary completion rate (% of relevant age group)	..	..	77	70
Adult literacy rate (% of population ages 15+)	..	..	78	78
Family planning and maternal health				
Total fertility rate (births per woman)	4.7		2.8	
Adolescent fertility (births per 1,000 women ages 15–19)	..		113	
Women married by age 18 (% of women ages 20–24)	..		..	
Contraceptive prevalence (% of women ages 15–49)	49		72	
Unmet need for contraception (% of women ages 15–49)	..		..	
Pregnant women receiving prenatal care (%)	72		90	
Births attended by skilled health staff (% of total)	..		74	
Maternal mortality ratio (per 100,000 live births)	..		170	
Labor force and employment dynamics				
Labor force participation (% of population ages 15+)	39	85	38	87
Women in the labor force (% of total labor force)	32		31	
Employment to population ratio (% ages 15+)	33	73	36	82
Vulnerable employment (% of employed ages 15+)	..	..	46	45
Employment in agriculture (% of employed ages 15+)	0	4	10	41
Employment in industry (% of employed ages 15+)	14	27	17	19
Employment in service (% of employed ages 15+)	86	69	52	33
Wage and salaried workers (% of employed ages 15+)	51	57	52	50
Self-employed workers (% of employed ages 15+)	45	37	39	38
Unpaid family workers (% of employed ages 15+)	..	..	9	12
Women in nonagricultural wage employment (%)	..		..	
Children in employment (% of children ages 7–14)	..	..	4	16
Unemployment (% of labor force ages 15+)	15	9	5	5
Long-term unemployment (% of total unemployment)	..	..	..	..
Youth unemployment (% of labor force ages 15–24)	35	36	16	11
Maternity leave (weeks)	12		12	
Maternal leave benefits (% of wages paid)	60		60	
Women's political participation				
Seats held by women in national parliament (%)	15		19	
Women in managerial positions (%)	..		..	

Niger

Sub-Saharan Africa		**Low income**

Population (millions)	14	Population living on less	
GNI ($ billions)	4.0	than $1.25 a day (%)	65.9
GNI per capita ($)	280		

	1990		2007	
	Female	Male	Female	Male
Demography				
Sex ratio at birth (females per 1,000 males)	958		958	
Life expectancy at birth (years)	45	48	56	58
Child mortality rate (per 1,000)	*232*	*212*	*135*	*138*
Female-headed households (%)	*10*		*19*	
Education				
Gross primary enrollment (% of relevant age group)	20	33	46	61
Gross secondary enrollment (% of relevant age group)	3	9	8	13
Gross tertiary enrollment (% of relevant age group)	..	..	1	2
Primary completion rate (% of relevant age group)	11	21	32	47
Adult literacy rate (% of population ages 15+)	..	..	*15*	*43*
Family planning and maternal health				
Total fertility rate (births per woman)	7.9		7.0	
Adolescent fertility (births per 1,000 women ages 15–19)	..		196	
Women married by age 18 (% of women ages 20–24)	*84*		..	
Contraceptive prevalence (% of women ages 15–49)	4		11	
Unmet need for contraception (% of women ages 15–49)	19		16	
Pregnant women receiving prenatal care (%)	*30*		*46*	
Births attended by skilled health staff (% of total)	*15*		*33*	
Maternal mortality ratio (per 100,000 live births)	..		*1,800*	
Labor force and employment dynamics				
Labor force participation (% of population ages 15+)	41	87	39	88
Women in the labor force (% of total labor force)	33		31	
Employment to population ratio (% ages 15+)	*39*	*82*	*38*	*83*
Vulnerable employment (% of employed ages 15+)	..	..	..	..
Employment in agriculture (% of employed ages 15+)	..	..	..	..
Employment in industry (% of employed ages 15+)	..	..	..	..
Employment in service (% of employed ages 15+)	..	..	..	..
Wage and salaried workers (% of employed ages 15+)	..	..	..	..
Self-employed workers (% of employed ages 15+)	..	..	..	..
Unpaid family workers (% of employed ages 15+)	..	..	..	..
Women in nonagricultural wage employment (%)	11		..	
Children in employment (% of children ages 7–14)	..	..	..	..
Unemployment (% of labor force ages 15+)	..	..	..	..
Long-term unemployment (% of total unemployment)	..	..	..	..
Youth unemployment (% of labor force ages 15–24)	..	..	..	..
Maternity leave (weeks)	14		*14*	
Maternal leave benefits (% of wages paid)	50		*50*	
Women's political participation				
Seats held by women in national parliament (%)	5		12	
Women in managerial positions (%)	..		..	

Nigeria

Population (millions)	148	Population living on less	
GNI ($ billions)	136.3	than $1.25 a day (%)	64.4
GNI per capita ($)	920		

	1990		2007	
	Female	Male	Female	Male
Demography				
Sex ratio at birth (females per 1,000 males)	966		966	
Life expectancy at birth (years)	49	46	47	46
Child mortality rate (per 1,000)	102	118	57	57
Female-headed households (%)	14		17	
Education				
Gross primary enrollment (% of relevant age group)	73	96	89	104
Gross secondary enrollment (% of relevant age group)	20	26	28	35
Gross tertiary enrollment (% of relevant age group)	..	..	8	12
Primary completion rate (% of relevant age group)	..	..	65	80
Adult literacy rate (% of population ages 15+)	44	68	64	80
Family planning and maternal health				
Total fertility rate (births per woman)	6.7		5.3	
Adolescent fertility (births per 1,000 women ages 15–19)	..		126	
Women married by age 18 (% of women ages 20–24)	52		43	
Contraceptive prevalence (% of women ages 15–49)	6		13	
Unmet need for contraception (% of women ages 15–49)	21		17	
Pregnant women receiving prenatal care (%)	57		58	
Births attended by skilled health staff (% of total)	33		35	
Maternal mortality ratio (per 100,000 live births)	..		1,100	
Labor force and employment dynamics				
Labor force participation (% of population ages 15+)	37	75	39	71
Women in the labor force (% of total labor force)	34		36	
Employment to population ratio (% ages 15+)	35	70	37	66
Vulnerable employment (% of employed ages 15+)	..	..	..	..
Employment in agriculture (% of employed ages 15+)	..	..	..	..
Employment in industry (% of employed ages 15+)	..	..	..	..
Employment in service (% of employed ages 15+)	..	..	..	..
Wage and salaried workers (% of employed ages 15+)	..	..	..	..
Self-employed workers (% of employed ages 15+)	..	..	..	..
Unpaid family workers (% of employed ages 15+)	..	..	..	..
Women in nonagricultural wage employment (%)	..		21	
Children in employment (% of children ages 7–14)	..	..	..	..
Unemployment (% of labor force ages 15+)	..	..	..	..
Long-term unemployment (% of total unemployment)	..	..	..	..
Youth unemployment (% of labor force ages 15–24)	..	..	..	..
Maternity leave (weeks)	12		12	
Maternal leave benefits (% of wages paid)	50		50	
Women's political participation				
Seats held by women in national parliament (%)	..		7	
Women in managerial positions (%)	..		..	

Northern Mariana Islands

High income

Population (thousands)	84	Population living on less
GNI ($ billions)	..	than $1.25 a day (%) ..
GNI per capita ($)	..	

	1990		2007	
	Female	Male	Female	Male
Demography				
Sex ratio at birth (females per 1,000 males)	..		..	
Life expectancy at birth (years)	..	..	..	..
Child mortality rate (per 1,000)	..	..	..	..
Female-headed households (%)	..		..	
Education				
Gross primary enrollment (% of relevant age group)	..	..	..	..
Gross secondary enrollment (% of relevant age group)	..	..	..	..
Gross tertiary enrollment (% of relevant age group)	..	..	..	..
Primary completion rate (% of relevant age group)	..	..	..	..
Adult literacy rate (% of population ages 15+)	..	..	..	..
Family planning and maternal health				
Total fertility rate (births per woman)	..		..	
Adolescent fertility (births per 1,000 women ages 15–19)	..		..	
Women married by age 18 (% of women ages 20–24)	..		..	
Contraceptive prevalence (% of women ages 15–49)	..		..	
Unmet need for contraception (% of women ages 15–49)	..		..	
Pregnant women receiving prenatal care (%)	..		..	
Births attended by skilled health staff (% of total)	..		..	
Maternal mortality ratio (per 100,000 live births)	..		..	
Labor force and employment dynamics				
Labor force participation (% of population ages 15+)	..	..	..	..
Women in the labor force (% of total labor force)	..		..	
Employment to population ratio (% ages 15+)	..	..	..	..
Vulnerable employment (% of employed ages 15+)	..	..	..	..
Employment in agriculture (% of employed ages 15+)	..	..	..	..
Employment in industry (% of employed ages 15+)	..	..	..	..
Employment in service (% of employed ages 15+)	..	..	..	..
Wage and salaried workers (% of employed ages 15+)	..	..	..	..
Self-employed workers (% of employed ages 15+)	..	..	..	..
Unpaid family workers (% of employed ages 15+)	..	..	..	..
Women in nonagricultural wage employment (%)	..		59	
Children in employment (% of children ages 7–14)	..	..	..	..
Unemployment (% of labor force ages 15+)	..	..	4	5
Long-term unemployment (% of total unemployment)	..	..	..	..
Youth unemployment (% of labor force ages 15–24)	..	..	..	..
Maternity leave (weeks)	..		..	
Maternal leave benefits (% of wages paid)	..		..	
Women's political participation				
Seats held by women in national parliament (%)	..		..	
Women in managerial positions (%)	..		..	

Norway

High income

Population (millions)	4.7	Population living on less	
GNI ($ billions)	364.3	than $1.25 a day (%)	..
GNI per capita ($)	77,370		

	1990		2007	
	Female	Male	Female	Male
Demography				
Sex ratio at birth (females per 1,000 males)	946		946	
Life expectancy at birth (years)	80	73	83	78
Child mortality rate (per 1,000)	..	..	..	..
Female-headed households (%)	..			
Education				
Gross primary enrollment (% of relevant age group)	100	100	98	98
Gross secondary enrollment (% of relevant age group)	103	99	112	113
Gross tertiary enrollment (% of relevant age group)	..	..	94	61
Primary completion rate (% of relevant age group)	96	95	97	95
Adult literacy rate (% of population ages 15+)	..	..	..	..
Family planning and maternal health				
Total fertility rate (births per woman)	1.9		1.9	
Adolescent fertility (births per 1,000 women ages 15–19)	..		8	
Women married by age 18 (% of women ages 20–24)	..		..	
Contraceptive prevalence (% of women ages 15–49)	74		..	
Unmet need for contraception (% of women ages 15–49)	..		..	
Pregnant women receiving prenatal care (%)	..		..	
Births attended by skilled health staff (% of total)	100		..	
Maternal mortality ratio (per 100,000 live births)	..		7	
Labor force and employment dynamics				
Labor force participation (% of population ages 15+)	57	73	62	71
Women in the labor force (% of total labor force)	45		47	
Employment to population ratio (% ages 15+)	54	66	61	69
Vulnerable employment (% of employed ages 15+)	..	..	3	8
Employment in agriculture (% of employed ages 15+)	4	8	2	5
Employment in industry (% of employed ages 15+)	11	35	8	32
Employment in service (% of employed ages 15+)	85	56	90	63
Wage and salaried workers (% of employed ages 15+)	93	85	95	89
Self-employed workers (% of employed ages 15+)	5	13	4	11
Unpaid family workers (% of employed ages 15+)	3	2	0	0
Women in nonagricultural wage employment (%)	47		49	
Children in employment (% of children ages 7–14)	..	..	..	..
Unemployment (% of labor force ages 15+)	5	6	2	3
Long-term unemployment (% of total unemployment)	23	19	7	10
Youth unemployment (% of labor force ages 15–24)	11	12	12	13
Maternity leave (weeks)	18		47	
Maternal leave benefits (% of wages paid)	100		90	
Women's political participation				
Seats held by women in national parliament (%)	36		38	
Women in managerial positions (%)	..		30	

Oman

Population (millions)	2.6
GNI ($ billions)	32.8
GNI per capita ($)	12,860

Population living on less than $1.25 a day (%)	..

	1990		2007	
	Female	Male	Female	Male
Demography				
Sex ratio at birth (females per 1,000 males)	952		952	
Life expectancy at birth (years)	72	68	77	74
Child mortality rate (per 1,000)	..	..	..	..
Female-headed households (%)		..		..
Education				
Gross primary enrollment (% of relevant age group)	79	86	81	80
Gross secondary enrollment (% of relevant age group)	33	45	88	91
Gross tertiary enrollment (% of relevant age group)	..	..	28	23
Primary completion rate (% of relevant age group)	62	67	88	88
Adult literacy rate (% of population ages 15+)	..	..	77	89
Family planning and maternal health				
Total fertility rate (births per woman)	6.5		3.0	
Adolescent fertility (births per 1,000 women ages 15–19)	..		10	
Women married by age 18 (% of women ages 20–24)	..		..	
Contraceptive prevalence (% of women ages 15–49)	9		..	
Unmet need for contraception (% of women ages 15–49)	..		..	
Pregnant women receiving prenatal care (%)	88		..	
Births attended by skilled health staff (% of total)	87		98	
Maternal mortality ratio (per 100,000 live births)	..		64	
Labor force and employment dynamics				
Labor force participation (% of population ages 15+)	20	81	26	77
Women in the labor force (% of total labor force)	14		20	
Employment to population ratio (% ages 15+)	17	76	23	71
Vulnerable employment (% of employed ages 15+)	..	..	..	..
Employment in agriculture (% of employed ages 15+)	5	10	..	..
Employment in industry (% of employed ages 15+)	7	8	..	..
Employment in service (% of employed ages 15+)	86	81	..	..
Wage and salaried workers (% of employed ages 15+)	91	85	..	..
Self-employed workers (% of employed ages 15+)	6	14	..	..
Unpaid family workers (% of employed ages 15+)	..	..	..	..
Women in nonagricultural wage employment (%)	19		..	
Children in employment (% of children ages 7–14)	..	..	..	..
Unemployment (% of labor force ages 15+)	..	..	..	..
Long-term unemployment (% of total unemployment)	..	..	..	..
Youth unemployment (% of labor force ages 15–24)	..	..	..	..
Maternity leave (weeks)	..		..	
Maternal leave benefits (% of wages paid)	..		..	
Women's political participation				
Seats held by women in national parliament (%)	..		0	
Women in managerial positions (%)	..		..	

Pakistan

South Asia   **Low income**

Population (millions)	162	Population living on less
GNI ($ billions)	140.2	than $1.25 a day (%) 22.6
GNI per capita ($)	860	

	1990		2007	
	Female	Male	Female	Male
Demography				
Sex ratio at birth (females per 1,000 males)	952		952	
Life expectancy at birth (years)	60	60	66	65
Child mortality rate (per 1,000)	37	22	22	14
Female-headed households (%)	7		10	
Education				
Gross primary enrollment (% of relevant age group)	33	64	73	94
Gross secondary enrollment (% of relevant age group)	13	30	28	37
Gross tertiary enrollment (% of relevant age group)	..	..	5	6
Primary completion rate (% of relevant age group)	..	..	53	70
Adult literacy rate (% of population ages 15+)	..	..	40	68
Family planning and maternal health				
Total fertility rate (births per woman)	6.1		3.9	
Adolescent fertility (births per 1,000 women ages 15–19)	..		36	
Women married by age 18 (% of women ages 20–24)	32		..	
Contraceptive prevalence (% of women ages 15–49)	15		30	
Unmet need for contraception (% of women ages 15–49)	32		25	
Pregnant women receiving prenatal care (%)	27		61	
Births attended by skilled health staff (% of total)	19		39	
Maternal mortality ratio (per 100,000 live births)	..		320	
Labor force and employment dynamics				
Labor force participation (% of population ages 15+)	11	86	21	85
Women in the labor force (% of total labor force)	11		19	
Employment to population ratio (% ages 15+)	12	81	19	81
Vulnerable employment (% of employed ages 15+)	..	..	75	58
Employment in agriculture (% of employed ages 15+)	72	48	67	38
Employment in industry (% of employed ages 15+)	14	21	15	21
Employment in service (% of employed ages 15+)	14	31	18	41
Wage and salaried workers (% of employed ages 15+)	..	..	25	41
Self-employed workers (% of employed ages 15+)	..	..	14	41
Unpaid family workers (% of employed ages 15+)	..	..	62	19
Women in nonagricultural wage employment (%)	7		11	
Children in employment (% of children ages 7–14)	..	..	..	..
Unemployment (% of labor force ages 15+)	1	3	8	5
Long-term unemployment (% of total unemployment)	..	..	..	..
Youth unemployment (% of labor force ages 15–24)	1	6	15	11
Maternity leave (weeks)	12		12	
Maternal leave benefits (% of wages paid)	100		100	
Women's political participation				
Seats held by women in national parliament (%)	10		21	
Women in managerial positions (%)	..		..	

Palau

East Asia & Pacific		Upper middle income	

		Population living on less	
Population (thousands)	20	than $1.25 a day (%)	..
GNI ($ millions)	166.8		
GNI per capita ($)	8,270		

	1990		2007	
	Female	Male	Female	Male
Demography				
Sex ratio at birth (females per 1,000 males)	..		..	
Life expectancy at birth (years)	75	63	72	66
Child mortality rate (per 1,000)	..	..	..	..
Female-headed households (%)	..		..	
Education				
Gross primary enrollment (% of relevant age group)	..	..	101	107
Gross secondary enrollment (% of relevant age group)	..	..	105	96
Gross tertiary enrollment (% of relevant age group)	..	..	..	..
Primary completion rate (% of relevant age group)	..	..	..	..
Adult literacy rate (% of population ages 15+)	..	..	..	..
Family planning and maternal health				
Total fertility rate (births per woman)	2.8		..	
Adolescent fertility (births per 1,000 women ages 15–19)	..		..	
Women married by age 18 (% of women ages 20–24)	..		..	
Contraceptive prevalence (% of women ages 15–49)	47		..	
Unmet need for contraception (% of women ages 15–49)	..		..	
Pregnant women receiving prenatal care (%)	..		..	
Births attended by skilled health staff (% of total)	99		..	
Maternal mortality ratio (per 100,000 live births)	..		..	
Labor force and employment dynamics				
Labor force participation (% of population ages 15+)	..	..	..	..
Women in the labor force (% of total labor force)	..		..	
Employment to population ratio (% ages 15+)	..	..	..	..
Vulnerable employment (% of employed ages 15+)	..	..	..	..
Employment in agriculture (% of employed ages 15+)	..	..	..	..
Employment in industry (% of employed ages 15+)	..	..	..	..
Employment in service (% of employed ages 15+)	..	..	..	..
Wage and salaried workers (% of employed ages 15+)	..	..	..	..
Self-employed workers (% of employed ages 15+)	..	..	..	..
Unpaid family workers (% of employed ages 15+)	..	..	..	..
Women in nonagricultural wage employment (%)	..		..	
Children in employment (% of children ages 7–14)	..	..	..	..
Unemployment (% of labor force ages 15+)	..	..	..	..
Long-term unemployment (% of total unemployment)	..	..	..	..
Youth unemployment (% of labor force ages 15–24)	..	..	..	..
Maternity leave (weeks)	..		..	
Maternal leave benefits (% of wages paid)	..		..	
Women's political participation				
Seats held by women in national parliament (%)	..		0	
Women in managerial positions (%)	..		..	

Panama

Latin America & Caribbean		Upper middle income	

		Population living on less	
Population (millions)	3.3	than $1.25 a day (%)	
GNI ($ billions)	18.4		9.5
GNI per capita ($)	5,500		

	1990		2007	
	Female	Male	Female	Male
Demography				
Sex ratio at birth (females per 1,000 males)	952		952	
Life expectancy at birth (years)	75	70	78	73
Child mortality rate (per 1,000)	..	..	..	..
Female-headed households (%)	..		..	
Education				
Gross primary enrollment (% of relevant age group)	104	109	111	114
Gross secondary enrollment (% of relevant age group)	63	59	73	68
Gross tertiary enrollment (% of relevant age group)	..	..	56	35
Primary completion rate (% of relevant age group)	..	..	99	98
Adult literacy rate (% of population ages 15+)	88	89	93	94
Family planning and maternal health				
Total fertility rate (births per woman)	3.0		2.6	
Adolescent fertility (births per 1,000 women ages 15–19)	..		83	
Women married by age 18 (% of women ages 20–24)	..		..	
Contraceptive prevalence (% of women ages 15–49)	..		..	
Unmet need for contraception (% of women ages 15–49)	..		..	
Pregnant women receiving prenatal care (%)	..		..	
Births attended by skilled health staff (% of total)	86		91	
Maternal mortality ratio (per 100,000 live births)	..		130	
Labor force and employment dynamics				
Labor force participation (% of population ages 15+)	37	81	48	80
Women in the labor force (% of total labor force)	31		37	
Employment to population ratio (% ages 15+)	29	70	43	76
Vulnerable employment (% of employed ages 15+)	15	40	24	30
Employment in agriculture (% of employed ages 15+)	3	38	4	22
Employment in industry (% of employed ages 15+)	11	16	9	22
Employment in service (% of employed ages 15+)	87	46	86	56
Wage and salaried workers (% of employed ages 15+)	84	57	75	66
Self-employed workers (% of employed ages 15+)	14	38	21	32
Unpaid family workers (% of employed ages 15+)	2	6	4	2
Women in nonagricultural wage employment (%)	45		43	
Children in employment (% of children ages 7–14)	..	..	2	8
Unemployment (% of labor force ages 15+)	23	13	9	5
Long-term unemployment (% of total unemployment)	27	21	..	..
Youth unemployment (% of labor force ages 15–24)	41	26	30	19
Maternity leave (weeks)	14		14	
Maternal leave benefits (% of wages paid)	100		100	
Women's political participation				
Seats held by women in national parliament (%)	8		17	
Women in managerial positions (%)	..		40	

Papua New Guinea

Low income

Population (millions)	6.3	Population living on less
GNI ($ billions)	5.4	than $1.25 a day (%) ..
GNI per capita ($)	850	

	1990		2007	
	Female	Male	Female	Male
Demography				
Sex ratio at birth (females per 1,000 males)	926		926	
Life expectancy at birth (years)	58	52	60	55
Child mortality rate (per 1,000)	..	..	..	..
Female-headed households (%)	..		..	
Education				
Gross primary enrollment (% of relevant age group)	59	71	50	60
Gross secondary enrollment (% of relevant age group)	8	14	..	..
Gross tertiary enrollment (% of relevant age group)	..	..	..	..
Primary completion rate (% of relevant age group)	43	54	..	..
Adult literacy rate (% of population ages 15+)	..	..	53	62
Family planning and maternal health				
Total fertility rate (births per woman)	4.8		3.8	
Adolescent fertility (births per 1,000 women ages 15–19)	..		51	
Women married by age 18 (% of women ages 20–24)	..		..	
Contraceptive prevalence (% of women ages 15–49)	..		..	
Unmet need for contraception (% of women ages 15–49)	..		..	
Pregnant women receiving prenatal care (%)	..		..	
Births attended by skilled health staff (% of total)	..		42	
Maternal mortality ratio (per 100,000 live births)	..		470	
Labor force and employment dynamics				
Labor force participation (% of population ages 15+)	71	75	71	73
Women in the labor force (% of total labor force)	47		49	
Employment to population ratio (% ages 15+)	68	73	69	72
Vulnerable employment (% of employed ages 15+)	..	..	..	..
Employment in agriculture (% of employed ages 15+)	..	..	..	..
Employment in industry (% of employed ages 15+)	..	..	..	..
Employment in service (% of employed ages 15+)	..	..	..	..
Wage and salaried workers (% of employed ages 15+)	..	..	..	..
Self-employed workers (% of employed ages 15+)	..	..	..	..
Unpaid family workers (% of employed ages 15+)	..	..	..	..
Women in nonagricultural wage employment (%)	28		..	
Children in employment (% of children ages 7–14)	..	..	..	
Unemployment (% of labor force ages 15+)	6	9	..	..
Long-term unemployment (% of total unemployment)	..	..	..	..
Youth unemployment (% of labor force ages 15–24)	..	..	..	..
Maternity leave (weeks)	6		6	
Maternal leave benefits (% of wages paid)	0		0	
Women's political participation				
Seats held by women in national parliament (%)	0		1	
Women in managerial positions (%)	..		..	

Paraguay

Latin America & Caribbean   **Lower middle income**

Population (millions)	6.1	Population living on less
GNI ($ billions)	10.5	than $1.25 a day (%)
GNI per capita ($)	1,710	6.5

	1990		2007	
	Female	Male	Female	Male
Demography				
Sex ratio at birth (females per 1,000 males)	952		952	
Life expectancy at birth (years)	70	66	74	70
Child mortality rate (per 1,000)	12	10	..	..
Female-headed households (%)	17		..	
Education				
Gross primary enrollment (% of relevant age group)	102	106	110	113
Gross secondary enrollment (% of relevant age group)	31	30	67	66
Gross tertiary enrollment (% of relevant age group)	..	..	27	24
Primary completion rate (% of relevant age group)	65	65	96	94
Adult literacy rate (% of population ages 15+)	89	92	93	96
Family planning and maternal health				
Total fertility rate (births per woman)	4.5		3.1	
Adolescent fertility (births per 1,000 women ages 15–19)	..		72	
Women married by age 18 (% of women ages 20–24)	24		..	
Contraceptive prevalence (% of women ages 15–49)	48		73	
Unmet need for contraception (% of women ages 15–49)	15		..	
Pregnant women receiving prenatal care (%)	84		94	
Births attended by skilled health staff (% of total)	66		77	
Maternal mortality ratio (per 100,000 live births)	..		150	
Labor force and employment dynamics				
Labor force participation (% of population ages 15+)	52	83	71	84
Women in the labor force (% of total labor force)	38		45	
Employment to population ratio (% ages 15+)	45	78	65	81
Vulnerable employment (% of employed ages 15+)	31	17	50	45
Employment in agriculture (% of employed ages 15+)	1	3	20	39
Employment in industry (% of employed ages 15+)	16	36	10	19
Employment in service (% of employed ages 15+)	84	61	70	42
Wage and salaried workers (% of employed ages 15+)	67	69	47	49
Self-employed workers (% of employed ages 15+)	33	31	44	40
Unpaid family workers (% of employed ages 15+)	0	0	9	11
Women in nonagricultural wage employment (%)	41		43	
Children in employment (% of children ages 7–14)	..	..	8	23
Unemployment (% of labor force ages 15+)	6	7	8	4
Long-term unemployment (% of total unemployment)	..	..	..	..
Youth unemployment (% of labor force ages 15–24)	17	15	21	12
Maternity leave (weeks)	12		12	
Maternal leave benefits (% of wages paid)	50		50	
Women's political participation				
Seats held by women in national parliament (%)	6		10	
Women in managerial positions (%)	..		..	

Peru

Latin America & Caribbean		Lower middle income	

Population (millions)	28	Population living on less	
GNI ($ billions)	95.0	than $1.25 a day (%)	7.9
GNI per capita ($)	3,410		

	1990		2007	
	Female	Male	Female	Male
Demography				
Sex ratio at birth (females per 1,000 males)	952		952	
Life expectancy at birth (years)	68	63	74	69
Child mortality rate (per 1,000)	31	29	8	11
Female-headed households (%)	15		22	
Education				
Gross primary enrollment (% of relevant age group)	117	120	117	116
Gross secondary enrollment (% of relevant age group)	65	69	96	93
Gross tertiary enrollment (% of relevant age group)	..	..	36	34
Primary completion rate (% of relevant age group)	..	..	101	101
Adult literacy rate (% of population ages 15+)	82	93	85	95
Family planning and maternal health				
Total fertility rate (births per woman)	3.9		2.5	
Adolescent fertility (births per 1,000 women ages 15–19)	..		60	
Women married by age 18 (% of women ages 20–24)	18		..	
Contraceptive prevalence (% of women ages 15–49)	59		71	
Unmet need for contraception (% of women ages 15–49)	16		8	
Pregnant women receiving prenatal care (%)	64		91	
Births attended by skilled health staff (% of total)	80		71	
Maternal mortality ratio (per 100,000 live births)	..		240	
Labor force and employment dynamics				
Labor force participation (% of population ages 15+)	48	76	64	82
Women in the labor force (% of total labor force)	39		44	
Employment to population ratio (% ages 15+)	46	71	60	77
Vulnerable employment (% of employed ages 15+)	46	30	47	33
Employment in agriculture (% of employed ages 15+)	1	2	0	1
Employment in industry (% of employed ages 15+)	20	32	13	31
Employment in service (% of employed ages 15+)	80	66	86	68
Wage and salaried workers (% of employed ages 15+)	53	63	49	58
Self-employed workers (% of employed ages 15+)	38	34	41	37
Unpaid family workers (% of employed ages 15+)	9	3	10	5
Women in nonagricultural wage employment (%)	29		36	
Children in employment (% of children ages 7–14)	..	..	..	..
Unemployment (% of labor force ages 15+)	11	7	8	6
Long-term unemployment (% of total unemployment)	..	..	..	..
Youth unemployment (% of labor force ages 15–24)	20	13	21	21
Maternity leave (weeks)	12		13	
Maternal leave benefits (% of wages paid)	100		100	
Women's political participation				
Seats held by women in national parliament (%)	6		29	
Women in managerial positions (%)	..		23	

Philippines

East Asia & Pacific		Lower middle income	

Population (millions)	88	Population living on less	
GNI ($ billions)	142.1	than $1.25 a day (%)	22.6
GNI per capita ($)	1,620		

	1990		2007	
	Female	Male	Female	Male
Demography				
Sex ratio at birth (females per 1,000 males)	943		943	
Life expectancy at birth (years)	68	64	74	70
Child mortality rate (per 1,000)	25	28	9	14
Female-headed households (%)	14		15	
Education				
Gross primary enrollment (% of relevant age group)	109	111	109	110
Gross secondary enrollment (% of relevant age group)	72	70	88	79
Gross tertiary enrollment (% of relevant age group)	..	..	32	25
Primary completion rate (% of relevant age group)	..	..	97	90
Adult literacy rate (% of population ages 15+)	93	94	94	93
Family planning and maternal health				
Total fertility rate (births per woman)	4.3		3.2	
Adolescent fertility (births per 1,000 women ages 15–19)	..		47	
Women married by age 18 (% of women ages 20–24)	14		14	
Contraceptive prevalence (% of women ages 15–49)	40		51	
Unmet need for contraception (% of women ages 15–49)	26		17	
Pregnant women receiving prenatal care (%)	83		88	
Births attended by skilled health staff (% of total)	53		60	
Maternal mortality ratio (per 100,000 live births)	..		230	
Labor force and employment dynamics				
Labor force participation (% of population ages 15+)	47	83	50	80
Women in the labor force (% of total labor force)	37		38	
Employment to population ratio (% ages 15+)	42	76	47	75
Vulnerable employment (% of employed ages 15+)	..	..	47	44
Employment in agriculture (% of employed ages 15+)	31	53	25	45
Employment in industry (% of employed ages 15+)	13	16	12	17
Employment in service (% of employed ages 15+)	56	31	64	39
Wage and salaried workers (% of employed ages 15+)	..	..	51	51
Self-employed workers (% of employed ages 15+)	..	..	31	40
Unpaid family workers (% of employed ages 15+)	..	..	18	9
Women in nonagricultural wage employment (%)	40		42	
Children in employment (% of children ages 7–14)	..	..	..	..
Unemployment (% of labor force ages 15+)	10	7	6	6
Long-term unemployment (% of total unemployment)	..	..	..	..
Youth unemployment (% of labor force ages 15–24)	19	13	19	15
Maternity leave (weeks)	14		9	
Maternal leave benefits (% of wages paid)	100		100	
Women's political participation				
Seats held by women in national parliament (%)	9		22	
Women in managerial positions (%)	..		..	

Poland

Europe & Central Asia		Upper middle income

		Population living on less	
Population (millions)	38	than $1.25 a day (%)	2.0
GNI ($ billions)	375.3		
GNI per capita ($)	9,850		

	1990		2007	
	Female	Male	Female	Male
Demography				
Sex ratio at birth (females per 1,000 males)	945		945	
Life expectancy at birth (years)	76	67	80	71
Child mortality rate (per 1,000)	..	..	..	..
Female-headed households (%)	..		..	
Education				
Gross primary enrollment (% of relevant age group)	97	100	97	98
Gross secondary enrollment (% of relevant age group)	90	86	99	100
Gross tertiary enrollment (% of relevant age group)	..	..	77	55
Primary completion rate (% of relevant age group)	..	..	..	..
Adult literacy rate (% of population ages 15+)	..	..	99	100
Family planning and maternal health				
Total fertility rate (births per woman)	2.0		1.3	
Adolescent fertility (births per 1,000 women ages 15–19)	..		13	
Women married by age 18 (% of women ages 20–24)	..		..	
Contraceptive prevalence (% of women ages 15–49)	49		..	
Unmet need for contraception (% of women ages 15–49)	..		..	
Pregnant women receiving prenatal care (%)	..		..	
Births attended by skilled health staff (% of total)	..		100	
Maternal mortality ratio (per 100,000 live births)	..		8	
Labor force and employment dynamics				
Labor force participation (% of population ages 15+)	55	72	47	61
Women in the labor force (% of total labor force)	45		45	
Employment to population ratio (% ages 15+)	47	62	42	56
Vulnerable employment (% of employed ages 15+)	28	28	18	21
Employment in agriculture (% of employed ages 15+)	..	..	17	18
Employment in industry (% of employed ages 15+)	..	..	17	39
Employment in service (% of employed ages 15+)	..	..	66	43
Wage and salaried workers (% of employed ages 15+)	71	69	79	75
Self-employed workers (% of employed ages 15+)	21	26	15	23
Unpaid family workers (% of employed ages 15+)	8	6	6	3
Women in nonagricultural wage employment (%)	47		47	
Children in employment (% of children ages 7–14)	..	..	..	..
Unemployment (% of labor force ages 15+)	15	12	10	9
Long-term unemployment (% of total unemployment)	36	33	46	46
Youth unemployment (% of labor force ages 15–24)	30	26	39	37
Maternity leave (weeks)	16		16	
Maternal leave benefits (% of wages paid)	100		100	
Women's political participation				
Seats held by women in national parliament (%)	14		20	
Women in managerial positions (%)	..		34	

Portugal

Population (millions)	11	Population living on less
GNI ($ billions)	201.1	than $1.25 a day (%) ..
GNI per capita ($)	18,950	

	1990		2007	
	Female	Male	Female	Male
Demography				
Sex ratio at birth (females per 1,000 males)	943		943	
Life expectancy at birth (years)	77	70	82	75
Child mortality rate (per 1,000)	..	..	..	..
Female-headed households (%)	..		..	
Education				
Gross primary enrollment (% of relevant age group)	119	124	112	118
Gross secondary enrollment (% of relevant age group)	59	59	102	94
Gross tertiary enrollment (% of relevant age group)	..	..	61	48
Primary completion rate (% of relevant age group)	94	93	107	102
Adult literacy rate (% of population ages 15+)	85	92	93	97
Family planning and maternal health				
Total fertility rate (births per woman)	1.4		1.3	
Adolescent fertility (births per 1,000 women ages 15–19)	..		13	
Women married by age 18 (% of women ages 20–24)	..		..	
Contraceptive prevalence (% of women ages 15–49)	..		..	
Unmet need for contraception (% of women ages 15–49)	..		..	
Pregnant women receiving prenatal care (%)	..		..	
Births attended by skilled health staff (% of total)	98		..	
Maternal mortality ratio (per 100,000 live births)	..		11	
Labor force and employment dynamics				
Labor force participation (% of population ages 15+)	50	73	56	70
Women in the labor force (% of total labor force)	43		46	
Employment to population ratio (% ages 15+)	48	71	51	65
Vulnerable employment (% of employed ages 15+)	21	18	19	18
Employment in agriculture (% of employed ages 15+)	21	16	13	11
Employment in industry (% of employed ages 15+)	26	41	19	41
Employment in service (% of employed ages 15+)	53	44	68	48
Wage and salaried workers (% of employed ages 15+)	76	74	77	74
Self-employed workers (% of employed ages 15+)	22	25	21	25
Unpaid family workers (% of employed ages 15+)	2	1	2	1
Women in nonagricultural wage employment (%)	43		47	
Children in employment (% of children ages 7–14)	..	..	..	..
Unemployment (% of labor force ages 15+)	7	3	10	7
Long-term unemployment (% of total unemployment)	49	38	47	48
Youth unemployment (% of labor force ages 15–24)	13	7	19	14
Maternity leave (weeks)	12		17	
Maternal leave benefits (% of wages paid)	100		100	
Women's political participation				
Seats held by women in national parliament (%)	8		21	
Women in managerial positions (%)	..		32	

Puerto Rico

Population (millions)	3.9	Population living on less	
GNI ($ billions)	..	than $1.25 a day (%)	..
GNI per capita ($)	..		

	1990		2007	
	Female	Male	Female	Male
Demography				
Sex ratio at birth (females per 1,000 males)	950		950	
Life expectancy at birth (years)	79	71	83	74
Child mortality rate (per 1,000)	..	..	..	..
Female-headed households (%)	..		..	
Education				
Gross primary enrollment (% of relevant age group)	..	..	..	..
Gross secondary enrollment (% of relevant age group)	..	..	..	..
Gross tertiary enrollment (% of relevant age group)	..	..	..	..
Primary completion rate (% of relevant age group)	..	..	..	..
Adult literacy rate (% of population ages 15+)	90	90	..	..
Family planning and maternal health				
Total fertility rate (births per woman)	2.2		1.8	
Adolescent fertility (births per 1,000 women ages 15–19)	..		47	
Women married by age 18 (% of women ages 20–24)	..		..	
Contraceptive prevalence (% of women ages 15–49)	..		..	
Unmet need for contraception (% of women ages 15–49)	..		..	
Pregnant women receiving prenatal care (%)	..		..	
Births attended by skilled health staff (% of total)	..		100	
Maternal mortality ratio (per 100,000 live births)	..		18	
Labor force and employment dynamics				
Labor force participation (% of population ages 15+)	31	61	38	58
Women in the labor force (% of total labor force)	36		42	
Employment to population ratio (% ages 15+)	27	51	35	51
Vulnerable employment (% of employed ages 15+)	..	..	..	..
Employment in agriculture (% of employed ages 15+)	0	6	0	3
Employment in industry (% of employed ages 15+)	21	27	11	25
Employment in service (% of employed ages 15+)	79	68	89	72
Wage and salaried workers (% of employed ages 15+)	92	80	91	80
Self-employed workers (% of employed ages 15+)	6	20	9	21
Unpaid family workers (% of employed ages 15+)	2	0	0	0
Women in nonagricultural wage employment (%)	47		41	
Children in employment (% of children ages 7–14)	..	..	..	..
Unemployment (% of labor force ages 15+)	11	18	10	12
Long-term unemployment (% of total unemployment)	..	..	..	..
Youth unemployment (% of labor force ages 15–24)	28	33	21	25
Maternity leave (weeks)	..		..	
Maternal leave benefits (% of wages paid)	..		..	
Women's political participation				
Seats held by women in national parliament (%)	..		..	
Women in managerial positions (%)	..		41	

Qatar

Population (thousands)	836	Population living on less
GNI ($ billions)	..	than $1.25 a day (%) ..
GNI per capita ($)	..	

	1990		2007	
	Female	Male	Female	Male
Demography				
Sex ratio at birth (females per 1,000 males)	952		952	
Life expectancy at birth (years)	72	68	76	75
Child mortality rate (per 1,000)	..	..	..	..
Female-headed households (%)	..		..	
Education				
Gross primary enrollment (% of relevant age group)	103	111	109	110
Gross secondary enrollment (% of relevant age group)	87	80	102	105
Gross tertiary enrollment (% of relevant age group)	..	..	27	9
Primary completion rate (% of relevant age group)	72	67	103	105
Adult literacy rate (% of population ages 15+)	..	..	90	94
Family planning and maternal health				
Total fertility rate (births per woman)	4.3		2.7	
Adolescent fertility (births per 1,000 women ages 15–19)	..		17	
Women married by age 18 (% of women ages 20–24)	..		..	
Contraceptive prevalence (% of women ages 15–49)	32		..	
Unmet need for contraception (% of women ages 15–49)	..		..	
Pregnant women receiving prenatal care (%)	94		..	
Births attended by skilled health staff (% of total)	..		..	
Maternal mortality ratio (per 100,000 live births)	..		12	
Labor force and employment dynamics				
Labor force participation (% of population ages 15+)	30	93	41	92
Women in the labor force (% of total labor force)	11		15	
Employment to population ratio (% ages 15+)	29	91	40	91
Vulnerable employment (% of employed ages 15+)	..	..	0	1
Employment in agriculture (% of employed ages 15+)	..	..	0	3
Employment in industry (% of employed ages 15+)	..	..	3	48
Employment in service (% of employed ages 15+)	..	..	97	49
Wage and salaried workers (% of employed ages 15+)	..	..	100	99
Self-employed workers (% of employed ages 15+)	..	..	0	1
Unpaid family workers (% of employed ages 15+)	..	..	0	0
Women in nonagricultural wage employment (%)	..		16	
Children in employment (% of children ages 7–14)	..	..	..	..
Unemployment (% of labor force ages 15+)	..	..	..	..
Long-term unemployment (% of total unemployment)	..	..	..	..
Youth unemployment (% of labor force ages 15–24)	..	..	..	..
Maternity leave (weeks)	8		7	
Maternal leave benefits (% of wages paid)	100		100	
Women's political participation				
Seats held by women in national parliament (%)	..		0	
Women in managerial positions (%)	..		..	

Romania

Europe & Central Asia   **Upper middle income**

Population (millions)	22	Population living on less	
GNI ($ billions)	137.7	than $1.25 a day (%)	2.0
GNI per capita ($)	6,390		

	1990		2007	
	Female	**Male**	**Female**	**Male**
Demography				
Sex ratio at birth (females per 1,000 males)	943		941	
Life expectancy at birth (years)	73	67	76	69
Child mortality rate (per 1,000)	..	..	..	..
Female-headed households (%)	..		..	
Education				
Gross primary enrollment (% of relevant age group)	98	99	104	105
Gross secondary enrollment (% of relevant age group)	100	103	86	86
Gross tertiary enrollment (% of relevant age group)	..	..	59	46
Primary completion rate (% of relevant age group)	100	100	101	101
Adult literacy rate (% of population ages 15+)	95	99	97	98
Family planning and maternal health				
Total fertility rate (births per woman)	1.8		1.3	
Adolescent fertility (births per 1,000 women ages 15–19)	..		32	
Women married by age 18 (% of women ages 20–24)	..		..	
Contraceptive prevalence (% of women ages 15–49)	57		70	
Unmet need for contraception (% of women ages 15–49)	..		..	
Pregnant women receiving prenatal care (%)	..		94	
Births attended by skilled health staff (% of total)	99		98	
Maternal mortality ratio (per 100,000 live births)	..		24	
Labor force and employment dynamics				
Labor force participation (% of population ages 15+)	55	67	46	60
Women in the labor force (% of total labor force)	47		45	
Employment to population ratio (% ages 15+)	51	63	44	56
Vulnerable employment (% of employed ages 15+)	11	7	33	32
Employment in agriculture (% of employed ages 15+)	34	25	33	31
Employment in industry (% of employed ages 15+)	37	49	25	35
Employment in service (% of employed ages 15+)	29	26	42	34
Wage and salaried workers (% of employed ages 15+)	68	81	67	66
Self-employed workers (% of employed ages 15+)	32	19	14	28
Unpaid family workers (% of employed ages 15+)	0	0	20	7
Women in nonagricultural wage employment (%)	42		47	
Children in employment (% of children ages 7–14)	..	..	..	..
Unemployment (% of labor force ages 15+)	..	..	5	7
Long-term unemployment (% of total unemployment)	..	..	..	..
Youth unemployment (% of labor force ages 15–24)	..	..	18	21
Maternity leave (weeks)	16		18	
Maternal leave benefits (% of wages paid)	..		85	
Women's political participation				
Seats held by women in national parliament (%)	34		11	
Women in managerial positions (%)	..		31	

Russian Federation

Population (millions)	142	Population living on less	
GNI ($ billions)	1,069.8	than $1.25 a day (%)	2.0
GNI per capita ($)	7,530		

	1990		2007	
	Female	**Male**	**Female**	**Male**
Demography				
Sex ratio at birth (females per 1,000 males)	947		942	
Life expectancy at birth (years)	74	64	74	62
Child mortality rate (per 1,000)	..	..	..	..
Female-headed households (%)	..		..	
Education				
Gross primary enrollment (% of relevant age group)	106	106	96	96
Gross secondary enrollment (% of relevant age group)	96	94	83	85
Gross tertiary enrollment (% of relevant age group)	..	..	83	61
Primary completion rate (% of relevant age group)	..	..	..	..
Adult literacy rate (% of population ages 15+)	97	99	99	100
Family planning and maternal health				
Total fertility rate (births per woman)	1.9		1.4	
Adolescent fertility (births per 1,000 women ages 15–19)	..		28	
Women married by age 18 (% of women ages 20–24)	..		..	
Contraceptive prevalence (% of women ages 15–49)	34		..	
Unmet need for contraception (% of women ages 15–49)	..		..	
Pregnant women receiving prenatal care (%)	..		..	
Births attended by skilled health staff (% of total)	..		100	
Maternal mortality ratio (per 100,000 live births)	..		28	
Labor force and employment dynamics				
Labor force participation (% of population ages 15+)	60	76	57	69
Women in the labor force (% of total labor force)	49		49	
Employment to population ratio (% ages 15+)	52	65	54	65
Vulnerable employment (% of employed ages 15+)	1	1	6	6
Employment in agriculture (% of employed ages 15+)	..	..	8	12
Employment in industry (% of employed ages 15+)	..	..	21	38
Employment in service (% of employed ages 15+)	..	..	71	50
Wage and salaried workers (% of employed ages 15+)	94	90	93	92
Self-employed workers (% of employed ages 15+)	6	10	7	8
Unpaid family workers (% of employed ages 15+)	0	0	0	0
Women in nonagricultural wage employment (%)	50		51	
Children in employment (% of children ages 7–14)	..	..	..	..
Unemployment (% of labor force ages 15+)	5	5	6	6
Long-term unemployment (% of total unemployment)	15	10	..	..
Youth unemployment (% of labor force ages 15–24)	16	17	..	..
Maternity leave (weeks)	20		20	
Maternal leave benefits (% of wages paid)	100		100	
Women's political participation				
Seats held by women in national parliament (%)	..		10	
Women in managerial positions (%)	..		39	

Rwanda

        Low income

Population (millions)	9.7	Population living on less
GNI ($ billions)	3.1	than $1.25 a day (%) 76.6
GNI per capita ($)	320	

	1990		2007	
	Female	Male	Female	Male
Demography				
Sex ratio at birth (females per 1,000 males)	990		990	
Life expectancy at birth (years)	34	30	48	45
Child mortality rate (per 1,000)	73	87	87	90
Female-headed households (%)	21		34	
Education				
Gross primary enrollment (% of relevant age group)	67	73	149	146
Gross secondary enrollment (% of relevant age group)	7	9	17	19
Gross tertiary enrollment (% of relevant age group)	..	..	2	3
Primary completion rate (% of relevant age group)	32	41	35	36
Adult literacy rate (% of population ages 15+)	..	..	..	..
Family planning and maternal health				
Total fertility rate (births per woman)	7.4		5.9	
Adolescent fertility (births per 1,000 women ages 15–19)	..		40	
Women married by age 18 (% of women ages 20–24)	15		..	
Contraceptive prevalence (% of women ages 15–49)	21		17	
Unmet need for contraception (% of women ages 15–49)	39		38	
Pregnant women receiving prenatal care (%)	94		94	
Births attended by skilled health staff (% of total)	26		39	
Maternal mortality ratio (per 100,000 live births)	..		1,300	
Labor force and employment dynamics				
Labor force participation (% of population ages 15+)	86	88	81	79
Women in the labor force (% of total labor force)	52		53	
Employment to population ratio (% ages 15+)	86	88	81	79
Vulnerable employment (% of employed ages 15+)	..	..	..	..
Employment in agriculture (% of employed ages 15+)	96	83	..	..
Employment in industry (% of employed ages 15+)	1	5	..	..
Employment in service (% of employed ages 15+)	3	11	..	..
Wage and salaried workers (% of employed ages 15+)	..	..	..	..
Self-employed workers (% of employed ages 15+)	..	..	..	..
Unpaid family workers (% of employed ages 15+)	..	..	..	..
Women in nonagricultural wage employment (%)	..		..	
Children in employment (% of children ages 7–14)	..	..	..	..
Unemployment (% of labor force ages 15+)	0	1	..	..
Long-term unemployment (% of total unemployment)	..	..	..	..
Youth unemployment (% of labor force ages 15–24)	1	1	..	..
Maternity leave (weeks)	12		12	
Maternal leave benefits (% of wages paid)	33		67	
Women's political participation				
Seats held by women in national parliament (%)	17		49	
Women in managerial positions (%)	..		..	

Samoa

East Asia & Pacific	Lower middle income

Population (thousands)	181	Population living on less
GNI ($ millions)	489.1	than $1.25 a day (%) ..
GNI per capita ($)	2,700	

	1990		2007	
	Female	Male	Female	Male
Demography				
Sex ratio at birth (females per 1,000 males)	926		926	
Life expectancy at birth (years)	69	62	75	69
Child mortality rate (per 1,000)	..	..	..	..
Female-headed households (%)	..		..	
Education				
Gross primary enrollment (% of relevant age group)	126	116	95	96
Gross secondary enrollment (% of relevant age group)	38	31	86	76
Gross tertiary enrollment (% of relevant age group)	..	..	..	..
Primary completion rate (% of relevant age group)	..	..	98	98
Adult literacy rate (% of population ages 15+)	97	98	98	99
Family planning and maternal health				
Total fertility rate (births per woman)	4.7		3.9	
Adolescent fertility (births per 1,000 women ages 15–19)	..		27	
Women married by age 18 (% of women ages 20–24)	..		..	
Contraceptive prevalence (% of women ages 15–49)	..		..	
Unmet need for contraception (% of women ages 15–49)	..		..	
Pregnant women receiving prenatal care (%)	..		..	
Births attended by skilled health staff (% of total)	76		100	
Maternal mortality ratio (per 100,000 live births)	..		..	
Labor force and employment dynamics				
Labor force participation (% of population ages 15+)	40	77	41	76
Women in the labor force (% of total labor force)	32		32	
Employment to population ratio (% ages 15+)	..	..	..	..
Vulnerable employment (% of employed ages 15+)	..	..	..	..
Employment in agriculture (% of employed ages 15+)	..	..	..	..
Employment in industry (% of employed ages 15+)	..	..	..	..
Employment in service (% of employed ages 15+)	..	..	..	..
Wage and salaried workers (% of employed ages 15+)	..	..	..	..
Self-employed workers (% of employed ages 15+)	..	..	..	..
Unpaid family workers (% of employed ages 15+)	..	..	..	..
Women in nonagricultural wage employment (%)	32		..	
Children in employment (% of children ages 7–14)	..	..	..	..
Unemployment (% of labor force ages 15+)	..	..	..	..
Long-term unemployment (% of total unemployment)	..	..	..	..
Youth unemployment (% of labor force ages 15–24)	..	..	..	..
Maternity leave (weeks)	..		..	
Maternal leave benefits (% of wages paid)	..		..	
Women's political participation				
Seats held by women in national parliament (%)	0		6	
Women in managerial positions (%)	..		..	

San Marino

Population (thousands)	31	Population living on less	
GNI ($ billions)	1.4	than $1.25 a day (%)	..
GNI per capita ($)	46,770		

	1990		2007	
	Female	Male	Female	Male
Demography				
Sex ratio at birth (females per 1,000 males)	..		..	
Life expectancy at birth (years)	..	..	85	79
Child mortality rate (per 1,000)	..	..	..	..
Female-headed households (%)	..		..	
Education				
Gross primary enrollment (% of relevant age group)	..	..	..	..
Gross secondary enrollment (% of relevant age group)	..	..	..	..
Gross tertiary enrollment (% of relevant age group)	..	..	..	..
Primary completion rate (% of relevant age group)	..	..	..	..
Adult literacy rate (% of population ages 15+)	..	..	..	..
Family planning and maternal health				
Total fertility rate (births per woman)	..		..	
Adolescent fertility (births per 1,000 women ages 15–19)	..		..	
Women married by age 18 (% of women ages 20–24)	..		..	
Contraceptive prevalence (% of women ages 15–49)	..		..	
Unmet need for contraception (% of women ages 15–49)	..		..	
Pregnant women receiving prenatal care (%)	..		..	
Births attended by skilled health staff (% of total)	..		..	
Maternal mortality ratio (per 100,000 live births)	..		..	
Labor force and employment dynamics				
Labor force participation (% of population ages 15+)	..	..	..	..
Women in the labor force (% of total labor force)	..		..	
Employment to population ratio (% ages 15+)	..	..	..	..
Vulnerable employment (% of employed ages 15+)	..	..	..	..
Employment in agriculture (% of employed ages 15+)	3	2	0	1
Employment in industry (% of employed ages 15+)	32	52	24	52
Employment in service (% of employed ages 15+)	66	46	76	47
Wage and salaried workers (% of employed ages 15+)	..	..	93	89
Self-employed workers (% of employed ages 15+)	..	..	7	11
Unpaid family workers (% of employed ages 15+)	..	..	0	0
Women in nonagricultural wage employment (%)	40		42	
Children in employment (% of children ages 7–14)	..	..	..	..
Unemployment (% of labor force ages 15+)	..	..	..	..
Long-term unemployment (% of total unemployment)	..	..	..	..
Youth unemployment (% of labor force ages 15–24)	..	..	..	..
Maternity leave (weeks)	..		20	
Maternal leave benefits (% of wages paid)	..		100	
Women's political participation				
Seats held by women in national parliament (%)	12		12	
Women in managerial positions (%)	..		..	

São Tomé and Príncipe

Population (thousands)	158	Population living on less
GNI ($ millions)	138.2	than $1.25 a day (%) ..
GNI per capita ($)	870	

	1990		2007	
	Female	Male	Female	Male
Demography				
Sex ratio at birth (females per 1,000 males)	971		971	
Life expectancy at birth (years)	64	61	67	64
Child mortality rate (per 1,000)	..	..	..	..
Female-headed households (%)	..		..	
Education				
Gross primary enrollment (% of relevant age group)	130	142	129	132
Gross secondary enrollment (% of relevant age group)	37	42	48	45
Gross tertiary enrollment (% of relevant age group)	..	..	..	..
Primary completion rate (% of relevant age group)	..	..	77	74
Adult literacy rate (% of population ages 15+)	62	85	83	93
Family planning and maternal health				
Total fertility rate (births per woman)	5.4		3.9	
Adolescent fertility (births per 1,000 women ages 15–19)	..		66	
Women married by age 18 (% of women ages 20–24)	..		..	
Contraceptive prevalence (% of women ages 15–49)	..		30	
Unmet need for contraception (% of women ages 15–49)	..		..	
Pregnant women receiving prenatal care (%)	..		97	
Births attended by skilled health staff (% of total)	..		81	
Maternal mortality ratio (per 100,000 live births)	..		..	
Labor force and employment dynamics				
Labor force participation (% of population ages 15+)	37	78	43	71
Women in the labor force (% of total labor force)	33		39	
Employment to population ratio (% ages 15+)	..	..	..	..
Vulnerable employment (% of employed ages 15+)	30	26	..	..
Employment in agriculture (% of employed ages 15+)	..	..	..	..
Employment in industry (% of employed ages 15+)	..	..	..	..
Employment in service (% of employed ages 15+)	..	..	..	..
Wage and salaried workers (% of employed ages 15+)	69	72	..	..
Self-employed workers (% of employed ages 15+)	29	26	..	..
Unpaid family workers (% of employed ages 15+)	1	1	..	..
Women in nonagricultural wage employment (%)	..		38	
Children in employment (% of children ages 7–14)	..	..	..	..
Unemployment (% of labor force ages 15+)	..	..	25	11
Long-term unemployment (% of total unemployment)	..	..	..	..
Youth unemployment (% of labor force ages 15–24)	..	..	..	..
Maternity leave (weeks)	10		10	
Maternal leave benefits (% of wages paid)	100		100	
Women's political participation				
Seats held by women in national parliament (%)	12		2	
Women in managerial positions (%)	..		..	

Saudi Arabia

High income

Population (millions)	24	Population living on less
GNI ($ billions)	373.7	than $1.25 a day (%) ..
GNI per capita ($)	15,470	

	1990		2007	
	Female	Male	Female	Male
Demography				
Sex ratio at birth (females per 1,000 males)	971		971	
Life expectancy at birth (years)	70	66	75	71
Child mortality rate (per 1,000)	..	..	4	3
Female-headed households (%)	..		..	
Education				
Gross primary enrollment (% of relevant age group)	67	79	96	100
Gross secondary enrollment (% of relevant age group)	37	49	86	94
Gross tertiary enrollment (% of relevant age group)	..	..	36	25
Primary completion rate (% of relevant age group)	50	57	91	96
Adult literacy rate (% of population ages 15+)	57	80	79	89
Family planning and maternal health				
Total fertility rate (births per woman)	5.9		3.4	
Adolescent fertility (births per 1,000 women ages 15–19)	..		28	
Women married by age 18 (% of women ages 20–24)	..		..	
Contraceptive prevalence (% of women ages 15–49)	..		..	
Unmet need for contraception (% of women ages 15–49)	..		..	
Pregnant women receiving prenatal care (%)			..	
Births attended by skilled health staff (% of total)	..		96	
Maternal mortality ratio (per 100,000 live births)	..		18	
Labor force and employment dynamics				
Labor force participation (% of population ages 15+)	15	80	19	80
Women in the labor force (% of total labor force)	11		15	
Employment to population ratio (% ages 15+)	14	77	18	76
Vulnerable employment (% of employed ages 15+)	..	..	..	..
Employment in agriculture (% of employed ages 15+)	..	..	0	5
Employment in industry (% of employed ages 15+)	..	..	1	11
Employment in service (% of employed ages 15+)	..	..	99	85
Wage and salaried workers (% of employed ages 15+)	..	..	..	..
Self-employed workers (% of employed ages 15+)	..	..	..	..
Unpaid family workers (% of employed ages 15+)	..	..	..	..
Women in nonagricultural wage employment (%)	..		13	
Children in employment (% of children ages 7–14)	..	..	..	..
Unemployment (% of labor force ages 15+)	..	..	13	4
Long-term unemployment (% of total unemployment)	..	..	..	..
Youth unemployment (% of labor force ages 15–24)	..	..	..	..
Maternity leave (weeks)	10		10	
Maternal leave benefits (% of wages paid)	50		75	
Women's political participation				
Seats held by women in national parliament (%)	..		0	
Women in managerial positions (%)	..		..	

Senegal

Sub-Saharan Africa   **Low income**

Population (millions)	12	Population living on less
GNI ($ billions)	10.3	than $1.25 a day (%) 33.5
GNI per capita ($)	830	

	1990		2007	
	Female	Male	Female	Male
Demography				
Sex ratio at birth (females per 1,000 males)	969		969	
Life expectancy at birth (years)	58	56	65	61
Child mortality rate (per 1,000)	80	96	69	69
Female-headed households (%)	16		23	
Education				
Gross primary enrollment (% of relevant age group)	46	64	84	84
Gross secondary enrollment (% of relevant age group)	10	20	20	27
Gross tertiary enrollment (% of relevant age group)	..	..	..	..
Primary completion rate (% of relevant age group)	33	52	47	51
Adult literacy rate (% of population ages 15+)	18	37	33	52
Family planning and maternal health				
Total fertility rate (births per woman)	6.5		5.1	
Adolescent fertility (births per 1,000 women ages 15-19)	..		87	
Women married by age 18 (% of women ages 20-24)	48		..	
Contraceptive prevalence (% of women ages 15-49)	7		12	
Unmet need for contraception (% of women ages 15-49)	29		32	
Pregnant women receiving prenatal care (%)	74		87	
Births attended by skilled health staff (% of total)	47		52	
Maternal mortality ratio (per 100,000 live births)	..		980	
Labor force and employment dynamics				
Labor force participation (% of population ages 15+)	61	90	62	86
Women in the labor force (% of total labor force)	40		42	
Employment to population ratio (% ages 15+)	56	77	57	75
Vulnerable employment (% of employed ages 15+)	91	77	..	..
Employment in agriculture (% of employed ages 15+)	..	..	..	..
Employment in industry (% of employed ages 15+)	..	..	..	..
Employment in service (% of employed ages 15+)	..	..	..	..
Wage and salaried workers (% of employed ages 15+)	8	14	..	..
Self-employed workers (% of employed ages 15+)	59	53	..	..
Unpaid family workers (% of employed ages 15+)	32	25	..	..
Women in nonagricultural wage employment (%)	..		..	
Children in employment (% of children ages 7-14)	..	..	13	24
Unemployment (% of labor force ages 15+)	..	..	..	..
Long-term unemployment (% of total unemployment)	..	..	..	..
Youth unemployment (% of labor force ages 15-24)	..	..	..	..
Maternity leave (weeks)	14		14	
Maternal leave benefits (% of wages paid)	100		100	
Women's political participation				
Seats held by women in national parliament (%)	13		22	
Women in managerial positions (%)	..		..	

Serbia

Europe & Central Asia		Upper middle income	

Population (millions)	7.4	Population living on less	
GNI ($ billions)	33.5	than $1.25 a day (%)	..
GNI per capita ($)	4,540		

	1990		2007	
	Female	Male	Female	Male
Demography				
Sex ratio at birth (females per 1,000 males)	926		926	
Life expectancy at birth (years)	74	69	76	71
Child mortality rate (per 1,000)	..	..	3	4
Female-headed households (%)	..		29	
Education				
Gross primary enrollment (% of relevant age group)	..	..	97	97
Gross secondary enrollment (% of relevant age group)	..	..	89	87
Gross tertiary enrollment (% of relevant age group)	..	..	..	..
Primary completion rate (% of relevant age group)	..	..	..	..
Adult literacy rate (% of population ages 15+)	..	..	..	..
Family planning and maternal health				
Total fertility rate (births per woman)	1.8		1.4	
Adolescent fertility (births per 1,000 women ages 15–19)	..		24	
Women married by age 18 (% of women ages 20–24)	..		..	
Contraceptive prevalence (% of women ages 15–49)	..		41	
Unmet need for contraception (% of women ages 15–49)	..		29	
Pregnant women receiving prenatal care (%)	..		98	
Births attended by skilled health staff (% of total)	..		99	
Maternal mortality ratio (per 100,000 live births)	..		..	
Labor force and employment dynamics				
Labor force participation (% of population ages 15+)	..	..	43	60
Women in the labor force (% of total labor force)	..		43	
Employment to population ratio (% ages 15+)	..	..	..	..
Vulnerable employment (% of employed ages 15+)	..	..	20	25
Employment in agriculture (% of employed ages 15+)	..	..	20	21
Employment in industry (% of employed ages 15+)	..	..	20	37
Employment in service (% of employed ages 15+)	..	..	60	42
Wage and salaried workers (% of employed ages 15+)	..	..	77	70
Self-employed workers (% of employed ages 15+)	..	..	11	27
Unpaid family workers (% of employed ages 15+)	..	..	12	3
Women in nonagricultural wage employment (%)	..		42	
Children in employment (% of children ages 7–14)	..	..	7	7
Unemployment (% of labor force ages 15+)	..	..	21	16
Long-term unemployment (% of total unemployment)	..	..	82	79
Youth unemployment (% of labor force ages 15–24)	..	..	..	..
Maternity leave (weeks)	..		..	
Maternal leave benefits (% of wages paid)	..		..	
Women's political participation				
Seats held by women in national parliament (%)	..		20	
Women in managerial positions (%)	..		..	

Seychelles

Sub-Saharan Africa

Upper middle income

Population (thousands)	85	Population living on less	
GNI ($ millions)	761.8	than $1.25 a day (%)	..
GNI per capita ($)	8,960		

	1990		2007	
	Female	Male	Female	Male
Demography				
Sex ratio at birth (females per 1,000 males)	..		..	
Life expectancy at birth (years)	74	67	78	69
Child mortality rate (per 1,000)	..	..	..	..
Female-headed households (%)	..		..	
Education				
Gross primary enrollment (% of relevant age group)	..	..	125	126
Gross secondary enrollment (% of relevant age group)	..	..	119	105
Gross tertiary enrollment (% of relevant age group)	..	..	..	..
Primary completion rate (% of relevant age group)	..	..	118	111
Adult literacy rate (% of population ages 15+)	85	83	..	..
Family planning and maternal health				
Total fertility rate (births per woman)	2.8		2.1	
Adolescent fertility (births per 1,000 women ages 15–19)	..		..	
Women married by age 18 (% of women ages 20–24)	..		..	
Contraceptive prevalence (% of women ages 15–49)	..		..	
Unmet need for contraception (% of women ages 15–49)	..		..	
Pregnant women receiving prenatal care (%)	..		..	
Births attended by skilled health staff (% of total)	..		..	
Maternal mortality ratio (per 100,000 live births)	..		..	
Labor force and employment dynamics				
Labor force participation (% of population ages 15+)	..	..	..	..
Women in the labor force (% of total labor force)	..		..	
Employment to population ratio (% ages 15+)	..	..	..	..
Vulnerable employment (% of employed ages 15+)	..	..	..	..
Employment in agriculture (% of employed ages 15+)	..	..	..	..
Employment in industry (% of employed ages 15+)	..	..	..	..
Employment in service (% of employed ages 15+)	..	..	..	..
Wage and salaried workers (% of employed ages 15+)	86	79	..	..
Self-employed workers (% of employed ages 15+)	6	15	..	..
Unpaid family workers (% of employed ages 15+)	..	..	..	..
Women in nonagricultural wage employment (%)	49		..	
Children in employment (% of children ages 7–14)	..	..	..	..
Unemployment (% of labor force ages 15+)	41	28	5	6
Long-term unemployment (% of total unemployment)	..	..	..	..
Youth unemployment (% of labor force ages 15–24)	..	..	..	..
Maternity leave (weeks)	14		14	
Maternal leave benefits (% of wages paid)	..		..	
Women's political participation				
Seats held by women in national parliament (%)	16		24	
Women in managerial positions (%)	..		..	

Sierra Leone

Sub-Saharan Africa | **Low income**

Population (millions)	5.8	Population living on less
GNI ($ billions)	1.5	than $1.25 a day (%) 53.4
GNI per capita ($)	260	

	1990		2007	
	Female	Male	Female	Male
Demography				
Sex ratio at birth (females per 1,000 males)	971		971	
Life expectancy at birth (years)	40	38	44	41
Child mortality rate (per 1,000)	..	..	124	134
Female-headed households (%)	..		..	
Education				
Gross primary enrollment (% of relevant age group)	47	68	139	155
Gross secondary enrollment (% of relevant age group)	12	23	26	37
Gross tertiary enrollment (% of relevant age group)	..	..	..	..
Primary completion rate (% of relevant age group)	..	..	70	92
Adult literacy rate (% of population ages 15+)	..	..	27	50
Family planning and maternal health				
Total fertility rate (births per woman)	6.5		6.5	
Adolescent fertility (births per 1,000 women ages 15–19)	..		160	
Women married by age 18 (% of women ages 20–24)	..		..	
Contraceptive prevalence (% of women ages 15–49)	..		5	
Unmet need for contraception (% of women ages 15–49)	..		..	
Pregnant women receiving prenatal care (%)	..		81	
Births attended by skilled health staff (% of total)	..		43	
Maternal mortality ratio (per 100,000 live births)	..		2,100	
Labor force and employment dynamics				
Labor force participation (% of population ages 15+)	66	65	65	67
Women in the labor force (% of total labor force)	52		50	
Employment to population ratio (% ages 15+)	65	62	63	64
Vulnerable employment (% of employed ages 15+)	..	..	..	..
Employment in agriculture (% of employed ages 15+)	..	..	..	..
Employment in industry (% of employed ages 15+)	..	..	..	..
Employment in service (% of employed ages 15+)	..	..	..	..
Wage and salaried workers (% of employed ages 15+)	..	..	4	11
Self-employed workers (% of employed ages 15+)	..	..	..	..
Unpaid family workers (% of employed ages 15+)	..	..	22	15
Women in nonagricultural wage employment (%)	..		23	
Children in employment (% of children ages 7–14)	..	..	62	64
Unemployment (% of labor force ages 15+)	..	..	2	5
Long-term unemployment (% of total unemployment)	..	..	..	..
Youth unemployment (% of labor force ages 15–24)	..	..	..	..
Maternity leave (weeks)	..		..	
Maternal leave benefits (% of wages paid)	..		..	
Women's political participation				
Seats held by women in national parliament (%)	..		13	
Women in managerial positions (%)	..		..	

Singapore

Population (millions)	4.6	Population living on less
GNI ($ billions)	148.4	than $1.25 a day (%) ..
GNI per capita ($)	32,340	

	1990		2007	
	Female	Male	Female	Male
Demography				
Sex ratio at birth (females per 1,000 males)	932		932	
Life expectancy at birth (years)	77	72	83	78
Child mortality rate (per 1,000)	..	..	..	..
Female-headed households (%)	..		..	
Education				
Gross primary enrollment (% of relevant age group)	102	105	..	..
Gross secondary enrollment (% of relevant age group)	..	..	..	..
Gross tertiary enrollment (% of relevant age group)	..	..	..	..
Primary completion rate (% of relevant age group)	..	..	..	..
Adult literacy rate (% of population ages 15+)	83	95	92	97
Family planning and maternal health				
Total fertility rate (births per woman)	1.9		1.3	
Adolescent fertility (births per 1,000 women ages 15-19)	..		5	
Women married by age 18 (% of women ages 20-24)	..		..	
Contraceptive prevalence (% of women ages 15-49)	65		..	
Unmet need for contraception (% of women ages 15-49)	..		..	
Pregnant women receiving prenatal care (%)	..		..	
Births attended by skilled health staff (% of total)	..		100	
Maternal mortality ratio (per 100,000 live births)	..		14	
Labor force and employment dynamics				
Labor force participation (% of population ages 15+)	51	79	54	76
Women in the labor force (% of total labor force)	39		41	
Employment to population ratio (% ages 15+)	50	79	51	74
Vulnerable employment (% of employed ages 15+)	6	10	7	12
Employment in agriculture (% of employed ages 15+)	0	0	0	0
Employment in industry (% of employed ages 15+)	33	37	21	36
Employment in service (% of employed ages 15+)	67	63	79	63
Wage and salaried workers (% of employed ages 15+)	92	83	90	81
Self-employed workers (% of employed ages 15+)	6	17	9	19
Unpaid family workers (% of employed ages 15+)	2	0	1	0
Women in nonagricultural wage employment (%)	43		50	
Children in employment (% of children ages 7-14)	..	..	..	..
Unemployment (% of labor force ages 15+)	2	2	4	4
Long-term unemployment (% of total unemployment)	..	..	..	..
Youth unemployment (% of labor force ages 15-24)	6	5	6	4
Maternity leave (weeks)	8		8	
Maternal leave benefits (% of wages paid)	100		100	
Women's political participation				
Seats held by women in national parliament (%)	5		25	
Women in managerial positions (%)	..		26	

Slovak Republic

Population (millions)	5.4	Population living on less
GNI ($ billions)	63.3	than $1.25 a day (%) ..
GNI per capita ($)	11,720	

	1990		2007	
	Female	Male	Female	Male
Demography				
Sex ratio at birth (females per 1,000 males)	957		947	
Life expectancy at birth (years)	75	67	78	71
Child mortality rate (per 1,000)	..	..	..	..
Female-headed households (%)	..		..	
Education				
Gross primary enrollment (% of relevant age group)	..	..	99	101
Gross secondary enrollment (% of relevant age group)	..	..	96	95
Gross tertiary enrollment (% of relevant age group)	..	..	53	38
Primary completion rate (% of relevant age group)	..	..	92	94
Adult literacy rate (% of population ages 15+)	..	..	..	..
Family planning and maternal health				
Total fertility rate (births per woman)	2.1		1.3	
Adolescent fertility (births per 1,000 women ages 15–19)	..		20	
Women married by age 18 (% of women ages 20–24)	..		..	
Contraceptive prevalence (% of women ages 15–49)	74		..	
Unmet need for contraception (% of women ages 15–49)	..		..	
Pregnant women receiving prenatal care (%)	..		..	
Births attended by skilled health staff (% of total)	..		100	
Maternal mortality ratio (per 100,000 live births)	..		6	
Labor force and employment dynamics				
Labor force participation (% of population ages 15+)	66	79	52	69
Women in the labor force (% of total labor force)	47		45	
Employment to population ratio (% ages 15+)	50	62	45	62
Vulnerable employment (% of employed ages 15+)	..	..	5	13
Employment in agriculture (% of employed ages 15+)	..	..	3	6
Employment in industry (% of employed ages 15+)	..	..	25	50
Employment in service (% of employed ages 15+)	..	..	72	44
Wage and salaried workers (% of employed ages 15+)	..	..	92	83
Self-employed workers (% of employed ages 15+)	..	..	7	17
Unpaid family workers (% of employed ages 15+)	..	..	0	0
Women in nonagricultural wage employment (%)	49		50	
Children in employment (% of children ages 7–14)	..	..	..	..
Unemployment (% of labor force ages 15+)	12	13	13	10
Long-term unemployment (% of total unemployment)	..	..	69	72
Youth unemployment (% of labor force ages 15–24)	..	..	29	31
Maternity leave (weeks)	..		28	
Maternal leave benefits (% of wages paid)	..		55	
Women's political participation				
Seats held by women in national parliament (%)	..		19	
Women in managerial positions (%)	..		35	

Slovenia

High income

Population (millions)	2.0	Population living on less than $1.25 a day (%)		
GNI ($ billions)	43.4			2.0
GNI per capita ($)	21,510			

	1990		2007	
	Female	Male	Female	Male
Demography				
Sex ratio at birth (females per 1,000 males)	949		949	
Life expectancy at birth (years)	77	69	82	74
Child mortality rate (per 1,000)	..	..	..	..
Female-headed households (%)	..		..	
Education				
Gross primary enrollment (% of relevant age group)	..	..	100	100
Gross secondary enrollment (% of relevant age group)	..	..	95	95
Gross tertiary enrollment (% of relevant age group)	..	..	99	68
Primary completion rate (% of relevant age group)	..	..	99	100
Adult literacy rate (% of population ages 15+)	99	100	100	100
Family planning and maternal health				
Total fertility rate (births per woman)	1.5		1.4	
Adolescent fertility (births per 1,000 women ages 15-19)	..		7	
Women married by age 18 (% of women ages 20-24)	..		..	
Contraceptive prevalence (% of women ages 15-49)	..		..	
Unmet need for contraception (% of women ages 15-49)	..		..	
Pregnant women receiving prenatal care (%)	98		..	
Births attended by skilled health staff (% of total)	100		100	
Maternal mortality ratio (per 100,000 live births)	..		6	
Labor force and employment dynamics				
Labor force participation (% of population ages 15+)	60	76	52	65
Women in the labor force (% of total labor force)	46		46	
Employment to population ratio (% ages 15+)	51	62	49	63
Vulnerable employment (% of employed ages 15+)	10	14	13	14
Employment in agriculture (% of employed ages 15+)	10	11	9	9
Employment in industry (% of employed ages 15+)	36	52	25	47
Employment in service (% of employed ages 15+)	54	37	65	43
Wage and salaried workers (% of employed ages 15+)	88	82	86	82
Self-employed workers (% of employed ages 15+)	8	16	7	15
Unpaid family workers (% of employed ages 15+)	5	2	7	3
Women in nonagricultural wage employment (%)	48		48	
Children in employment (% of children ages 7-14)	..	..	..	..
Unemployment (% of labor force ages 15+)	8	10	6	4
Long-term unemployment (% of total unemployment)	50	57	..	..
Youth unemployment (% of labor force ages 15-24)	28	37	12	11
Maternity leave (weeks)	..		15	
Maternal leave benefits (% of wages paid)	.. -		100	
Women's political participation				
Seats held by women in national parliament (%)	..		12	
Women in managerial positions (%)	..		33	

Solomon Islands

Population (thousands)	495	Population living on less
GNI ($ millions)	373.8	than $1.25 a day (%) ..
GNI per capita ($)	750	

	1990		2007	
	Female	**Male**	**Female**	**Male**
Demography				
Sex ratio at birth (females per 1,000 males)	917		917	
Life expectancy at birth (years)	58	57	64	63
Child mortality rate (per 1,000)	..	..	..	..
Female-headed households (%)	..		..	
Education				
Gross primary enrollment (% of relevant age group)	80	93	98	102
Gross secondary enrollment (% of relevant age group)	11	17	27	32
Gross tertiary enrollment (% of relevant age group)	..	..	..	..
Primary completion rate (% of relevant age group)	..	..	..	..
Adult literacy rate (% of population ages 15+)	..	..	..	..
Family planning and maternal health				
Total fertility rate (births per woman)	5.8		3.9	
Adolescent fertility (births per 1,000 women ages 15–19)	..		41	
Women married by age 18 (% of women ages 20–24)	..		..	
Contraceptive prevalence (% of women ages 15–49)	..		..	
Unmet need for contraception (% of women ages 15–49)	..		..	
Pregnant women receiving prenatal care (%)	..		..	
Births attended by skilled health staff (% of total)	..		..	
Maternal mortality ratio (per 100,000 live births)	..		220	
Labor force and employment dynamics				
Labor force participation (% of population ages 15+)	59	82	54	81
Women in the labor force (% of total labor force)	40		39	
Employment to population ratio (% ages 15+)	55	79	51	78
Vulnerable employment (% of employed ages 15+)	..	..	..	..
Employment in agriculture (% of employed ages 15+)	..	..	..	..
Employment in industry (% of employed ages 15+)	..	..	..	..
Employment in service (% of employed ages 15+)	..	..	..	..
Wage and salaried workers (% of employed ages 15+)	..	..	..	..
Self-employed workers (% of employed ages 15+)	..	..	..	..
Unpaid family workers (% of employed ages 15+)	..	..	..	..
Women in nonagricultural wage employment (%)	..		..	
Children in employment (% of children ages 7–14)	..	..	..	..
Unemployment (% of labor force ages 15+)	..	..	..	..
Long-term unemployment (% of total unemployment)	..	..	..	..
Youth unemployment (% of labor force ages 15–24)	..	..	..	..
Maternity leave (weeks)	12		12	
Maternal leave benefits (% of wages paid)	25		25	
Women's political participation				
Seats held by women in national parliament (%)	0		0	
Women in managerial positions (%)	..		..	

Somalia

Sub-Saharan Africa   **Low income**

Population (millions)	8.7	Population living on less
GNI ($ billions)	..	than $1.25 a day (%) ..
GNI per capita ($)	..	

	1990		2007	
	Female	**Male**	**Female**	**Male**
Demography				
Sex ratio at birth (females per 1,000 males)	971		971	
Life expectancy at birth (years)	43	40	49	47
Child mortality rate (per 1,000)	..	..	54	53
Female-headed households (%)	..		..	
Education				
Gross primary enrollment (% of relevant age group)	..	..	9	16
Gross secondary enrollment (% of relevant age group)	..	..	..	..
Gross tertiary enrollment (% of relevant age group)	..	..	..	..
Primary completion rate (% of relevant age group)	..	..	..	..
Adult literacy rate (% of population ages 15+)	..	..	..	..
Family planning and maternal health				
Total fertility rate (births per woman)	6.8		6.0	
Adolescent fertility (births per 1,000 women ages 15–19)	..		66	
Women married by age 18 (% of women ages 20–24)	..		..	
Contraceptive prevalence (% of women ages 15–49)	1		15	
Unmet need for contraception (% of women ages 15–49)	..		..	
Pregnant women receiving prenatal care (%)	..		26	
Births attended by skilled health staff (% of total)	..		33	
Maternal mortality ratio (per 100,000 live births)	..		1,400	
Labor force and employment dynamics				
Labor force participation (% of population ages 15+)	52	89	54	89
Women in the labor force (% of total labor force)	38		39	
Employment to population ratio (% ages 15+)	49	82	51	82
Vulnerable employment (% of employed ages 15+)	..	..	..	..
Employment in agriculture (% of employed ages 15+)	..	..	..	..
Employment in industry (% of employed ages 15+)	..	..	..	..
Employment in service (% of employed ages 15+)	..	..	..	..
Wage and salaried workers (% of employed ages 15+)	..	..	..	..
Self-employed workers (% of employed ages 15+)	..	..	..	..
Unpaid family workers (% of employed ages 15+)	..	..	..	..
Women in nonagricultural wage employment (%)	22		..	
Children in employment (% of children ages 7–14)	..	..	42	46
Unemployment (% of labor force ages 15+)	..	..	..	..
Long-term unemployment (% of total unemployment)	..	..	..	..
Youth unemployment (% of labor force ages 15–24)	..	..	..	..
Maternity leave (weeks)	14		14	
Maternal leave benefits (% of wages paid)	50		50	
Women's political participation				
Seats held by women in national parliament (%)	4		8	
Women in managerial positions (%)	..		..	

South Africa

Sub-Saharan Africa			Upper middle income	

Population (millions)	48	Population living on less		
GNI ($ billions)	273.9	than $1.25 a day (%)		26.2
GNI per capita ($)	5,720			

	1990		2007	
	Female	Male	Female	Male
Demography				
Sex ratio at birth (females per 1,000 males)	971		971	
Life expectancy at birth (years)	65	58	52	49
Child mortality rate (per 1,000)	..	..	9	13
Female-headed households (%)	..		..	
Education				
Gross primary enrollment (% of relevant age group)	106	107	101	105
Gross secondary enrollment (% of relevant age group)	71	61	99	93
Gross tertiary enrollment (% of relevant age group)	..	..	17	14
Primary completion rate (% of relevant age group)	80	71	92	92
Adult literacy rate (% of population ages 15+)	..	..	87	89
Family planning and maternal health				
Total fertility rate (births per woman)	3.5		2.7	
Adolescent fertility (births per 1,000 women ages 15–19)	..		61	
Women married by age 18 (% of women ages 20–24)	..		..	
Contraceptive prevalence (% of women ages 15–49)	57		60	
Unmet need for contraception (% of women ages 15–49)	..		..	
Pregnant women receiving prenatal care (%)	..		92	
Births attended by skilled health staff (% of total)	..		92	
Maternal mortality ratio (per 100,000 live births)	..		400	
Labor force and employment dynamics				
Labor force participation (% of population ages 15+)	44	64	47	60
Women in the labor force (% of total labor force)	42		45	
Employment to population ratio (% ages 15+)	31	49	34	48
Vulnerable employment (% of employed ages 15+)	..	..	3	2
Employment in agriculture (% of employed ages 15+)	..	..	7	13
Employment in industry (% of employed ages 15+)	..	..	14	33
Employment in service (% of employed ages 15+)	..	..	79	54
Wage and salaried workers (% of employed ages 15+)	..	..	81	84
Self-employed workers (% of employed ages 15+)	..	..	18	16
Unpaid family workers (% of employed ages 15+)	..	..	1	0
Women in nonagricultural wage employment (%)	..		43	
Children in employment (% of children ages 7–14)	..	..	..	..
Unemployment (% of labor force ages 15+)	..	..	27	20
Long-term unemployment (% of total unemployment)	..	..	..	..
Youth unemployment (% of labor force ages 15–24)	..	..	65	56
Maternity leave (weeks)	..		16	
Maternal leave benefits (% of wages paid)	..		60	
Women's political participation				
Seats held by women in national parliament (%)	3		33	
Women in managerial positions (%)	..		..	

Spain

High income

Population (millions)	45	Population living on less
GNI ($ billions)	1,314.5	than $1.25 a day (%)
GNI per capita ($)	29,290	

	1990		2007	
	Female	**Male**	**Female**	**Male**
Demography				
Sex ratio at birth (females per 1,000 males)	940		940	
Life expectancy at birth (years)	81	73	84	78
Child mortality rate (per 1,000)	..	..	..	..
Female-headed households (%)	..		..	
Education				
Gross primary enrollment (% of relevant age group)	106	108	104	106
Gross secondary enrollment (% of relevant age group)	105	99	122	115
Gross tertiary enrollment (% of relevant age group)	..	..	74	61
Primary completion rate (% of relevant age group)	103	104	99	99
Adult literacy rate (% of population ages 15+)	95	98	97	99
Family planning and maternal health				
Total fertility rate (births per woman)	1.3		1.4	
Adolescent fertility (births per 1,000 women ages 15–19)	..		9	
Women married by age 18 (% of women ages 20–24)	..		..	
Contraceptive prevalence (% of women ages 15–49)	..		..	
Unmet need for contraception (% of women ages 15–49)	..		..	
Pregnant women receiving prenatal care (%)	..		..	
Births attended by skilled health staff (% of total)	..		..	
Maternal mortality ratio (per 100,000 live births)	..		4	
Labor force and employment dynamics				
Labor force participation (% of population ages 15+)	34	69	47	68
Women in the labor force (% of total labor force)	34		41	
Employment to population ratio (% ages 15+)	26	60	42	64
Vulnerable employment (% of employed ages 15+)	24	20	10	13
Employment in agriculture (% of employed ages 15+)	10	13	4	6
Employment in industry (% of employed ages 15+)	17	41	12	41
Employment in service (% of employed ages 15+)	73	47	84	52
Wage and salaried workers (% of employed ages 15+)	73	74	87	79
Self-employed workers (% of employed ages 15+)	16	23	12	20
Unpaid family workers (% of employed ages 15+)	11	3	2	1
Women in nonagricultural wage employment (%)	32		43	
Children in employment (% of children ages 7–14)	..	..	..	..
Unemployment (% of labor force ages 15+)	24	12	11	6
Long-term unemployment (% of total unemployment)	62	46	31	24
Youth unemployment (% of labor force ages 15–24)	40	23	24	17
Maternity leave (weeks)	16		16	
Maternal leave benefits (% of wages paid)	75		100	
Women's political participation				
Seats held by women in national parliament (%)	15		36	
Women in managerial positions (%)	..		30	

Sri Lanka

South Asia			Lower middle income	

Population (millions)	20	Population living on less than $1.25 a day (%)	14.0
GNI ($ billions)	30.8		
GNI per capita ($)	1,540		

	1990		2007	
	Female	Male	Female	Male
Demography				
Sex ratio at birth (females per 1,000 males)	962		962	
Life expectancy at birth (years)	74	67	76	69
Child mortality rate (per 1,000)	10	10	..	..
Female-headed households (%)	..		..	
Education				
Gross primary enrollment (% of relevant age group)	111	115	108	108
Gross secondary enrollment (% of relevant age group)	74	68	88	86
Gross tertiary enrollment (% of relevant age group)	..	..	..	..
Primary completion rate (% of relevant age group)	99	98	107	106
Adult literacy rate (% of population ages 15+)	..	..	89	93
Family planning and maternal health				
Total fertility rate (births per woman)	2.5		1.9	
Adolescent fertility (births per 1,000 women ages 15–19)	..		25	
Women married by age 18 (% of women ages 20–24)	14		..	
Contraceptive prevalence (% of women ages 15–49)	66		68	
Unmet need for contraception (% of women ages 15–49)	..		..	
Pregnant women receiving prenatal care (%)	80		99	
Births attended by skilled health staff (% of total)	94		99	
Maternal mortality ratio (per 100,000 live births)	..		58	
Labor force and employment dynamics				
Labor force participation (% of population ages 15+)	46	79	43	75
Women in the labor force (% of total labor force)	36		37	
Employment to population ratio (% ages 15+)	33	71	39	72
Vulnerable employment (% of employed ages 15+)	..	..	44	39
Employment in agriculture (% of employed ages 15+)	43	37	..	..
Employment in industry (% of employed ages 15+)	22	19	..	..
Employment in service (% of employed ages 15+)	32	38	..	..
Wage and salaried workers (% of employed ages 15+)	..	..	55	57
Self-employed workers (% of employed ages 15+)	..	..	23	38
Unpaid family workers (% of employed ages 15+)	..	..	22	4
Women in nonagricultural wage employment (%)	39		45	
Children in employment (% of children ages 7–14)	..	..	..	..
Unemployment (% of labor force ages 15+)	24	9	9	4
Long-term unemployment (% of total unemployment)	..	..	..	..
Youth unemployment (% of labor force ages 15–24)	47	23	37	20
Maternity leave (weeks)	12		12	
Maternal leave benefits (% of wages paid)	100		100	
Women's political participation				
Seats held by women in national parliament (%)	5		5	
Women in managerial positions (%)	..		21	

St. Kitts and Nevis

Latin America & Caribbean		Upper middle income

Population (thousands)	49	Population living on less
GNI ($ millions)	487.5	than $1.25 a day (%)
GNI per capita ($)	9,990	..

	1990		2007	
	Female	Male	Female	Male
Demography				
Sex ratio at birth (females per 1,000 males)	..		..	
Life expectancy at birth (years)	69	65	..	..
Child mortality rate (per 1,000)	..	..	..	..
Female-headed households (%)	..		..	
Education				
Gross primary enrollment (% of relevant age group)	120	118	94	93
Gross secondary enrollment (% of relevant age group)	90	81	100	110
Gross tertiary enrollment (% of relevant age group)	..	..	..	..
Primary completion rate (% of relevant age group)	..	..	95	97
Adult literacy rate (% of population ages 15+)	..	..	..	..
Family planning and maternal health				
Total fertility rate (births per woman)	2.7		..	
Adolescent fertility (births per 1,000 women ages 15–19)	..		..	
Women married by age 18 (% of women ages 20–24)	..		..	
Contraceptive prevalence (% of women ages 15–49)	..		54	
Unmet need for contraception (% of women ages 15–49)	..		..	
Pregnant women receiving prenatal care (%)	100		100	
Births attended by skilled health staff (% of total)	..		100	
Maternal mortality ratio (per 100,000 live births)	..		..	
Labor force and employment dynamics				
Labor force participation (% of population ages 15+)	..	..	..	..
Women in the labor force (% of total labor force)	..		..	
Employment to population ratio (% ages 15+)	..	..	..	..
Vulnerable employment (% of employed ages 15+)	12	12	..	..
Employment in agriculture (% of employed ages 15+)	..	..	..	..
Employment in industry (% of employed ages 15+)	..	..	..	..
Employment in service (% of employed ages 15+)	..	..	..	..
Wage and salaried workers (% of employed ages 15+)	84	81	..	..
Self-employed workers (% of employed ages 15+)	13	16	..	..
Unpaid family workers (% of employed ages 15+)	1	1	..	..
Women in nonagricultural wage employment (%)	..		..	
Children in employment (% of children ages 7–14)	..	..	..	..
Unemployment (% of labor force ages 15+)	..	..	..	..
Long-term unemployment (% of total unemployment)	..	..	..	..
Youth unemployment (% of labor force ages 15–24)	..	..	..	..
Maternity leave (weeks)	..		13	
Maternal leave benefits (% of wages paid)	..		60	
Women's political participation				
Seats held by women in national parliament (%)	7		7	
Women in managerial positions (%)	..		..	

St. Lucia

Latin America & Caribbean   **Upper middle income**

Population (thousands)	168	Population living on less
GNI ($ millions)	927.6	than $1.25 a day (%) ..
GNI per capita ($)	5,520	

	1990		2007	
	Female	Male	Female	Male
Demography				
Sex ratio at birth (females per 1,000 males)	971		971	
Life expectancy at birth (years)	73	69	76	73
Child mortality rate (per 1,000)	..	..	..	..
Female-headed households (%)	..		..	
Education				
Gross primary enrollment (% of relevant age group)	134	143	108	111
Gross secondary enrollment (% of relevant age group)	60	40	99	88
Gross tertiary enrollment (% of relevant age group)	..	..	12	5
Primary completion rate (% of relevant age group)	121	122	109	122
Adult literacy rate (% of population ages 15+)	..	..	..	..
Family planning and maternal health				
Total fertility rate (births per woman)	3.3		*2.1*	
Adolescent fertility (births per 1,000 women ages 15–19)	..		60	
Women married by age 18 (% of women ages 20–24)	..		..	
Contraceptive prevalence (% of women ages 15–49)	47		..	
Unmet need for contraception (% of women ages 15–49)	..		..	
Pregnant women receiving prenatal care (%)	100		*99*	
Births attended by skilled health staff (% of total)	..		*100*	
Maternal mortality ratio (per 100,000 live births)	..		..	
Labor force and employment dynamics				
Labor force participation (% of population ages 15+)	47	78	52	79
Women in the labor force (% of total labor force)	39		41	
Employment to population ratio (% ages 15+)	..	..	..	..
Vulnerable employment (% of employed ages 15+)	21	25	..	..
Employment in agriculture (% of employed ages 15+)	15	30	9	14
Employment in industry (% of employed ages 15+)	19	24	11	23
Employment in service (% of employed ages 15+)	64	43	68	47
Wage and salaried workers (% of employed ages 15+)	74	57	..	..
Self-employed workers (% of employed ages 15+)	21	38	..	..
Unpaid family workers (% of employed ages 15+)	4	2	..	..
Women in nonagricultural wage employment (%)	50		47	
Children in employment (% of children ages 7–14)	..	..	..	..
Unemployment (% of labor force ages 15+)	22	12	25	17
Long-term unemployment (% of total unemployment)	..	..	..	..
Youth unemployment (% of labor force ages 15–24)	35	23	49	32
Maternity leave (weeks)	13		*12*	
Maternal leave benefits (% of wages paid)	60		65	
Women's political participation				
Seats held by women in national parliament (%)	0		6	
Women in managerial positions (%)	..		..	

St. Vincent & Grenadines

Latin America & Caribbean			Upper middle income	

Population (thousands)	120	Population living on less			
GNI ($ millions)	506.9	than $1.25 a day (%)			..
GNI per capita ($)	4,210				

	1990		2007	
	Female	Male	Female	Male
Demography				
Sex ratio at birth (females per 1,000 males)	971		971	
Life expectancy at birth (years)	72	67	74	69
Child mortality rate (per 1,000)	..	..	..	..
Female-headed households (%)	..		..	
Education				
Gross primary enrollment (% of relevant age group)	115	116	100	105
Gross secondary enrollment (% of relevant age group)	65	52	83	67
Gross tertiary enrollment (% of relevant age group)	..	..	..	..
Primary completion rate (% of relevant age group)	..	..	104	81
Adult literacy rate (% of population ages 15+)	..	..	..	..
Family planning and maternal health				
Total fertility rate (births per woman)	3.0		2.2	
Adolescent fertility (births per 1,000 women ages 15–19)	..		64	
Women married by age 18 (% of women ages 20–24)	..		..	
Contraceptive prevalence (% of women ages 15–49)	58		48	
Unmet need for contraception (% of women ages 15–49)	..		..	
Pregnant women receiving prenatal care (%)	..		95	
Births attended by skilled health staff (% of total)	..		100	
Maternal mortality ratio (per 100,000 live births)	..		..	
Labor force and employment dynamics				
Labor force participation (% of population ages 15+)	45	81	54	80
Women in the labor force (% of total labor force)	36		40	
Employment to population ratio (% ages 15+)	..	..	..	..
Vulnerable employment (% of employed ages 15+)	17	22	..	..
Employment in agriculture (% of employed ages 15+)	14	31	..	..
Employment in industry (% of employed ages 15+)	11	27	..	..
Employment in service (% of employed ages 15+)	75	42	..	..
Wage and salaried workers (% of employed ages 15+)	79	71	..	..
Self-employed workers (% of employed ages 15+)	18	27	..	..
Unpaid family workers (% of employed ages 15+)	3	2	..	..
Women in nonagricultural wage employment (%)	..		..	
Children in employment (% of children ages 7–14)	..	..	..	
Unemployment (% of labor force ages 15+)	22	18	..	..
Long-term unemployment (% of total unemployment)	..	..	..	..
Youth unemployment (% of labor force ages 15–24)	43	33	..	..
Maternity leave (weeks)	..		13	
Maternal leave benefits (% of wages paid)	..		65	
Women's political participation				
Seats held by women in national parliament (%)	10		18	
Women in managerial positions (%)	..		..	

Sudan

<table>
<tr><td>Sub-Saharan Africa</td><td colspan="4" align="right">Lower middle income</td></tr>
</table>

Population (millions)	39	Population living on less		
GNI ($ billions)	36.7	than $1.25 a day (%)		..
GNI per capita ($)	950			

	1990		2007	
	Female	Male	Female	Male
Demography				
Sex ratio at birth (females per 1,000 males)	949		949	
Life expectancy at birth (years)	54	51	60	57
Child mortality rate (per 1,000)	63	62	30	38
Female-headed households (%)	..		19	
Education				
Gross primary enrollment (% of relevant age group)	42	55	67	76
Gross secondary enrollment (% of relevant age group)	18	23	34	37
Gross tertiary enrollment (% of relevant age group)	..	..	..	..
Primary completion rate (% of relevant age group)	37	47	46	54
Adult literacy rate (% of population ages 15+)	..	..	..	..
Family planning and maternal health				
Total fertility rate (births per woman)	5.9		4.2	
Adolescent fertility (births per 1,000 women ages 15–19)	..		57	
Women married by age 18 (% of women ages 20–24)	27		..	
Contraceptive prevalence (% of women ages 15–49)	9		8	
Unmet need for contraception (% of women ages 15–49)	..		6	
Pregnant women receiving prenatal care (%)	70		70	
Births attended by skilled health staff (% of total)	69		49	
Maternal mortality ratio (per 100,000 live births)	..		450	
Labor force and employment dynamics				
Labor force participation (% of population ages 15+)	24	78	31	72
Women in the labor force (% of total labor force)	23		30	
Employment to population ratio (% ages 15+)	21	71	28	67
Vulnerable employment (% of employed ages 15+)	..	..	..	..
Employment in agriculture (% of employed ages 15+)	..	..	..	..
Employment in industry (% of employed ages 15+)	..	..	..	..
Employment in service (% of employed ages 15+)	..	..	..	..
Wage and salaried workers (% of employed ages 15+)	..	..	..	..
Self-employed workers (% of employed ages 15+)	..	..	..	..
Unpaid family workers (% of employed ages 15+)	..	..	..	..
Women in nonagricultural wage employment (%)	22		..	
Children in employment (% of children ages 7–14)	..	..	..	..
Unemployment (% of labor force ages 15+)	..	..	..	..
Long-term unemployment (% of total unemployment)	..	..	..	..
Youth unemployment (% of labor force ages 15–24)	..	..	..	..
Maternity leave (weeks)	..		8	
Maternal leave benefits (% of wages paid)	..		100	
Women's political participation				
Seats held by women in national parliament (%)	..		18	
Women in managerial positions (%)	..		..	

Suriname

Latin America & Caribbean   **Upper middle income**

Population (thousands)	458	Population living on less
GNI ($ billions)	2.2	than $1.25 a day (%)
GNI per capita ($)	4,730	..

	1990		2007	
	Female	Male	Female	Male
Demography				
Sex ratio at birth (females per 1,000 males)	926		926	
Life expectancy at birth (years)	71	66	74	67
Child mortality rate (per 1,000)	..	..	..	..
Female-headed households (%)	..		..	
Education				
Gross primary enrollment (% of relevant age group)	113	102	118	120
Gross secondary enrollment (% of relevant age group)	62	50	93	67
Gross tertiary enrollment (% of relevant age group)	..	..	..	..
Primary completion rate (% of relevant age group)	..	..	91	77
Adult literacy rate (% of population ages 15+)	..	..	88	93
Family planning and maternal health				
Total fertility rate (births per woman)	2.8		2.4	
Adolescent fertility (births per 1,000 women ages 15–19)	..		39	
Women married by age 18 (% of women ages 20–24)	..		..	
Contraceptive prevalence (% of women ages 15–49)	..		46	
Unmet need for contraception (% of women ages 15–49)	..		..	
Pregnant women receiving prenatal care (%)	..		90	
Births attended by skilled health staff (% of total)	91		90	
Maternal mortality ratio (per 100,000 live births)	..		72	
Labor force and employment dynamics				
Labor force participation (% of population ages 15+)	37	68	37	65
Women in the labor force (% of total labor force)	36		37	
Employment to population ratio (% ages 15+)	30	60	30	59
Vulnerable employment (% of employed ages 15+)	..	..	..	..
Employment in agriculture (% of employed ages 15+)	2	5	..	..
Employment in industry (% of employed ages 15+)	8	27	..	..
Employment in service (% of employed ages 15+)	87	65	..	..
Wage and salaried workers (% of employed ages 15+)	..	..	..	..
Self-employed workers (% of employed ages 15+)	..	..	..	..
Unpaid family workers (% of employed ages 15+)	..	..	..	..
Women in nonagricultural wage employment (%)	39		..	
Children in employment (% of children ages 7–14)	..	..	..	
Unemployment (% of labor force ages 15+)	20	13	..	..
Long-term unemployment (% of total unemployment)	..	..	..	..
Youth unemployment (% of labor force ages 15–24)	47	29	..	..
Maternity leave (weeks)	..		..	
Maternal leave benefits (% of wages paid)	..		..	
Women's political participation				
Seats held by women in national parliament (%)	8		26	
Women in managerial positions (%)	..		..	

Swaziland

Sub-Saharan Africa			Lower middle income	

Population (millions)	1.1	Population living on less than $1.25 a day (%)	62.9
GNI ($ billions)	2.9		
GNI per capita ($)	2,560		

	1990		2007	
	Female	Male	Female	Male
Demography				
Sex ratio at birth (females per 1,000 males)	971		971	
Life expectancy at birth (years)	60	56	39	40
Child mortality rate (per 1,000)	..	..	30	32
Female-headed households (%)	..		48	
Education				
Gross primary enrollment (% of relevant age group)	94	94	102	110
Gross secondary enrollment (% of relevant age group)	39	41	47	47
Gross tertiary enrollment (% of relevant age group)	..	..	4	4
Primary completion rate (% of relevant age group)	65	59	69	64
Adult literacy rate (% of population ages 15+)	..	..	..	..
Family planning and maternal health				
Total fertility rate (births per woman)	5.6		3.6	
Adolescent fertility (births per 1,000 women ages 15–19)	..		33	
Women married by age 18 (% of women ages 20–24)	..		..	
Contraceptive prevalence (% of women ages 15–49)	20		51	
Unmet need for contraception (% of women ages 15–49)	..		24	
Pregnant women receiving prenatal care (%)	..		85	
Births attended by skilled health staff (% of total)	..		69	
Maternal mortality ratio (per 100,000 live births)	..		390	
Labor force and employment dynamics				
Labor force participation (% of population ages 15+)	66	79	62	69
Women in the labor force (% of total labor force)	51		50	
Employment to population ratio (% ages 15+)	49	61	47	55
Vulnerable employment (% of employed ages 15+)	..	..	..	..
Employment in agriculture (% of employed ages 15+)	..	..	..	..
Employment in industry (% of employed ages 15+)	..	..	..	..
Employment in service (% of employed ages 15+)	..	..	..	..
Wage and salaried workers (% of employed ages 15+)	..	..	..	..
Self-employed workers (% of employed ages 15+)	..	..	..	..
Unpaid family workers (% of employed ages 15+)	..	..	..	..
Women in nonagricultural wage employment (%)	35		..	
Children in employment (% of children ages 7–14)	..	..	..	..
Unemployment (% of labor force ages 15+)	..	..	..	..
Long-term unemployment (% of total unemployment)	..	..	..	..
Youth unemployment (% of labor force ages 15–24)	..	..	..	..
Maternity leave (weeks)	12		12	
Maternal leave benefits (% of wages paid)	0		0	
Women's political participation				
Seats held by women in national parliament (%)	4		11	
Women in managerial positions (%)	..		..	

Sweden

High income

Population (millions)	9.1
GNI ($ billions)	437.9
GNI per capita ($)	47,870

Population living on less
than $1.25 a day (%) ..

	1990		2007	
	Female	Male	Female	Male
Demography				
Sex ratio at birth (females per 1,000 males)	944		944	
Life expectancy at birth (years)	80	75	83	79
Child mortality rate (per 1,000)	..	..	..	..
Female-headed households (%)	..		..	
Education				
Gross primary enrollment (% of relevant age group)	100	99	95	96
Gross secondary enrollment (% of relevant age group)	92	88	103	104
Gross tertiary enrollment (% of relevant age group)	..	..	96	62
Primary completion rate (% of relevant age group)	96	97	..	..
Adult literacy rate (% of population ages 15+)	..	..	..	..
Family planning and maternal health				
Total fertility rate (births per woman)	2.1		1.9	
Adolescent fertility (births per 1,000 women ages 15–19)	..		4	
Women married by age 18 (% of women ages 20–24)	..		..	
Contraceptive prevalence (% of women ages 15–49)	..		..	
Unmet need for contraception (% of women ages 15–49)	..		..	
Pregnant women receiving prenatal care (%)			..	
Births attended by skilled health staff (% of total)	100		..	
Maternal mortality ratio (per 100,000 live births)	..		3	
Labor force and employment dynamics				
Labor force participation (% of population ages 15+)	63	72	61	69
Women in the labor force (% of total labor force)	48		47	
Employment to population ratio (% ages 15+)	61	69	57	65
Vulnerable employment (% of employed ages 15+)	..	..	..	..
Employment in agriculture (% of employed ages 15+)	2	5	1	3
Employment in industry (% of employed ages 15+)	14	43	9	34
Employment in service (% of employed ages 15+)	84	52	90	63
Wage and salaried workers (% of employed ages 15+)	95	87	94	85
Self-employed workers (% of employed ages 15+)	..	..	..	..
Unpaid family workers (% of employed ages 15+)	1	0	0	0
Women in nonagricultural wage employment (%)	51		50	
Children in employment (% of children ages 7–14)	..	..	..	
Unemployment (% of labor force ages 15+)	2	2	6	6
Long-term unemployment (% of total unemployment)	12	12	11	15
Youth unemployment (% of labor force ages 15–24)	5	5	22	23
Maternity leave (weeks)	12		14	
Maternal leave benefits (% of wages paid)	90		80	
Women's political participation				
Seats held by women in national parliament (%)	38		47	
Women in managerial positions (%)	..		30	

Switzerland

Population (millions)	7.6	Population living on less	
GNI ($ billions)	459.2	than $1.25 a day (%)	..
GNI per capita ($)	60,820		

	1990		2007	
	Female	Male	Female	Male
Demography				
Sex ratio at birth (females per 1,000 males)	951		951	
Life expectancy at birth (years)	81	74	84	79
Child mortality rate (per 1,000)	..	..	..	..
Female-headed households (%)	..		..	
Education				
Gross primary enrollment (% of relevant age group)	90	88	97	98
Gross secondary enrollment (% of relevant age group)	96	102	90	95
Gross tertiary enrollment (% of relevant age group)	..	..	43	48
Primary completion rate (% of relevant age group)	52	52	89	88
Adult literacy rate (% of population ages 15+)	..	..	..	..
Family planning and maternal health				
Total fertility rate (births per woman)	1.6		1.5	
Adolescent fertility (births per 1,000 women ages 15–19)	..		4	
Women married by age 18 (% of women ages 20–24)	..		..	
Contraceptive prevalence (% of women ages 15–49)	..		..	
Unmet need for contraception (% of women ages 15–49)	..		..	
Pregnant women receiving prenatal care (%)	..		..	
Births attended by skilled health staff (% of total)	..		100	
Maternal mortality ratio (per 100,000 live births)	..		5	
Labor force and employment dynamics				
Labor force participation (% of population ages 15+)	49	79	60	75
Women in the labor force (% of total labor force)	39		46	
Employment to population ratio (% ages 15+)	56	80	57	72
Vulnerable employment (% of employed ages 15+)	11	8	11	10
Employment in agriculture (% of employed ages 15+)	4	5	3	5
Employment in industry (% of employed ages 15+)	18	41	11	32
Employment in service (% of employed ages 15+)	78	54	86	63
Wage and salaried workers (% of employed ages 15+)	86	84	86	82
Self-employed workers (% of employed ages 15+)	8	14	11	16
Unpaid family workers (% of employed ages 15+)	6	2	3	2
Women in nonagricultural wage employment (%)	43		47	
Children in employment (% of children ages 7–14)	..	..	..	..
Unemployment (% of labor force ages 15+)	2	1	5	3
Long-term unemployment (% of total unemployment)	18	16	43	38
Youth unemployment (% of labor force ages 15–24)	3	3	9	9
Maternity leave (weeks)	8		14	
Maternal leave benefits (% of wages paid)	100		80	
Women's political participation				
Seats held by women in national parliament (%)	14		30	
Women in managerial positions (%)	..		28	

Syrian Arab Republic

Middle East & North Africa　　　　　**Lower middle income**

Population (millions)	20	Population living on less
GNI ($ billions)	35.3	than $1.25 a day (%)
GNI per capita ($)	1,780	..

	1990		2007	
	Female	Male	Female	Male
Demography				
Sex ratio at birth (females per 1,000 males)	952		952	
Life expectancy at birth (years)	70	67	76	72
Child mortality rate (per 1,000)	..	..	3	5
Female-headed households (%)	..		..	
Education				
Gross primary enrollment (% of relevant age group)	95	106	123	129
Gross secondary enrollment (% of relevant age group)	43	59	71	73
Gross tertiary enrollment (% of relevant age group)	..	..	..	..
Primary completion rate (% of relevant age group)	83	94	113	116
Adult literacy rate (% of population ages 15+)	..	..	76	90
Family planning and maternal health				
Total fertility rate (births per woman)	5.4		3.1	
Adolescent fertility (births per 1,000 women ages 15–19)	..		35	
Women married by age 18 (% of women ages 20–24)	..		..	
Contraceptive prevalence (% of women ages 15–49)	40		58	
Unmet need for contraception (% of women ages 15–49)	..		..	
Pregnant women receiving prenatal care (%)	51		84	
Births attended by skilled health staff (% of total)	77		93	
Maternal mortality ratio (per 100,000 live births)	..		130	
Labor force and employment dynamics				
Labor force participation (% of population ages 15+)	18	81	21	78
Women in the labor force (% of total labor force)	18		21	
Employment to population ratio (% ages 15+)	16	77	17	73
Vulnerable employment (% of employed ages 15+)	..	..	..	..
Employment in agriculture (% of employed ages 15+)	54	23	49	23
Employment in industry (% of employed ages 15+)	8	28	8	29
Employment in service (% of employed ages 15+)	38	49	43	48
Wage and salaried workers (% of employed ages 15+)	..	..	..	..
Self-employed workers (% of employed ages 15+)	..	..	..	..
Unpaid family workers (% of employed ages 15+)	..	..	..	..
Women in nonagricultural wage employment (%)	11		10	
Children in employment (% of children ages 7–14)	..	..	4	9
Unemployment (% of labor force ages 15+)	14	5	21	8
Long-term unemployment (% of total unemployment)	..	..	..	..
Youth unemployment (% of labor force ages 15–24)	..	..	..	..
Maternity leave (weeks)	7		7	
Maternal leave benefits (% of wages paid)	70		70	
Women's political participation				
Seats held by women in national parliament (%)	9		12	
Women in managerial positions (%)	..		..	

Tajikistan

Europe & Central Asia		Low income

		Population living on less
Population (millions)	6.7	than $1.25 a day (%)	21.5
GNI ($ billions)	3.1		
GNI per capita ($)	460		

	1990		2007	
	Female	Male	Female	Male
Demography				
Sex ratio at birth (females per 1,000 males)	952		952	
Life expectancy at birth (years)	66	61	69	64
Child mortality rate (per 1,000)	..	..	13	18
Female-headed households (%)	..		..	
Education				
Gross primary enrollment (% of relevant age group)	90	92	98	102
Gross secondary enrollment (% of relevant age group)	..	..	76	91
Gross tertiary enrollment (% of relevant age group)	..	..	11	29
Primary completion rate (% of relevant age group)	..	..	104	108
Adult literacy rate (% of population ages 15+)	97	99	100	100
Family planning and maternal health				
Total fertility rate (births per woman)	5.1		3.3	
Adolescent fertility (births per 1,000 women ages 15–19)	..		28	
Women married by age 18 (% of women ages 20–24)	..		..	
Contraceptive prevalence (% of women ages 15–49)	..		38	
Unmet need for contraception (% of women ages 15–49)	..		..	
Pregnant women receiving prenatal care (%)	..		80	
Births attended by skilled health staff (% of total)	..		83	
Maternal mortality ratio (per 100,000 live births)	..		170	
Labor force and employment dynamics				
Labor force participation (% of population ages 15+)	75	84	56	67
Women in the labor force (% of total labor force)	48		47	
Employment to population ratio (% ages 15+)	49	60	50	59
Vulnerable employment (% of employed ages 15+)	..	..	..	..
Employment in agriculture (% of employed ages 15+)	..	..	59	69
Employment in industry (% of employed ages 15+)	..	..	..	..
Employment in service (% of employed ages 15+)	..	..	..	..
Wage and salaried workers (% of employed ages 15+)	..	..	..	..
Self-employed workers (% of employed ages 15+)	..	..	..	..
Unpaid family workers (% of employed ages 15+)	..	..	..	..
Women in nonagricultural wage employment (%)	40		..	
Children in employment (% of children ages 7–14)	..	..	9	9
Unemployment (% of labor force ages 15+)	..	..	..	..
Long-term unemployment (% of total unemployment)	..	..	..	..
Youth unemployment (% of labor force ages 15–24)	..	..	..	..
Maternity leave (weeks)	..		20	
Maternal leave benefits (% of wages paid)	..		..	
Women's political participation				
Seats held by women in national parliament (%)	..		18	
Women in managerial positions (%)	..		..	

Tanzania

Sub-Saharan Africa		Low income

Population (millions)	40	Population living on less	
GNI ($ billions)	16.3	than $1.25 a day (%)	88.5
GNI per capita ($)	410		

	1990		2007	
	Female	Male	Female	Male
Demography				
Sex ratio at birth (females per 1,000 males)	971		971	
Life expectancy at birth (years)	53	49	54	51
Child mortality rate (per 1,000)	57	63	52	56
Female-headed households (%)	19		25	
Education				
Gross primary enrollment (% of relevant age group)	69	70	113	112
Gross secondary enrollment (% of relevant age group)	4	6	..	..
Gross tertiary enrollment (% of relevant age group)	..	..	1	2
Primary completion rate (% of relevant age group)	63	62	109	115
Adult literacy rate (% of population ages 15+)	48	71	66	79
Family planning and maternal health				
Total fertility rate (births per woman)	6.1		5.2	
Adolescent fertility (births per 1,000 women ages 15–19)	..		121	
Women married by age 18 (% of women ages 20–24)	37		..	
Contraceptive prevalence (% of women ages 15–49)	10		26	
Unmet need for contraception (% of women ages 15–49)	28		22	
Pregnant women receiving prenatal care (%)	62		78	
Births attended by skilled health staff (% of total)	53		43	
Maternal mortality ratio (per 100,000 live births)	..		950	
Labor force and employment dynamics				
Labor force participation (% of population ages 15+)	89	93	87	90
Women in the labor force (% of total labor force)	50		50	
Employment to population ratio (% ages 15+)	86	90	76	81
Vulnerable employment (% of employed ages 15+)	..	..	93	82
Employment in agriculture (% of employed ages 15+)	90	78	..	..
Employment in industry (% of employed ages 15+)	1	7	..	..
Employment in service (% of employed ages 15+)	8	15	..	..
Wage and salaried workers (% of employed ages 15+)	..	..	6	15
Self-employed workers (% of employed ages 15+)	..	..	81	75
Unpaid family workers (% of employed ages 15+)	..	..	13	10
Women in nonagricultural wage employment (%)	..		..	
Children in employment (% of children ages 7–14)	..	..	..	..
Unemployment (% of labor force ages 15+)	4	3	..	..
Long-term unemployment (% of total unemployment)	..	..	..	..
Youth unemployment (% of labor force ages 15–24)	..	..	..	..
Maternity leave (weeks)	..		12	
Maternal leave benefits (% of wages paid)	..		100	
Women's political participation				
Seats held by women in national parliament (%)	..		30	
Women in managerial positions (%)	..		..	

Thailand

East Asia & Pacific		Lower middle income	

Population (millions)	64	Population living on less than $1.25 a day (%)	
GNI ($ billions)	217.2		2.0
GNI per capita ($)	3,400		

	1990		2007	
	Female	Male	Female	Male
Demography				
Sex ratio at birth (females per 1,000 males)	952		952	
Life expectancy at birth (years)	71	64	75	66
Child mortality rate (per 1,000)	*12*	*11*	..	..
Female-headed households (%)	..		*30*	
Education				
Gross primary enrollment (% of relevant age group)	*112*	*115*	106	106
Gross secondary enrollment (% of relevant age group)	31	30	88	79
Gross tertiary enrollment (% of relevant age group)	..	..	55	44
Primary completion rate (% of relevant age group)	..	..	104	99
Adult literacy rate (% of population ages 15+)	..	..	93	96
Family planning and maternal health				
Total fertility rate (births per woman)	2.1		1.9	
Adolescent fertility (births per 1,000 women ages 15–19)	..		42	
Women married by age 18 (% of women ages 20–24)	*21*		..	
Contraceptive prevalence (% of women ages 15–49)	*74*		77	
Unmet need for contraception (% of women ages 15–49)	..		..	
Pregnant women receiving prenatal care (%)	..		98	
Births attended by skilled health staff (% of total)	69		97	
Maternal mortality ratio (per 100,000 live births)	..		*110*	
Labor force and employment dynamics				
Labor force participation (% of population ages 15+)	76	87	66	81
Women in the labor force (% of total labor force)	47		47	
Employment to population ratio (% ages 15+)	71	84	65	80
Vulnerable employment (% of employed ages 15+)	74	67	56	51
Employment in agriculture (% of employed ages 15+)	65	63	*41*	*44*
Employment in industry (% of employed ages 15+)	12	16	*19*	*22*
Employment in service (% of employed ages 15+)	23	21	*41*	*34*
Wage and salaried workers (% of employed ages 15+)	26	31	42	45
Self-employed workers (% of employed ages 15+)	18	42	28	41
Unpaid family workers (% of employed ages 15+)	56	27	30	14
Women in nonagricultural wage employment (%)	45		47	
Children in employment (% of children ages 7–14)	..	..	14	16
Unemployment (% of labor force ages 15+)	2	2	1	1
Long-term unemployment (% of total unemployment)	..	..	..	..
Youth unemployment (% of labor force ages 15–24)	4	4	5	5
Maternity leave (weeks)	12		*13*	
Maternal leave benefits (% of wages paid)	100		*100*	
Women's political participation				
Seats held by women in national parliament (%)	3		9	
Women in managerial positions (%)	..		*26*	

Timor-Leste

Population (millions)	1.1	Population living on less
GNI ($ billions)	1.6	than $1.25 a day (%) 52.9
GNI per capita ($)	1,510	

	1990		2007	
	Female	Male	Female	Male
Demography				
Sex ratio at birth (females per 1,000 males)	952		952	
Life expectancy at birth (years)	48	46	62	60
Child mortality rate (per 1,000)	..	..	..	..
Female-headed households (%)	..		..	
Education				
Gross primary enrollment (% of relevant age group)	..	..	88	93
Gross secondary enrollment (% of relevant age group)	..	..	53	53
Gross tertiary enrollment (% of relevant age group)	..	..	..	..
Primary completion rate (% of relevant age group)	..	..	69	69
Adult literacy rate (% of population ages 15+)	..	..	..	..
Family planning and maternal health				
Total fertility rate (births per woman)	5.5		6.5	
Adolescent fertility (births per 1,000 women ages 15–19)	..		54	
Women married by age 18 (% of women ages 20–24)	..		..	
Contraceptive prevalence (% of women ages 15–49)	..		20	
Unmet need for contraception (% of women ages 15–49)	..		..	
Pregnant women receiving prenatal care (%)	..		61	
Births attended by skilled health staff (% of total)	..		18	
Maternal mortality ratio (per 100,000 live births)	..		380	
Labor force and employment dynamics				
Labor force participation (% of population ages 15+)	52	81	58	83
Women in the labor force (% of total labor force)	38		40	
Employment to population ratio (% ages 15+)	49	78	55	80
Vulnerable employment (% of employed ages 15+)	..	..	..	..
Employment in agriculture (% of employed ages 15+)	..	..	..	..
Employment in industry (% of employed ages 15+)	..	..	..	..
Employment in service (% of employed ages 15+)	..	..	..	..
Wage and salaried workers (% of employed ages 15+)	..	..	..	..
Self-employed workers (% of employed ages 15+)	..	..	..	..
Unpaid family workers (% of employed ages 15+)	..	..	..	..
Women in nonagricultural wage employment (%)	..		..	
Children in employment (% of children ages 7–14)	..	..	..	..
Unemployment (% of labor force ages 15+)	..	..	..	..
Long-term unemployment (% of total unemployment)	..	..	..	..
Youth unemployment (% of labor force ages 15–24)	..	..	..	..
Maternity leave (weeks)	..		..	
Maternal leave benefits (% of wages paid)	..		..	
Women's political participation				
Seats held by women in national parliament (%)	..		28	
Women in managerial positions (%)	..		..	

Togo

Sub-Saharan Africa   **Low income**

Population (millions)	6.6	Population living on less
GNI ($ billions)	2.4	than $1.25 a day (%) 38.7
GNI per capita ($)	360	

	1990		2007	
	Female	Male	Female	Male
Demography				
Sex ratio at birth (females per 1,000 males)	982		982	
Life expectancy at birth (years)	60	56	60	57
Child mortality rate (per 1,000)	90	75	43	55
Female-headed households (%)	..		..	
Education				
Gross primary enrollment (% of relevant age group)	70	108	90	104
Gross secondary enrollment (% of relevant age group)	11	31	30	55
Gross tertiary enrollment (% of relevant age group)	..	..	..	..
Primary completion rate (% of relevant age group)	22	48	48	67
Adult literacy rate (% of population ages 15+)	..	..	..	..
Family planning and maternal health				
Total fertility rate (births per woman)	6.4		4.8	
Adolescent fertility (births per 1,000 women ages 15–19)	..		89	
Women married by age 18 (% of women ages 20–24)	44		..	
Contraceptive prevalence (% of women ages 15–49)	34		17	
Unmet need for contraception (% of women ages 15–49)	..		..	
Pregnant women receiving prenatal care (%)	43		84	
Births attended by skilled health staff (% of total)	31		62	
Maternal mortality ratio (per 100,000 live births)	..		510	
Labor force and employment dynamics				
Labor force participation (% of population ages 15+)	53	89	52	87
Women in the labor force (% of total labor force)	39		38	
Employment to population ratio (% ages 15+)	50	82	48	80
Vulnerable employment (% of employed ages 15+)	..	..	..	..
Employment in agriculture (% of employed ages 15+)	..	..	..	..
Employment in industry (% of employed ages 15+)	..	..	..	..
Employment in service (% of employed ages 15+)	..	..	..	..
Wage and salaried workers (% of employed ages 15+)	..	..	..	..
Self-employed workers (% of employed ages 15+)	..	..	..	..
Unpaid family workers (% of employed ages 15+)	..	..	..	..
Women in nonagricultural wage employment (%)	41		..	
Children in employment (% of children ages 7–14)	..	..	38	41
Unemployment (% of labor force ages 15+)	..	..	..	..
Long-term unemployment (% of total unemployment)	..	..	..	..
Youth unemployment (% of labor force ages 15–24)	..	..	..	..
Maternity leave (weeks)	..		14	
Maternal leave benefits (% of wages paid)	..		100	
Women's political participation				
Seats held by women in national parliament (%)	5		7	
Women in managerial positions (%)	..		..	

Tonga

East Asia & Pacific **Lower middle income**

		Population living on less	
Population (thousands)	102	than $1.25 a day (%)	..
GNI ($ millions)	253.6		
GNI per capita ($)	2,480		

	1990		2007	
	Female	Male	Female	Male
Demography				
Sex ratio at birth (females per 1,000 males)	952		952	
Life expectancy at birth (years)	71	69	74	72
Child mortality rate (per 1,000)	..	..	..	..
Female-headed households (%)	..		..	
Education				
Gross primary enrollment (% of relevant age group)	111	113	110	116
Gross secondary enrollment (% of relevant age group)	98	97	96	92
Gross tertiary enrollment (% of relevant age group)	..	..	8	5
Primary completion rate (% of relevant age group)	124	141	102	98
Adult literacy rate (% of population ages 15+)	..	..	99	99
Family planning and maternal health				
Total fertility rate (births per woman)	4.6		3.8	
Adolescent fertility (births per 1,000 women ages 15–19)	..		18	
Women married by age 18 (% of women ages 20–24)	..		..	
Contraceptive prevalence (% of women ages 15–49)	..		..	
Unmet need for contraception (% of women ages 15–49)	..		..	
Pregnant women receiving prenatal care (%)	..		..	
Births attended by skilled health staff (% of total)	92		98	
Maternal mortality ratio (per 100,000 live births)	..		..	
Labor force and employment dynamics				
Labor force participation (% of population ages 15+)	28	73	53	71
Women in the labor force (% of total labor force)	28		42	
Employment to population ratio (% ages 15+)	..	..	..	..
Vulnerable employment (% of employed ages 15+)	..	..	..	..
Employment in agriculture (% of employed ages 15+)	..	..	..	..
Employment in industry (% of employed ages 15+)	..	..	..	..
Employment in service (% of employed ages 15+)	..	..	..	..
Wage and salaried workers (% of employed ages 15+)	..	..	..	..
Self-employed workers (% of employed ages 15+)	..	..	..	..
Unpaid family workers (% of employed ages 15+)	..	..	..	..
Women in nonagricultural wage employment (%)	..		39	
Children in employment (% of children ages 7–14)	..	..	..	..
Unemployment (% of labor force ages 15+)	..	..	7	4
Long-term unemployment (% of total unemployment)	..	..	..	..
Youth unemployment (% of labor force ages 15–24)	..	..	..	..
Maternity leave (weeks)	..		..	
Maternal leave benefits (% of wages paid)	..		..	
Women's political participation				
Seats held by women in national parliament (%)	0		3	
Women in managerial positions (%)	..		..	

Trinidad and Tobago

High income

Population (millions)	1.3	Population living on less
GNI ($ billions)	19.3	than $1.25 a day (%) ..
GNI per capita ($)	14,480	

	1990		2007	
	Female	Male	Female	Male
Demography				
Sex ratio at birth (females per 1,000 males)	963		963	
Life expectancy at birth (years)	72	67	72	68
Child mortality rate (per 1,000)	3	3	..	
Female-headed households (%)	..		..	
Education				
Gross primary enrollment (% of relevant age group)	95	93	94	96
Gross secondary enrollment (% of relevant age group)	87	84	78	75
Gross tertiary enrollment (% of relevant age group)	..	..	13	10
Primary completion rate (% of relevant age group)	104	98	90	86
Adult literacy rate (% of population ages 15+)	96	98	98	99
Family planning and maternal health				
Total fertility rate (births per woman)	2.4		1.6	
Adolescent fertility (births per 1,000 women ages 15–19)	..		35	
Women married by age 18 (% of women ages 20–24)	34		..	
Contraceptive prevalence (% of women ages 15–49)	53		43	
Unmet need for contraception (% of women ages 15–49)	..		..	
Pregnant women receiving prenatal care (%)	98		96	
Births attended by skilled health staff (% of total)	98		98	
Maternal mortality ratio (per 100,000 live births)	..		45	
Labor force and employment dynamics				
Labor force participation (% of population ages 15+)	39	76	55	77
Women in the labor force (% of total labor force)	35		43	
Employment to population ratio (% ages 15+)	34	56	51	73
Vulnerable employment (% of employed ages 15+)	21	22	13	17
Employment in agriculture (% of employed ages 15+)	6	15	2	6
Employment in industry (% of employed ages 15+)	14	34	16	41
Employment in service (% of employed ages 15+)	80	51	82	52
Wage and salaried workers (% of employed ages 15+)	77	73	83	76
Self-employed workers (% of employed ages 15+)	16	24	14	23
Unpaid family workers (% of employed ages 15+)	7	3	2	0
Women in nonagricultural wage employment (%)	36		43	
Children in employment (% of children ages 7–14)	..	..	..	..
Unemployment (% of labor force ages 15+)	24	18	10	4
Long-term unemployment (% of total unemployment)	36	20	..	..
Youth unemployment (% of labor force ages 15–24)	43	33	..	..
Maternity leave (weeks)	13		13	
Maternal leave benefits (% of wages paid)	60		100	
Women's political participation				
Seats held by women in national parliament (%)	17		19	
Women in managerial positions (%)	..		..	

Tunisia

Middle East & North Africa	Lower middle income

		Population living on less	
Population (millions)	10	than $1.25 a day (%)	2.6
GNI ($ billions)	32.8		
GNI per capita ($)	3,210		

	1990		2007	
	Female	Male	Female	Male
Demography				
Sex ratio at birth (females per 1,000 males)	935		935	
Life expectancy at birth (years)	72	69	76	72
Child mortality rate (per 1,000)	19	19	..	..
Female-headed households (%)	..		..	
Education				
Gross primary enrollment (% of relevant age group)	105	119	107	110
Gross secondary enrollment (% of relevant age group)	38	50	89	81
Gross tertiary enrollment (% of relevant age group)	..	..	37	26
Primary completion rate (% of relevant age group)	75	85	117	122
Adult literacy rate (% of population ages 15+)	..	..	69	86
Family planning and maternal health				
Total fertility rate (births per woman)	3.5		2.0	
Adolescent fertility (births per 1,000 women ages 15–19)	..		7	
Women married by age 18 (% of women ages 20–24)	10		..	
Contraceptive prevalence (% of women ages 15–49)	50		..	
Unmet need for contraception (% of women ages 15–49)	..		..	
Pregnant women receiving prenatal care (%)	58		..	
Births attended by skilled health staff (% of total)	69		..	
Maternal mortality ratio (per 100,000 live births)	..		100	
Labor force and employment dynamics				
Labor force participation (% of population ages 15+)	21	76	26	71
Women in the labor force (% of total labor force)	22		26	
Employment to population ratio (% ages 15+)	17	64	21	62
Vulnerable employment (% of employed ages 15+)	..	..	..	..
Employment in agriculture (% of employed ages 15+)	..	..	..	..
Employment in industry (% of employed ages 15+)	..	..	..	..
Employment in service (% of employed ages 15+)	..	..	..	..
Wage and salaried workers (% of employed ages 15+)	59	69	..	..
Self-employed workers (% of employed ages 15+)	19	24	..	..
Unpaid family workers (% of employed ages 15+)	22	6	..	..
Women in nonagricultural wage employment (%)	..		25	
Children in employment (% of children ages 7–14)	..	..	..	..
Unemployment (% of labor force ages 15+)	22	15	17	13
Long-term unemployment (% of total unemployment)	..	..	..	..
Youth unemployment (% of labor force ages 15–24)	30	31	29	31
Maternity leave (weeks)	4		4	
Maternal leave benefits (% of wages paid)	67		67	
Women's political participation				
Seats held by women in national parliament (%)	4		23	
Women in managerial positions (%)	..		..	

Turkey

Europe & Central Asia	Upper middle income

Population (millions)	74	Population living on less than $1.25 a day (%)	2.7
GNI ($ billions)	593.0		
GNI per capita ($)	8,030		

	1990		2007	
	Female	Male	Female	Male
Demography				
Sex ratio at birth (females per 1,000 males)	952		952	
Life expectancy at birth (years)	68	64	74	69
Child mortality rate (per 1,000)	14	13	9	9
Female-headed households (%)	10		..	
Education				
Gross primary enrollment (% of relevant age group)	95	103	92	96
Gross secondary enrollment (% of relevant age group)	35	57	71	86
Gross tertiary enrollment (% of relevant age group)	..	..	30	39
Primary completion rate (% of relevant age group)	84	91	91	101
Adult literacy rate (% of population ages 15+)	69	90	81	96
Family planning and maternal health				
Total fertility rate (births per woman)	3.0		2.2	
Adolescent fertility (births per 1,000 women ages 15-19)	..		37	
Women married by age 18 (% of women ages 20-24)	23		..	
Contraceptive prevalence (% of women ages 15-49)	63		71	
Unmet need for contraception (% of women ages 15-49)	11		..	
Pregnant women receiving prenatal care (%)	62		81	
Births attended by skilled health staff (% of total)	76		83	
Maternal mortality ratio (per 100,000 live births)	..		44	
Labor force and employment dynamics				
Labor force participation (% of population ages 15+)	34	81	24	71
Women in the labor force (% of total labor force)	29		27	
Employment to population ratio (% ages 15+)	32	74	22	64
Vulnerable employment (% of employed ages 15+)	..	..	50	32
Employment in agriculture (% of employed ages 15+)	76	34	52	22
Employment in industry (% of employed ages 15+)	10	26	15	28
Employment in service (% of employed ages 15+)	14	41	33	50
Wage and salaried workers (% of employed ages 15+)	22	47	49	62
Self-employed workers (% of employed ages 15+)	9	41	13	33
Unpaid family workers (% of employed ages 15+)	69	13	38	6
Women in nonagricultural wage employment (%)	17		21	
Children in employment (% of children ages 7-14)	..	..	..	..
Unemployment (% of labor force ages 15+)	9	8	10	10
Long-term unemployment (% of total unemployment)	51	45	40	27
Youth unemployment (% of labor force ages 15-24)	15	17	19	19
Maternity leave (weeks)	12		16	
Maternal leave benefits (% of wages paid)	67		67	
Women's political participation				
Seats held by women in national parliament (%)	1		9	
Women in managerial positions (%)	..		6	

Turkmenistan

Europe & Central Asia   **Lower middle income**

Population (millions)	5.0	Population living on less
GNI ($ billions)	..	than $1.25 a day (%)
GNI per capita ($)	..	..

	1990		2007	
	Female	Male	Female	Male
Demography				
Sex ratio at birth (females per 1,000 males)	956		956	
Life expectancy at birth (years)	67	59	68	59
Child mortality rate (per 1,000)	..	..	..	..
Female-headed households (%)	..		..	
Education				
Gross primary enrollment (% of relevant age group)	..	..	..	..
Gross secondary enrollment (% of relevant age group)	..	..	..	..
Gross tertiary enrollment (% of relevant age group)	..	..	..	..
Primary completion rate (% of relevant age group)	..	..	..	..
Adult literacy rate (% of population ages 15+)	..	..	99	100
Family planning and maternal health				
Total fertility rate (births per woman)	4.2		2.5	
Adolescent fertility (births per 1,000 women ages 15–19)	..		16	
Women married by age 18 (% of women ages 20–24)	..		..	
Contraceptive prevalence (% of women ages 15–49)	..		48	
Unmet need for contraception (% of women ages 15–49)	..		..	
Pregnant women receiving prenatal care (%)	..		99	
Births attended by skilled health staff (% of total)	..		100	
Maternal mortality ratio (per 100,000 live births)	..		130	
Labor force and employment dynamics				
Labor force participation (% of population ages 15+)	63	75	59	71
Women in the labor force (% of total labor force)	47		47	
Employment to population ratio (% ages 15+)	51	62	54	63
Vulnerable employment (% of employed ages 15+)	..	..	..	..
Employment in agriculture (% of employed ages 15+)	..	..	..	..
Employment in industry (% of employed ages 15+)	..	..	..	..
Employment in service (% of employed ages 15+)	..	..	..	..
Wage and salaried workers (% of employed ages 15+)	..	..	..	..
Self-employed workers (% of employed ages 15+)	..	..	..	..
Unpaid family workers (% of employed ages 15+)	..	..	..	..
Women in nonagricultural wage employment (%)	..		..	
Children in employment (% of children ages 7–14)	..	..	..	..
Unemployment (% of labor force ages 15+)	..	..	..	..
Long-term unemployment (% of total unemployment)	..	..	..	..
Youth unemployment (% of labor force ages 15–24)	..	..	..	..
Maternity leave (weeks)	..		..	
Maternal leave benefits (% of wages paid)	..		..	
Women's political participation				
Seats held by women in national parliament (%)	26		16	
Women in managerial positions (%)	..		..	

Uganda

Sub-Saharan Africa				Low income

Population (millions)	31	Population living on less	
GNI ($ billions)	11.3	than $1.25 a day (%)	51.5
GNI per capita ($)	370		

	1990		2007	
	Female	Male	Female	Male
Demography				
Sex ratio at birth (females per 1,000 males)	971		971	
Life expectancy at birth (years)	52	48	52	51
Child mortality rate (per 1,000)	86	97	62	75
Female-headed households (%)	..		30	
Education				
Gross primary enrollment (% of relevant age group)	60	74	117	116
Gross secondary enrollment (% of relevant age group)	9	16	16	20
Gross tertiary enrollment (% of relevant age group)	..	..	3	4
Primary completion rate (% of relevant age group)	..	..	51	57
Adult literacy rate (% of population ages 15+)	45	68	66	82
Family planning and maternal health				
Total fertility rate (births per woman)	7.1		6.7	
Adolescent fertility (births per 1,000 women ages 15–19)	..		152	
Women married by age 18 (% of women ages 20–24)	53		..	
Contraceptive prevalence (% of women ages 15–49)	5		24	
Unmet need for contraception (% of women ages 15–49)	..		41	
Pregnant women receiving prenatal care (%)	87		94	
Births attended by skilled health staff (% of total)	38		42	
Maternal mortality ratio (per 100,000 live births)	..		550	
Labor force and employment dynamics				
Labor force participation (% of population ages 15+)	80	92	82	90
Women in the labor force (% of total labor force)	47		48	
Employment to population ratio (% ages 15+)	80	90	80	86
Vulnerable employment (% of employed ages 15+)	..	..	92	77
Employment in agriculture (% of employed ages 15+)	91	91	77	60
Employment in industry (% of employed ages 15+)	6	4	5	11
Employment in service (% of employed ages 15+)	3	5	18	29
Wage and salaried workers (% of employed ages 15+)	..	..	8	22
Self-employed workers (% of employed ages 15+)	..	..	52	68
Unpaid family workers (% of employed ages 15+)	..	..	41	10
Women in nonagricultural wage employment (%)	..		39	
Children in employment (% of children ages 7–14)	..	..	36	40
Unemployment (% of labor force ages 15+)	..	..	4	3
Long-term unemployment (% of total unemployment)	..	..	..	..
Youth unemployment (% of labor force ages 15–24)	..	..	..	..
Maternity leave (weeks)	8		8	
Maternal leave benefits (% of wages paid)	..		100	
Women's political participation				
Seats held by women in national parliament (%)	12		30	
Women in managerial positions (%)	..		..	

Ukraine

Europe & Central Asia		Lower middle income	

Population (millions)	47	Population living on less	
GNI ($ billions)	118.9	than $1.25 a day (%)	2.0
GNI per capita ($)	2,560		

	1990		2007	
	Female	Male	Female	Male
Demography				
Sex ratio at birth (females per 1,000 males)	944		939	
Life expectancy at birth (years)	75	66	74	63
Child mortality rate (per 1,000)	..	..	1	4
Female-headed households (%)	..		..	
Education				
Gross primary enrollment (% of relevant age group)	88	88	100	100
Gross secondary enrollment (% of relevant age group)	..	..	94	94
Gross tertiary enrollment (% of relevant age group)	..	..	85	68
Primary completion rate (% of relevant age group)	..	..	101	101
Adult literacy rate (% of population ages 15+)	..	..	100	100
Family planning and maternal health				
Total fertility rate (births per woman)	1.8		1.2	
Adolescent fertility (births per 1,000 women ages 15–19)	..		28	
Women married by age 18 (% of women ages 20–24)	..		..	
Contraceptive prevalence (% of women ages 15–49)	..		67	
Unmet need for contraception (% of women ages 15–49)	..		..	
Pregnant women receiving prenatal care (%)	..		99	
Births attended by skilled health staff (% of total)	..		99	
Maternal mortality ratio (per 100,000 live births)	..		18	
Labor force and employment dynamics				
Labor force participation (% of population ages 15+)	57	72	53	65
Women in the labor force (% of total labor force)	49		49	
Employment to population ratio (% ages 15+)	53	66	49	60
Vulnerable employment (% of employed ages 15+)	..	..	..	..
Employment in agriculture (% of employed ages 15+)	..	..	..	..
Employment in industry (% of employed ages 15+)	..	..	..	..
Employment in service (% of employed ages 15+)	..	..	..	..
Wage and salaried workers (% of employed ages 15+)	..	..	80	82
Self-employed workers (% of employed ages 15+)	..	..	20	18
Unpaid family workers (% of employed ages 15+)	..	..	0	0
Women in nonagricultural wage employment (%)	52		55	
Children in employment (% of children ages 7–14)	..	..	17	18
Unemployment (% of labor force ages 15+)	..	..	7	7
Long-term unemployment (% of total unemployment)	..	..	..	..
Youth unemployment (% of labor force ages 15–24)	..	..	14	15
Maternity leave (weeks)	..		18	
Maternal leave benefits (% of wages paid)	..		100	
Women's political participation				
Seats held by women in national parliament (%)	..		9	
Women in managerial positions (%)	..		39	

United Arab Emirates

High income

Population (millions)	4.4	Population living on less
GNI ($ billions)	103.7	than $1.25 a day (%) ..
GNI per capita ($)	26,270	

	1990		2007	
	Female	Male	Female	Male
Demography				
Sex ratio at birth (females per 1,000 males)	952		952	
Life expectancy at birth (years)	75	71	81	77
Child mortality rate (per 1,000)	..	..	..	..
Female-headed households (%)	..		..	
Education				
Gross primary enrollment (% of relevant age group)	113	116	106	107
Gross secondary enrollment (% of relevant age group)	69	60	94	91
Gross tertiary enrollment (% of relevant age group)	..	..	37	13
Primary completion rate (% of relevant age group)	96	98	106	103
Adult literacy rate (% of population ages 15+)	..	..	91	89
Family planning and maternal health				
Total fertility rate (births per woman)	4.3		2.3	
Adolescent fertility (births per 1,000 women ages 15–19)	..		18	
Women married by age 18 (% of women ages 20–24)	..		..	
Contraceptive prevalence (% of women ages 15–49)	..		..	
Unmet need for contraception (% of women ages 15–49)	..		..	
Pregnant women receiving prenatal care (%)	..		..	
Births attended by skilled health staff (% of total)	..		100	
Maternal mortality ratio (per 100,000 live births)	..		37	
Labor force and employment dynamics				
Labor force participation (% of population ages 15+)	25	92	40	93
Women in the labor force (% of total labor force)	10		15	
Employment to population ratio (% ages 15+)	25	90	37	90
Vulnerable employment (% of employed ages 15+)	..	..	..	..
Employment in agriculture (% of employed ages 15+)	..	..	..	..
Employment in industry (% of employed ages 15+)	..	..	..	..
Employment in service (% of employed ages 15+)	..	..	..	..
Wage and salaried workers (% of employed ages 15+)	..	..	99	97
Self-employed workers (% of employed ages 15+)	..	..	1	3
Unpaid family workers (% of employed ages 15+)	..	..	..	..
Women in nonagricultural wage employment (%)	..		..	
Children in employment (% of children ages 7–14)	..	..	..	..
Unemployment (% of labor force ages 15+)	..	..	7	3
Long-term unemployment (% of total unemployment)	..	..	..	..
Youth unemployment (% of labor force ages 15–24)	..	..	..	..
Maternity leave (weeks)	6		12	
Maternal leave benefits (% of wages paid)	100		100	
Women's political participation				
Seats held by women in national parliament (%)	0		23	
Women in managerial positions (%)	..		..	

United Kingdom

High income

Population (millions)	61
GNI ($ billions)	2,464.3
GNI per capita ($)	40,660

Population living on less
than $1.25 a day (%) ..

	1990		2007	
	Female	Male	Female	Male
Demography				
Sex ratio at birth (females per 1,000 males)	951		951	
Life expectancy at birth (years)	79	73	82	77
Child mortality rate (per 1,000)	..	..	..	..
Female-headed households (%)	..		..	
Education				
Gross primary enrollment (% of relevant age group)	106	105	106	105
Gross secondary enrollment (% of relevant age group)	85	82	99	97
Gross tertiary enrollment (% of relevant age group)	..	..	69	50
Primary completion rate (% of relevant age group)	..	..	..	..
Adult literacy rate (% of population ages 15+)	..	..	..	..
Family planning and maternal health				
Total fertility rate (births per woman)	1.8		1.9	
Adolescent fertility (births per 1,000 women ages 15–19)	..		24	
Women married by age 18 (% of women ages 20–24)	..		..	
Contraceptive prevalence (% of women ages 15–49)	82		..	
Unmet need for contraception (% of women ages 15–49)	..		..	
Pregnant women receiving prenatal care (%)	..		..	
Births attended by skilled health staff (% of total)	..		..	
Maternal mortality ratio (per 100,000 live births)	..		8	
Labor force and employment dynamics				
Labor force participation (% of population ages 15+)	53	75	56	70
Women in the labor force (% of total labor force)	43		46	
Employment to population ratio (% ages 15+)	49	68	53	66
Vulnerable employment (% of employed ages 15+)	..	..	..	..
Employment in agriculture (% of employed ages 15+)	1	3	1	2
Employment in industry (% of employed ages 15+)	17	44	9	33
Employment in service (% of employed ages 15+)	81	53	90	65
Wage and salaried workers (% of employed ages 15+)	91	80	92	82
Self-employed workers (% of employed ages 15+)	7	18	8	17
Unpaid family workers (% of employed ages 15+)	2	2	1	0
Women in nonagricultural wage employment (%)	48		50	
Children in employment (% of children ages 7–14)	..	..	..	..
Unemployment (% of labor force ages 15+)	7	7	5	6
Long-term unemployment (% of total unemployment)	24	42	18	30
Youth unemployment (% of labor force ages 15–24)	9	11	10	13
Maternity leave (weeks)	14		26	
Maternal leave benefits (% of wages paid)	90		90	
Women's political participation				
Seats held by women in national parliament (%)	6		20	
Women in managerial positions (%)	..		33	

United States

High income

	1990		2007	
	Female	Male	Female	Male

Population (millions) 302
GNI ($ billions) 13,886.4
GNI per capita ($) 46,040

Population living on less than $1.25 a day (%) ..

Demography

Sex ratio at birth (females per 1,000 males)	951		951	
Life expectancy at birth (years)	79	72	81	75
Child mortality rate (per 1,000)	..	..	..	..
Female-headed households (%)	..		..	

Education

Gross primary enrollment (% of relevant age group)	104	105	99	98
Gross secondary enrollment (% of relevant age group)	92	92	94	94
Gross tertiary enrollment (% of relevant age group)	..	..	96	68
Primary completion rate (% of relevant age group)	..	..	96	94
Adult literacy rate (% of population ages 15+)	..	..	..	..

Family planning and maternal health

Total fertility rate (births per woman)	2.1		2.1	
Adolescent fertility (births per 1,000 women ages 15–19)	..		42	
Women married by age 18 (% of women ages 20–24)	..		..	
Contraceptive prevalence (% of women ages 15–49)	71		..	
Unmet need for contraception (% of women ages 15–49)	..		..	
Pregnant women receiving prenatal care (%)	99		..	
Births attended by skilled health staff (% of total)	99		99	
Maternal mortality ratio (per 100,000 live births)	..		11	

Labor force and employment dynamics

Labor force participation (% of population ages 15+)	57	76	59	72
Women in the labor force (% of total labor force)	44		46	
Employment to population ratio (% ages 15+)	53	70	56	69
Vulnerable employment (% of employed ages 15+)	..	..	..	..
Employment in agriculture (% of employed ages 15+)	1	4	1	2
Employment in industry (% of employed ages 15+)	15	36	10	30
Employment in service (% of employed ages 15+)	84	60	90	68
Wage and salaried workers (% of employed ages 15+)	93	90	94	92
Self-employed workers (% of employed ages 15+)	6	10	6	8
Unpaid family workers (% of employed ages 15+)	1	0	0	0
Women in nonagricultural wage employment (%)	47		47	
Children in employment (% of children ages 7–14)	..	..	..	..
Unemployment (% of labor force ages 15+)	6	6	5	5
Long-term unemployment (% of total unemployment)	4	7	9	11
Youth unemployment (% of labor force ages 15–24)	11	12	10	12
Maternity leave (weeks)	12		12	
Maternal leave benefits (% of wages paid)	0		0	

Women's political participation

Seats held by women in national parliament (%)	7		16	
Women in managerial positions (%)	..		..	

Uruguay

Latin America & Caribbean		Upper middle income	

Population (millions)	3.3	Population living on less	
GNI ($ billions)	21.2	than $1.25 a day (%)	2.0
GNI per capita ($)	6,390		

	1990		2007	
	Female	Male	Female	Male
Demography				
Sex ratio at birth (females per 1,000 males)	952		952	
Life expectancy at birth (years)	76	69	80	72
Child mortality rate (per 1,000)	..	..	..	..
Female-headed households (%)	..		..	
Education				
Gross primary enrollment (% of relevant age group)	108	109	113	117
Gross secondary enrollment (% of relevant age group)	..	..	109	94
Gross tertiary enrollment (% of relevant age group)	..	..	58	35
Primary completion rate (% of relevant age group)	97	92	100	98
Adult literacy rate (% of population ages 15+)	..	..	98	97
Family planning and maternal health				
Total fertility rate (births per woman)	2.5		2.0	
Adolescent fertility (births per 1,000 women ages 15–19)	..		61	
Women married by age 18 (% of women ages 20–24)	..		..	
Contraceptive prevalence (% of women ages 15–49)	..		..	
Unmet need for contraception (% of women ages 15–49)	..		..	
Pregnant women receiving prenatal care (%)	..		..	
Births attended by skilled health staff (% of total)	..		99	
Maternal mortality ratio (per 100,000 live births)	..		20	
Labor force and employment dynamics				
Labor force participation (% of population ages 15+)	43	72	53	75
Women in the labor force (% of total labor force)	40		44	
Employment to population ratio (% ages 15+)	40	70	46	70
Vulnerable employment (% of employed ages 15+)	..	..	24	26
Employment in agriculture (% of employed ages 15+)	0	0	2	7
Employment in industry (% of employed ages 15+)	22	40	13	29
Employment in service (% of employed ages 15+)	78	60	86	64
Wage and salaried workers (% of employed ages 15+)	..	..	73	68
Self-employed workers (% of employed ages 15+)	..	..	24	31
Unpaid family workers (% of employed ages 15+)	..	..	3	1
Women in nonagricultural wage employment (%)	42		45	
Children in employment (% of children ages 7–14)	..	..	..	..
Unemployment (% of labor force ages 15+)	11	7	12	7
Long-term unemployment (% of total unemployment)	..	..	..	..
Youth unemployment (% of labor force ages 15–24)	27	21	35	25
Maternity leave (weeks)	12		12	
Maternal leave benefits (% of wages paid)	100		100	
Women's political participation				
Seats held by women in national parliament (%)	6		11	
Women in managerial positions (%)	..		35	

Uzbekistan

Europe & Central Asia				Low income

Population (millions)	27	Population living on less		
GNI ($ billions)	19.7	than $1.25 a day (%)		46.3
GNI per capita ($)	730			

	1990		2007	
	Female	Male	Female	Male
Demography				
Sex ratio at birth (females per 1,000 males)	953		953	
Life expectancy at birth (years)	72	66	70	64
Child mortality rate (per 1,000)	..	..	7	11
Female-headed households (%)	..		..	
Education				
Gross primary enrollment (% of relevant age group)	81	82	94	97
Gross secondary enrollment (% of relevant age group)	96	107	101	103
Gross tertiary enrollment (% of relevant age group)	..	..	8	11
Primary completion rate (% of relevant age group)	..	..	96	99
Adult literacy rate (% of population ages 15+)	..	..	..	..
Family planning and maternal health				
Total fertility rate (births per woman)	4.1		2.4	
Adolescent fertility (births per 1,000 women ages 15–19)	..		34	
Women married by age 18 (% of women ages 20–24)	..		..	
Contraceptive prevalence (% of women ages 15–49)	..		65	
Unmet need for contraception (% of women ages 15–49)	..		8	
Pregnant women receiving prenatal care (%)	..		99	
Births attended by skilled health staff (% of total)	..		100	
Maternal mortality ratio (per 100,000 live births)	..		24	
Labor force and employment dynamics				
Labor force participation (% of population ages 15+)	76	85	58	70
Women in the labor force (% of total labor force)	48		46	
Employment to population ratio (% ages 15+)	49	60	53	63
Vulnerable employment (% of employed ages 15+)	..	..	..	..
Employment in agriculture (% of employed ages 15+)	..	..	..	..
Employment in industry (% of employed ages 15+)	..	..	..	..
Employment in service (% of employed ages 15+)	..	..	..	..
Wage and salaried workers (% of employed ages 15+)	..	..	..	..
Self-employed workers (% of employed ages 15+)	..	..	..	..
Unpaid family workers (% of employed ages 15+)	..	..	..	..
Women in nonagricultural wage employment (%)	46		..	
Children in employment (% of children ages 7–14)	..	..	5	5
Unemployment (% of labor force ages 15+)	..	..	..	..
Long-term unemployment (% of total unemployment)	..	..	..	..
Youth unemployment (% of labor force ages 15–24)	..	..	..	..
Maternity leave (weeks)	..		18	
Maternal leave benefits (% of wages paid)	..		100	
Women's political participation				
Seats held by women in national parliament (%)	..		18	
Women in managerial positions (%)	..		..	

Vanuatu

Lower middle income

Population (thousands)	226	Population living on less
GNI ($ millions)	416.6	than $1.25 a day (%) ..
GNI per capita ($)	1,840	

	1990		2007	
	Female	Male	Female	Male
Demography				
Sex ratio at birth (females per 1,000 males)	935		935	
Life expectancy at birth (years)	65	62	72	68
Child mortality rate (per 1,000)	..	..	..	..
Female-headed households (%)		..		..
Education				
Gross primary enrollment (% of relevant age group)	95	97	107	110
Gross secondary enrollment (% of relevant age group)	15	19	37	43
Gross tertiary enrollment (% of relevant age group)	..	..	4	6
Primary completion rate (% of relevant age group)	..	..	86	87
Adult literacy rate (% of population ages 15+)	..	..	76	80
Family planning and maternal health				
Total fertility rate (births per woman)	4.9		3.7	
Adolescent fertility (births per 1,000 women ages 15–19)	..		44	
Women married by age 18 (% of women ages 20–24)	..		..	
Contraceptive prevalence (% of women ages 15–49)	15		..	
Unmet need for contraception (% of women ages 15–49)	..		..	
Pregnant women receiving prenatal care (%)	..		..	
Births attended by skilled health staff (% of total)	..		88	
Maternal mortality ratio (per 100,000 live births)	..		..	
Labor force and employment dynamics				
Labor force participation (% of population ages 15+)	80	89	79	88
Women in the labor force (% of total labor force)	46		47	
Employment to population ratio (% ages 15+)	..	..	..	..
Vulnerable employment (% of employed ages 15+)	..	..	..	..
Employment in agriculture (% of employed ages 15+)	..	..	..	..
Employment in industry (% of employed ages 15+)	..	..	..	..
Employment in service (% of employed ages 15+)	..	..	..	..
Wage and salaried workers (% of employed ages 15+)	..	..	..	..
Self-employed workers (% of employed ages 15+)	..	..	..	..
Unpaid family workers (% of employed ages 15+)	..	..	..	..
Women in nonagricultural wage employment (%)	..		..	
Children in employment (% of children ages 7–14)	..		..	
Unemployment (% of labor force ages 15+)	..	..	..	..
Long-term unemployment (% of total unemployment)	..	..	..	..
Youth unemployment (% of labor force ages 15–24)	..	..	..	..
Maternity leave (weeks)	..		12	
Maternal leave benefits (% of wages paid)	..		50	
Women's political participation				
Seats held by women in national parliament (%)	4		4	
Women in managerial positions (%)	..		..	

Venezuela, RB

Latin America & Caribbean		Upper middle income

Population (millions)	27	Population living on less than $1.25 a day (%)	3.5
GNI ($ billions)	207.6		
GNI per capita ($)	7,550		

	1990		2007	
	Female	Male	Female	Male
Demography				
Sex ratio at birth (females per 1,000 males)	952		952	
Life expectancy at birth (years)	74	68	77	71
Child mortality rate (per 1,000)	..	..	..	..
Female-headed households (%)	..		..	
Education				
Gross primary enrollment (% of relevant age group)	108	109	105	107
Gross secondary enrollment (% of relevant age group)	59	48	84	75
Gross tertiary enrollment (% of relevant age group)	..	..	41	38
Primary completion rate (% of relevant age group)	86	76	100	96
Adult literacy rate (% of population ages 15+)	89	91	95	95
Family planning and maternal health				
Total fertility rate (births per woman)	3.4		2.6	
Adolescent fertility (births per 1,000 women ages 15–19)	..		90	
Women married by age 18 (% of women ages 20–24)	..		..	
Contraceptive prevalence (% of women ages 15–49)	..		..	
Unmet need for contraception (% of women ages 15–49)	..		..	
Pregnant women receiving prenatal care (%)	..		..	
Births attended by skilled health staff (% of total)	..		95	
Maternal mortality ratio (per 100,000 live births)	..		57	
Labor force and employment dynamics				
Labor force participation (% of population ages 15+)	32	82	52	81
Women in the labor force (% of total labor force)	28		39	
Employment to population ratio (% ages 15+)	29	75	46	74
Vulnerable employment (% of employed ages 15+)	..	..	33	28
Employment in agriculture (% of employed ages 15+)	2	19	2	16
Employment in industry (% of employed ages 15+)	16	30	11	25
Employment in service (% of employed ages 15+)	82	52	86	59
Wage and salaried workers (% of employed ages 15+)	..	..	61	59
Self-employed workers (% of employed ages 15+)	..	..	38	41
Unpaid family workers (% of employed ages 15+)	..	..	2	1
Women in nonagricultural wage employment (%)	35		41	
Children in employment (% of children ages 7–14)	..	..	4	7
Unemployment (% of labor force ages 15+)	10	10	8	7
Long-term unemployment (% of total unemployment)	..	..	..	..
Youth unemployment (% of labor force ages 15–24)	..	..	35	24
Maternity leave (weeks)	18		18	
Maternal leave benefits (% of wages paid)	100		100	
Women's political participation				
Seats held by women in national parliament (%)	10		19	
Women in managerial positions (%)	..		..	

Vietnam

Population (millions)	85	Population living on less	
GNI ($ billions)	65.4	than $1.25 a day (%)	21.5
GNI per capita ($)	770		

	1990		2007	
	Female	**Male**	**Female**	**Male**
Demography				
Sex ratio at birth (females per 1,000 males)	952		952	
Life expectancy at birth (years)	68	64	76	72
Child mortality rate (per 1,000)	..	..	4	5
Female-headed households (%)	..		..	
Education				
Gross primary enrollment (% of relevant age group)	103	111	..	..
Gross secondary enrollment (% of relevant age group)	..	..	..	..
Gross tertiary enrollment (% of relevant age group)	..	..	..	..
Primary completion rate (% of relevant age group)	..	..	..	..
Adult literacy rate (% of population ages 15+)	83	93	..	..
Family planning and maternal health				
Total fertility rate (births per woman)	3.6		2.1	
Adolescent fertility (births per 1,000 women ages 15–19)	..		17	
Women married by age 18 (% of women ages 20–24)	..		..	
Contraceptive prevalence (% of women ages 15–49)	53		76	
Unmet need for contraception (% of women ages 15–49)	..		..	
Pregnant women receiving prenatal care (%)	..		91	
Births attended by skilled health staff (% of total)	..		88	
Maternal mortality ratio (per 100,000 live births)	..		150	
Labor force and employment dynamics				
Labor force participation (% of population ages 15+)	74	81	69	76
Women in the labor force (% of total labor force)	48		48	
Employment to population ratio (% ages 15+)	72	79	68	74
Vulnerable employment (% of employed ages 15+)	..	..	79	70
Employment in agriculture (% of employed ages 15+)	..	..	60	56
Employment in industry (% of employed ages 15+)	..	..	14	21
Employment in service (% of employed ages 15+)	..	..	26	23
Wage and salaried workers (% of employed ages 15+)	..	..	21	30
Self-employed workers (% of employed ages 15+)	..	..	32	51
Unpaid family workers (% of employed ages 15+)	..	..	47	19
Women in nonagricultural wage employment (%)	..		46	
Children in employment (% of children ages 7–14)	..	..	22	21
Unemployment (% of labor force ages 15+)	..	..	2	2
Long-term unemployment (% of total unemployment)	..	..	..	..
Youth unemployment (% of labor force ages 15–24)	..	..	5	4
Maternity leave (weeks)	..		20	
Maternal leave benefits (% of wages paid)	100		100	
Women's political participation				
Seats held by women in national parliament (%)	18		26	
Women in managerial positions (%)	..		..	

Virgin Islands (U.S.)

High income

Population (thousands)	108	Population living on less
GNI ($ billions)	..	than $1.25 a day (%) ..
GNI per capita ($)	..	

	1990		2007	
	Female	Male	Female	Male
Demography				
Sex ratio at birth (females per 1,000 males)	943		943	
Life expectancy at birth (years)	77	71	82	76
Child mortality rate (per 1,000)	..	..	..	..
Female-headed households (%)	..		..	
Education				
Gross primary enrollment (% of relevant age group)	..	..	..	..
Gross secondary enrollment (% of relevant age group)	..	..	..	..
Gross tertiary enrollment (% of relevant age group)	..	..	..	..
Primary completion rate (% of relevant age group)	..	..	..	..
Adult literacy rate (% of population ages 15+)	..	..	..	..
Family planning and maternal health				
Total fertility rate (births per woman)	2.6		1.9	
Adolescent fertility (births per 1,000 women ages 15–19)	..		31	
Women married by age 18 (% of women ages 20–24)	..		..	
Contraceptive prevalence (% of women ages 15–49)	..		..	
Unmet need for contraception (% of women ages 15–49)	..		..	
Pregnant women receiving prenatal care (%)	..		..	
Births attended by skilled health staff (% of total)	..		99	
Maternal mortality ratio (per 100,000 live births)	..		..	
Labor force and employment dynamics				
Labor force participation (% of population ages 15+)	62	70	58	62
Women in the labor force (% of total labor force)	49		52	
Employment to population ratio (% ages 15+)	..	..	..	..
Vulnerable employment (% of employed ages 15+)	..	..	..	..
Employment in agriculture (% of employed ages 15+)	..	..	..	..
Employment in industry (% of employed ages 15+)	..	..	..	..
Employment in service (% of employed ages 15+)	..	..	..	..
Wage and salaried workers (% of employed ages 15+)	..	..	..	..
Self-employed workers (% of employed ages 15+)	..	..	..	..
Unpaid family workers (% of employed ages 15+)	..	..	..	..
Women in nonagricultural wage employment (%)	..		..	
Children in employment (% of children ages 7–14)	..		..	
Unemployment (% of labor force ages 15+)	..	..	..	..
Long-term unemployment (% of total unemployment)	..	..	..	..
Youth unemployment (% of labor force ages 15–24)	..	..	..	..
Maternity leave (weeks)	..		..	
Maternal leave benefits (% of wages paid)	..		..	
Women's political participation				
Seats held by women in national parliament (%)	..		..	
Women in managerial positions (%)	..		..	

West Bank and Gaza

Middle East & North Africa	Lower middle income

Population (millions)	3.7	Population living on less	
GNI ($ billions)	4.5	than $1.25 a day (%)	..
GNI per capita ($)	1,290		

	1990		2007	
	Female	Male	Female	Male
Demography				
Sex ratio at birth (females per 1,000 males)	952		952	
Life expectancy at birth (years)	72	67	75	72
Child mortality rate (per 1,000)	..	..	3	3
Female-headed households (%)	..		..	
Education				
Gross primary enrollment (% of relevant age group)	..	..	80	80
Gross secondary enrollment (% of relevant age group)	..	..	95	90
Gross tertiary enrollment (% of relevant age group)	..	..	51	42
Primary completion rate (% of relevant age group)	..	..	83	83
Adult literacy rate (% of population ages 15+)	..	..	90	97
Family planning and maternal health				
Total fertility rate (births per woman)	6.3		4.6	
Adolescent fertility (births per 1,000 women ages 15–19)	..		79	
Women married by age 18 (% of women ages 20–24)	..		..	
Contraceptive prevalence (% of women ages 15–49)	..		50	
Unmet need for contraception (% of women ages 15–49)	..		..	
Pregnant women receiving prenatal care (%)	..		99	
Births attended by skilled health staff (% of total)	..		99	
Maternal mortality ratio (per 100,000 live births)	..		..	
Labor force and employment dynamics				
Labor force participation (% of population ages 15+)	10	67	14	67
Women in the labor force (% of total labor force)	12		17	
Employment to population ratio (% ages 15+)	8	50	11	52
Vulnerable employment (% of employed ages 15+)	..	..	47	34
Employment in agriculture (% of employed ages 15+)	..	..	34	12
Employment in industry (% of employed ages 15+)	..	..	8	28
Employment in service (% of employed ages 15+)	..	..	56	59
Wage and salaried workers (% of employed ages 15+)	..	..	55	60
Self-employed workers (% of employed ages 15+)	..	..	14	33
Unpaid family workers (% of employed ages 15+)	..	..	32	7
Women in nonagricultural wage employment (%)	..		17	
Children in employment (% of children ages 7–14)	..	..	..	..
Unemployment (% of labor force ages 15+)	..	..	19	22
Long-term unemployment (% of total unemployment)	..	..	..	..
Youth unemployment (% of labor force ages 15–24)	..	..	45	39
Maternity leave (weeks)	..		..	
Maternal leave benefits (% of wages paid)	..		..	
Women's political participation				
Seats held by women in national parliament (%)	..		..	
Women in managerial positions (%)	..		12	

Yemen, Rep.

Middle East & North Africa		Low income

		Population living on less	
Population (millions)	22	than $1.25 a day (%)	17.5
GNI ($ billions)	19.4		
GNI per capita ($)	870		

	1990		2007	
	Female	Male	Female	Male
Demography				
Sex ratio at birth (females per 1,000 males)	952		952	
Life expectancy at birth (years)	55	54	64	61
Child mortality rate (per 1,000)	47	41	11	10
Female-headed households (%)	12		..	
Education				
Gross primary enrollment (% of relevant age group)	..	..	74	100
Gross secondary enrollment (% of relevant age group)	..	..	30	61
Gross tertiary enrollment (% of relevant age group)	..	..	5	14
Primary completion rate (% of relevant age group)	..	..	46	74
Adult literacy rate (% of population ages 15+)	..	..	40	77
Family planning and maternal health				
Total fertility rate (births per woman)	8.0		5.5	
Adolescent fertility (births per 1,000 women ages 15–19)	..		71	
Women married by age 18 (% of women ages 20–24)	49		..	
Contraceptive prevalence (% of women ages 15–49)	10		28	
Unmet need for contraception (% of women ages 15–49)	..		..	
Pregnant women receiving prenatal care (%)	26		41	
Births attended by skilled health staff (% of total)	16		36	
Maternal mortality ratio (per 100,000 live births)	..		430	
Labor force and employment dynamics				
Labor force participation (% of population ages 15+)	15	70	22	66
Women in the labor force (% of total labor force)	17		24	
Employment to population ratio (% ages 15+)	14	63	20	58
Vulnerable employment (% of employed ages 15+)	..	..	..	..
Employment in agriculture (% of employed ages 15+)	83	44	..	..
Employment in industry (% of employed ages 15+)	2	14	..	..
Employment in service (% of employed ages 15+)	13	38	..	..
Wage and salaried workers (% of employed ages 15+)	..	..	..	..
Self-employed workers (% of employed ages 15+)	..	..	..	..
Unpaid family workers (% of employed ages 15+)	..	..	..	..
Women in nonagricultural wage employment (%)	..		..	
Children in employment (% of children ages 7–14)	..	..	..	..
Unemployment (% of labor force ages 15+)	..	..	..	..
Long-term unemployment (% of total unemployment)	..	..	..	..
Youth unemployment (% of labor force ages 15–24)	..	..	..	..
Maternity leave (weeks)	10		9	
Maternal leave benefits (% of wages paid)	70		100	
Women's political participation				
Seats held by women in national parliament (%)	4		0	
Women in managerial positions (%)	..		..	

Zambia

Population (millions)	12	Population living on less	
GNI ($ billions)	9.2	than $1.25 a day (%)	64.3
GNI per capita ($)	770		

	1990		2007	
	Female	**Male**	**Female**	**Male**
Demography				
Sex ratio at birth (females per 1,000 males)	971		971	
Life expectancy at birth (years)	50	46	42	42
Child mortality rate (per 1,000)	85	91	..	..
Female-headed households (%)	16		..	
Education				
Gross primary enrollment (% of relevant age group)	90	98	117	121
Gross secondary enrollment (% of relevant age group)	..	..	41	46
Gross tertiary enrollment (% of relevant age group)	..	..	..	..
Primary completion rate (% of relevant age group)	..	..	83	94
Adult literacy rate (% of population ages 15+)	57	73	61	81
Family planning and maternal health				
Total fertility rate (births per woman)	6.4		5.2	
Adolescent fertility (births per 1,000 women ages 15–19)	..		125	
Women married by age 18 (% of women ages 20–24)	43		..	
Contraceptive prevalence (% of women ages 15–49)	15		..	
Unmet need for contraception (% of women ages 15–49)	31		..	
Pregnant women receiving prenatal care (%)	92		..	
Births attended by skilled health staff (% of total)	51		..	
Maternal mortality ratio (per 100,000 live births)	..		830	
Labor force and employment dynamics				
Labor force participation (% of population ages 15+)	59	81	60	81
Women in the labor force (% of total labor force)	43		43	
Employment to population ratio (% ages 15+)	51	63	54	69
Vulnerable employment (% of employed ages 15+)	81	56	..	..
Employment in agriculture (% of employed ages 15+)	..	..	..	..
Employment in industry (% of employed ages 15+)	..	..	..	..
Employment in service (% of employed ages 15+)	..	..	..	..
Wage and salaried workers (% of employed ages 15+)	15	39	..	..
Self-employed workers (% of employed ages 15+)	26	31	..	..
Unpaid family workers (% of employed ages 15+)	56	28	..	..
Women in nonagricultural wage employment (%)	..		..	
Children in employment (% of children ages 7–14)	..	..	47	49
Unemployment (% of labor force ages 15+)	14	12	..	..
Long-term unemployment (% of total unemployment)	..	..	..	..
Youth unemployment (% of labor force ages 15–24)	21	21	..	..
Maternity leave (weeks)	12		12	
Maternal leave benefits (% of wages paid)	100		100	
Women's political participation				
Seats held by women in national parliament (%)	7		15	
Women in managerial positions (%)	..		..	

Zimbabwe

Sub-Saharan Africa   **Low income**

		Population living on less
Population (millions)	13	than $1.25 a day (%)
GNI ($ billions)	4.5	..
GNI per capita ($)	340	

	1990		2007	
	Female	Male	Female	Male
Demography				
Sex ratio at birth (females per 1,000 males)	980		980	
Life expectancy at birth (years)	64	59	43	44
Child mortality rate (per 1,000)	..	..	21	21
Female-headed households (%)	..		38	
Education				
Gross primary enrollment (% of relevant age group)	100	101	101	102
Gross secondary enrollment (% of relevant age group)	44	50	38	41
Gross tertiary enrollment (% of relevant age group)	..	..	3	4
Primary completion rate (% of relevant age group)	90	96	79	83
Adult literacy rate (% of population ages 15+)	79	89	88	94
Family planning and maternal health				
Total fertility rate (births per woman)	5.1		3.7	
Adolescent fertility (births per 1,000 women ages 15–19)	..		59	
Women married by age 18 (% of women ages 20–24)	33		..	
Contraceptive prevalence (% of women ages 15–49)	43		60	
Unmet need for contraception (% of women ages 15–49)	..		13	
Pregnant women receiving prenatal care (%)	91		94	
Births attended by skilled health staff (% of total)	70		69	
Maternal mortality ratio (per 100,000 live births)	..		880	
Labor force and employment dynamics				
Labor force participation (% of population ages 15+)	68	80	60	80
Women in the labor force (% of total labor force)	46		43	
Employment to population ratio (% ages 15+)	65	75	58	76
Vulnerable employment (% of employed ages 15+)	..	..	..	..
Employment in agriculture (% of employed ages 15+)	..	..	..	..
Employment in industry (% of employed ages 15+)	..	..	..	..
Employment in service (% of employed ages 15+)	..	..	..	..
Wage and salaried workers (% of employed ages 15+)	..	..	..	..
Self-employed workers (% of employed ages 15+)	..	..	..	..
Unpaid family workers (% of employed ages 15+)	..	..	..	..
Women in nonagricultural wage employment (%)	15		..	
Children in employment (% of children ages 7–14)	..	..	..	..
Unemployment (% of labor force ages 15+)	8	7	4	4
Long-term unemployment (% of total unemployment)	..	..	..	..
Youth unemployment (% of labor force ages 15–24)	14	16	..	..
Maternity leave (weeks)	12		13	
Maternal leave benefits (% of wages paid)	60		100	
Women's political participation				
Seats held by women in national parliament (%)	11		17	
Women in managerial positions (%)	..		..	

Glossary

Adolescent fertility is the number of births per 1,000 women ages 15–19. (United Nations Population Division)

Adult literacy rate is the percentage of people ages 15 and older that can, with understanding, both read and write a short, simple statement about their everyday life. (United Nations Educational, Scientific, and Cultural Organization Institute for Statistics)

Births attended by skilled health staff are the percentage of deliveries attended by personnel trained to give the necessary care to women during pregnancy, labor, and postpartum; to conduct deliveries on their own; and to care for newborns. (United Nations Children's Fund and Macro International)

Child mortality rate is the probability of dying between the ages of one and five, if subject to current age-specific mortality rates. The probability is expressed as a rate per 1,000. (Macro International)

Children in employment are children ages 7–14 involved in any economic activity for at least one hour during the reference week of the survey. (Understanding Children's Work)

Contraceptive prevalence is the percentage of women married or in-union ages 15–49 who are practicing, or whose sexual partners are practicing, any form of contraception. (United Nations Children's Fund and Macro International)

Employment in agriculture is the proportion of employment in agriculture—which covers division 1 of the International Standard Industrial Classification (ISIC) revision 2 or tabulation categories A and B (ISIC revision 3) and includes hunting, forestry, and fishing—in total employment. (International Labour Organization)

Employment in industry is the proportion of employment in industry—which covers divisions 2–5 of the International Standard Industrial Classification (ISIC) revision 2 or tabulation categories C–F (ISIC revision 3) and includes mining and quarrying (including oil production), manufacturing, construction, and public utilities (electricity, gas, and water)—in total employment. (International Labour Organization)

Employment in service is the proportion of employment in service—which covers divisions 6–9 of the International Standard Industrial Classification (ISIC) revision 2 or tabulation categories G–P (ISIC revision 3) and includes wholesale and retail trade and restaurants and hotels; transport, storage, and communications; financing, insurance, real estate, and business services; and community, social, and personal service—in total employment. (International Labour Organization)

Employment to population ratio is the proportion of the population ages 15 and older that is employed. (International Labour Organization)

Female-headed households is the percentage of households with a female head. (Macro International)

Glossary

GNI is gross national income. It is calculated as gross domestic product (GDP) plus net receipts of primary income (employee compensation and investment income) from abroad. GDP is the sum of value added by all resident producers plus any product taxes (less subsidies) not included in the valuation of output. (World Bank)

GNI per capita is gross national income (GNI) converted to U.S. dollars using the *World Bank Atlas* method divided by midyear population. GNI is the sum of value added by all resident producers plus any product taxes (less subsidies) not included in the valuation of output plus net receipts of primary income (compensation of employees and property income) from abroad. GNI, calculated in national currency, is usually converted to U.S. dollars at official exchange rates for comparisons across economies. The *World Bank Atlas* method is used to smooth fluctuations in prices and exchange rates. It averages the exchange rate for a given year and the two preceding years, adjusted for differences in rates of inflation between the country and the Euro zone, Japan, the United Kingdom, and the United States. (World Bank)

Gross primary enrollment is the ratio of total enrollment at the primary level, regardless of age, to the population of the age group that officially corresponds to primary education. (United Nations Educational, Scientific, and Cultural Organization Institute for Statistics)

Gross secondary enrollment is the ratio of total enrollment at the secondary level, regardless of age, to the population of the age group that officially corresponds to secondary education. (United Nations Educational, Scientific, and Cultural Organization Institute for Statistics)

Gross tertiary enrollment is the ratio of total enrollment at the tertiary level, regardless of age, to the population of the age group that officially corresponds to tertiary education. (United Nations Educational, Scientific, and Cultural Organization Institute for Statistics)

Labor force participation is the proportion of the population ages 15 and older that is economically active; that is, people who supply labor for the production of goods and services during a specified period. (International Labour Organization)

Life expectancy at birth is the number of years a newborn infant would live if prevailing patterns of mortality at the time of its birth were to stay the same throughout its life. (World Bank staff estimates from various sources including census reports, the United Nations Population Division's World Population Prospects, national statistical offices, household surveys conducted by national agencies, and Macro International.)

Long-term unemployment is people with continuous periods of unemployment extending for a year or longer as a share of the total unemployed. (International Labour Organization)

Maternal leave benefits are the percentage of the wage paid during maternity leave. (United Nations)

Maternal mortality ratio is the number of women who die from pregnancy-related causes during pregnancy and childbirth per 100,000 live births. (World Health Organization, United Nations Children's Fund, United Nations Population Fund and the World Bank)

Maternity leave is the number of weeks that maternity leave benefits are provided. (United Nations)

Population is the de facto definition of population, which counts all residents regardless of legal status or citizenship—except for refugees not permanently settled in the country of asylum, who are generally considered part of the population of their country of origin. (World Bank staff estimates from various sources including census reports, the United Nations Population Division's World Population Prospects, national statistical offices, household surveys conducted by national agencies, and Macro International)

Population living on less than $1.25 a day is the percentage of the population living on less than $1.25 a day at 2005 international prices. (World Bank)

Pregnant women receiving prenatal care are the percentage of women attended at least once during pregnancy by skilled health personnel for reasons related to pregnancy. (United Nations Children's Fund and Macro International)

Primary completion rate is the percentage of students completing the last year of primary school. It is calculated by dividing the total number of students in the last grade of primary school minus the number of repeaters in that grade by the total number of children of official completing age. (United Nations Educational, Scientific, and Cultural Organization Institute for Statistics)

Seats held by women in national parliament is the percentage of parliamentary seats in a single or lower chamber occupied by women. (Inter-Parliamentary Union)

Sex ratio at birth is the number of female births per 1,000 male births. (United Nations Population Division)

Self-employed workers are workers who—working on their own account, with one or a few partners, or in cooperative—hold the type of jobs defined as a "self-employment jobs." (International Labour Organization)

Total fertility rate is the number of children that would be born to a woman if she were to live to the end of her childbearing years and bear children in accordance with current age-specific fertility rates. (World Bank staff estimates from various sources including census reports, the United Nations Population Division's World Population Prospects, national statistical offices, household surveys conducted by national agencies, and Macro International.)

Unemployment is the share of the labor force without work but available for and seeking employment. Definitions of labor force and unemployment may differ by country. (International Labour Organization)

Glossary

Unmet need for contraception is the percentage of fertile, married women of reproductive age who do not want to become pregnant and are not using contraception. (Macro International)

Unpaid family workers are people who work without pay in a market-oriented establishment operated by a related person living in the same household. (International Labour Organization)

Vulnerable employment is unpaid family workers and own-account workers as a percentage of total employment. (International Labour Organization)

Wage and salaried workers are workers who hold the type of jobs defined as "paid employment jobs," where the incumbents hold explicit (written or oral) or implicit employment contracts that give them a basic remuneration that is not directly dependent on the revenue of the unit for which they work. (International Labour Organization)

Women in managerial positions is the share of women administrators and managers as a percentage of all workers in public sector and industry. (United Nations)

Women in nonagricultural wage employment is the share of female workers in the nonagricultural sector (industry and services) as a percentage of total employment in the nonagricultural sector. Industry includes mining and quarrying (including oil production), manufacturing, construction, electricity, gas, and water, corresponding to divisions 2–5 of the International Standard Industrial Classification (ISIC) revision 2 or tabulation categories C–F (ISIC revision 3). Services include wholesale and retail trade and restaurants and hotels; transport, storage, and communications; financing, insurance, real estate, and business services; and community, social, and personal services-corresponding to divisions 6–9 (ISIC revision 2) or tabulation categories G–P (ISIC revision 3). (International Labour Organization)

Women in the labor force is the share of women who are economically active in the total labor force. (International Labour Organization)

Women married by age 18 is the percentage of women ages 20–24 who were first married by age 18. (Macro International)

Youth unemployment is the share of the labor force ages 15–24 without work but available for and seeking employment. Definitions of labor force and unemployment may differ by country. (International Labour Organization)